Women With Intellectual Disabilities

Women With Intellectual Disabilities

Disabilities

Finding a Place in the World

Edited by Rannveig Traustadóttir
and Kelley Johnson

Jessica Kingsley Publishers
London and Philadelphia

First published in the United Kingdom in 2000 by
Jessica Kingsley Publishers Ltd
116 Pentonville Road,
London N1 9JB,
England
and
325 Chestnut Street,
Philadelphia, PA 19106,
USA.

www.jkp.com

Copyright © 2000 Jessica Kingsley Publishers

Library of Congress Cataloging-in-Publication Data
A CIP catalog record for this book is available from the Library of Congress

British Library Cataloguing in Publication Data
Women with intellectual disabilities : finding a place in
the world
1. Mentally handicapped women – Psychology 2. Mentally
handicapped women – Social conditions 3. Mentally
handicapped women – Case studies
I. Johnson, Kelley, 1947– II. Traustadóttir, Rannveig
362.3'082

ISBN 1 85302 846 0

Printed and Bound in Great Britain by
Athenaeum Press, Gateshead, Tyne and Wear

Contents

Acknowledgements   8

Finding a place…   9
Kelley Johnson, Australia and Rannveig Traustadóttir, Iceland

PART I: FINDING A PLACE IN FAMILIES   25

1. What is life like?   28
   Tamara Kainova with Maria Cerna, Czech Republic

2. Discovering a sister   34
   Rosemary West, Australia

3. Coming home   52
   Janka and Jana Hanková with Sonia Holubková, Slovakia

4. Unhappy families: Violence in the lives of girls
   and women   63
   Missy Morton, New Zealand

5. Life without parents: Experiences of older women
   with intellectual disabilities   69
   Christine Bigby, Australia

PART II: FINDING A PLACE IN RELATIONSHIPS   87

6. Family, marriage, friends and work: This is my life   90
   Janice Slattery with Kelley Johnson, Australia

7. Learning from and with women: The story of Jenny   106
   Kristjana Kristiansen, Norway

8. Friendship: Love or work?   118
   Rannveig Traustadóttir, Iceland

9. Consent, abuse and choices: Women with intellectual
   disabilities and sexuality   132
   Michelle McCarthy, England

PART III: FINDING A PLACE IN WORK   **157**

10. We like working   160
    Tamara Kainova with Maria Cerna, Czech Republic

11. Gina's story   162
    Sonia Teuben with Maude Davey, Australia

12. My leadership career   172
    Nancy Ward with Bonnie Shoultz, USA

13. The social meaning of work: Listening to women's
    own experiences   182
    Kristjana Kristiansen, Norway

14. Caring: A place in the world?   191
    Jan Walmsley, England

PART IV: FINDING A PLACE IN COMMUNITIES   **213**

15. My life in L'Arche   217
    Pat Felt with Pam Walker, USA

16. Intersecting cultures: Women of color
    with intellectual disabilities   229
    Susan O'Connor, Ellen Fisher and Debra Robinson, USA

17. Thirty nine months under the Disability
    Discrimination Act   239
    Amanda Millear with Kelley Johnson, Australia

18. Motherhood, family and community life   253
    Hanna Björg Sigurjónsdóttir and Rannveig Traustadóttir, Iceland

    …in the world   271
    Kelley Johnson, Australia and Rannveig Traustadóttir, Iceland

List of contributors   279
References   284
Subject Index   297
Name Index   301

For our mothers Eileen and Rúna

Acknowledgements

Many individuals and organizations have helped to create this book. We would particularly like to acknowledge the perseverance and creativity of the women from around the world who contributed their ideas, friendship and hard work to this book.

We would like to thank the following people who have provided support and advice during this five-year project: Back-to-Back Theatre Company, Geelong, Australia; Jan Carter, Deakin University, Australia; Jón Torfi Jónasson and Lilja Osk Ulvarsdóttir, University of Iceland; Margaret Thornton and Ian Freckelton, La Trobe University, Australia; Maria Nadazdyova, Department of Youth and Family Affairs, Slovakia; Alda Sveinsdottir, Iceland; Steve Taylor, Center on Human Policy, Syracuse University, USA; Tim Booth, University of Sheffield, England. Our very special thanks go to Spencer and Rúna for their constant support and encouragement.

A number of organizations and foundations provided financial support to the contributors, thus enabling us to pay for some of their work. In particular we would like to thank the Lance Reichstein Charitable Foundation that provided funding with which to pay some of the Australian contributors. The University of Iceland's Research Fund and the Icelandic Research Council provided research grants which made it possible to work on this project. The University of Iceland granted Rannveig a sabbatical in the spring of 1998 which enabled her to stay in Australia for a couple of months to work on the book. Deakin University provided office accommodation and support during her stay in Australia. The University of Iceland provided accommodation for Kelley during her visits to Iceland to work on this project.

We express our gratitude to Anna Einarsdóttir and Eyrún María Rúnarsdóttir, University of Iceland, for their support and invaluable assistance in editing and finalizing the manuscript. We would also like to thank Helen Parry at Jessica Kingsley Publishers for her patience and support and the staff of Arts Project Australia for assistance in locating the cover painting.

Finding a Place…

Kelley Johnson, Australia
and Rannveig Traustadóttir, Iceland

This book is written by, with and about women with intellectual disabilities, who come from eight different countries around the world. They all thought it was important that women write this book, because there are no books which tell the stories of women with intellectual disabilities. Some of these women have led very difficult lives, some have had joyful and very exciting ones. Other women with intellectual disabilities may find it helpful to read such stories. Also we thought that women who have not been labelled as having intellectual disabilities would also learn a lot from them. We hope that this book will help all of us understand each other better across the world.

All women share some aspects of their lives. All of us are concerned with things like our families, our friends, our work, and our communities. But women with intellectual disabilities have sometimes found it difficult to find a place in these areas of their lives. Sometimes this is because of the attitudes of other people, sometimes because of the kind of disability they have and sometimes it is because our communities do not provide the kinds of support women need to lead good lives. Sometimes the needs and wants of women with intellectual disabilities are not known by those around them because other people do not see them as *women*.

The stories in this book reveal that women with intellectual disabilities share some common concerns and ideas, but they also show that they are very different as individuals. Some women have written stories about their childhoods. Others have written about being a parent, a worker or a self-advocate. Some have written about their friends. There are also stories about getting older as a woman with intellectual disabilities, stories about sexuality and about the caring work that women do.

Some of these stories were written by women with intellectual disabilities alone. Some were written with another woman. Others were written by women who have not been labelled as having intellectual disabilities but who have spent time trying to understand some of the issues which affect the lives of this group. The women who have written stories for this book live far away from each other and some have never met.

Each story has been written in two ways. One is longer and may be more difficult to read. The other is short and in plain English. We did this because we know that some women find reading difficult. A flower sign separates the two different versions of each chapter.

It has taken a long time for these stories to be put together in a book. All the women who wrote them are excited that the book is coming out. We hope you enjoy it.

This is a women's book. Writing it has involved miracles of chance encounters, new friendships and continuing relationships among women across the world. The idea for the book originated with two women, one from Iceland and one from Australia. Then it developed through discussions with 23 others from 8 countries across the world.

The book was conceived over dinner in a small fish restaurant in Iceland. We had met at an international conference in Reykjavik which was concerned with sharing ideas and exploring new possibilities for people with intellectual disabilities living in the community as we entered the new millennium. The conference was great, but we were concerned that issues of gender and cultural difference were not reflected in the papers which were given. And, as usual, the voices of people with intellectual disabilities were marginalized. As we sat over dinner in the late night summer sunshine, our discussion moved from the conference to wider work issues. We found that although we lived on opposite sides of the world and knew little of each other's work, we had been developing similar work themes.

Both of us had been involved extensively with women with intellectual disabilities and we had both been outraged by the failure of those around them to recognize them as women or to take into account their concerns and desires. As advocates we had worked with them as they struggled to combat discrimination. As researchers we had repeatedly watched as their stated desires and needs were ignored by families and service providers while their gender (when it was acknowledged) was construed as a problem and a threat (Brantlinger 1995; Johnson 1998; Traustadóttir

1997). Their voices were neither recognized nor heard at an individual level or collectively. We thought that it was time to hear them.

Why this book?

The short answer to this question is 'because women with intellectual disabilities from different countries have not had a place where their stories can be heard'. We believe it is important to hear these stories because they reveal alarming gaps in our understanding of women's lives and because they challenge existing stereotypes of women with intellectual disabilities. This book also documents the struggles of a particular group of women in finding places in their communities and celebrates their achievements. Further, the book seeks to redress what we see as a failure by both feminist writers and people working within the disability movement to address issues which confront women with intellectual disabilities.

Including women with intellectual disabilities within feminism

Until relatively recently women's voices generally, their herstory, their contributions to public and private life, their places in their particular cultures and their stories have been excluded from public (or indeed private) consideration (Kirner and Rayner 1999). The development of feminism has done a great deal to remedy this situation. However, earlier feminist writings ignored culture, race, class, sexual orientation and disability; writing as if all women were the same. This meant that accounts of women's experiences were incomplete because important groups were missing. Over the past two decades there has been an increasing challenge to this hegemony of 'white, middle-class women' in feminist writing with the diversity of women's voices being heard more clearly and strongly (Asch and Fine 1988, 1992; hooks 1996; Morris 1991; Spelman 1988). This literature has ensured that differences between women, as well as commonality of issues, have been recognized increasingly as important ingredients in understanding the lives of women.

One of the last groups of women to find voices within feminist literature has been women with disabilities. Feminists with physical and sensory impairments (Keith 1994; Morris 1991) as well as non-disabled feminists (Traustadóttir 1990, 1998; Walmsley 1993, 1995) have expressed their deep concern that the voices of women with disabilities are silenced, even in feminist texts, so that their lives are unknown, their contributions are unrecognized and the effects of societal discrimination and inequality are ignored (Traustadóttir 1996). Women with disabilities have described their exclusion from the women's movement in terms of its physical and/or sensory inaccessibility (Israel 1985; Owen 1986, 1988) but the movement has also been criticized for ignoring or misunderstanding the issues facing women with disabilities (Keith 1992; Morris 1991, 1996; Walmsley 1993, 1995) and relegating them to the status of the 'other'.

Some feminist writers have sought to analyse the intersection between gender and disability and to ensure that the voices of women with disabilities are heard (Fine and Asch 1988; Keith 1992; Morris 1991; 1996). In line with other feminist writers and activists, they have politicized personal experience to make sense of their experiences of prejudice and discrimination. These books have made an important contribution to enriching our understanding of women's lives in general. However, they only address the lives of women with intellectual disabilities in a very marginalized fashion.

If we believe that feminist analysis and theory should include all the diversity of women's lives and experiences, it is important to examine why women with intellectual disabilities remain so marginal in the discussions of feminists, both those who are non-disabled and feminists with physical and sensory impairments. The key factor here may be that these writers theorize from their personal experience to develop insights into what it means to be a woman and have a disability. For women who have intellectual disabilities such theorizing has been more problematic. While there are currently many women with physical and sensory impairments who research, write and publish, there are very few women with intellectual disabilities writing about their lives. Some women are not able to explore or convey their experiences at all because of the nature of their disability and others find it difficult to do so. Further the intellectual and academic communities have not been accepting of women with intellectual disabilities and developmental impairment is more likely to restrict the possibilities of expressing experiences in a way that the gatekeepers of what is 'proper' find acceptable.

We argue that just as non-disabled feminists have ignored the lives of women with disabilities, so have women with physical and sensory impairments ignored the lives of women with intellectual disabilities. This book seeks to extend the dialogue between feminists and women with disabilities by including the voices of women with intellectual disabilities.

Including women with intellectual disabilities within the disability movement

It is not only feminist writers, scholars and activists who have ignored women with intellectual disabilities. Issues of importance for these women have also for the most part been ignored by the disability movement. Almost all writing about people with intellectual disabilities has assumed the irrelevance of gender as well as other social dimensions such as social class, race, ethnicity and sexual orientation. For example, Asch and Fine (1988, p.3) state that: 'Having a disability presumably eclipses these dimensions of social experiences. Even sensitive students of disability ... have focused on disability as a unitary concept and have taken it to be not merely "master" status, but apparently the exclusive status for disabled people.' Alternatively when the gender of women with intellectual disabilities has been an issue for those around them it has frequently been constituted as a problem to be managed (Johnson 1998).

There are at least two possible reasons why issues of gender have not been regarded as important within the disability movement. First, attitudes to gender reflect prevailing discourses about intellectual disability itself. The medical discourse constituted people with intellectual disabilities as sick and in need of medical attention. The label of intellectual disability and its permutations constituted their story. Within this discourse, interest in issues affecting women were restricted to a consideration of how identified 'syndromes' and 'disabilities' expressed themselves differentially in men and women and how they affected women's sexuality. The focus on women tended to be in terms of the possible social threat they posed through their capacity to have children (Brantlinger 1995; Rose 1979; Scheerenberger 1987; Wolfensberger 1975). These 'stories' objectified women with intellectual disabilities and validated a view of them as powerless and storyless. They did not constitute the women as having an internal life or desires.

While in some countries across the world this discourse has now been displaced, it continues to have an influential, though sometimes unacknowledged, impact on many women with intellectual disabilities. The movement away from a medical discourse to one which has focused on human rights has led to an increasing focus on how people with intellectual disabilities see the world and the impact of social inequalities and discrimination on their lives. However, while the focus on rights has had important and often very positive effects for people with intellectual disabilities, it has not managed to achieve goals of equal opportunities, independent living, economic self-sufficiency and full participation (Ramcharan *et al.* 1997). Nor have the concerns of women with intellectual disabilities received emphasis within the rights literature.

Second, while there is now an extensive literature by and about women with physical and sensory disabilities which includes anthologies of essays, poetry and first-person accounts (Browne, Connors and Stern 1985; Keith 1994; Saxton and Howe 1987; Wates and Jade 1999; Wilmuth and Holcomb 1993) as well as collections of scholarly writings analysing the experiences of women with disabilities (Deegan and Brooks 1985; Fine and Asch 1988; Morris 1996; Wendell 1996), this writing has only included issues affecting women with intellectual disabilities in marginal ways. None of the major writers are women with intellectual disabilities. This obviously influences the analysis. What does it mean for the development of disability theory and practice if a large and important group – people with intellectual disabilities – are missing from it (Chappell 1998)?

This book then aims to fill a gap in the disability literature which has failed to take account of the needs and voices of women with intellectual disabilities. It makes a strong case for the importance of considering these women and their worlds as important in disability writing and action.

Including women's voices from different cultures

In developing this book we have found only two other books which have included women with disabilities from different cultures and countries (Boylan 1991; Driedger, Feika and Batres 1996). Neither of these books included women with intellectual disabilities. So there has also been a lack of diversity in the voices of women with disabilities expressed across cultures. While some anthologies of writing by women with disabilities have included women from diverse minority cultures, they have focused on the experiences of women in one particular country. Both of us come from relatively small and somewhat marginalized countries and both of us have lived extensively in cultures different to our own. We have found that the power accorded by publishers, writers and policy developers to countries such as the UK and USA has frequently left the voices of women with disabilities from other countries silenced. This has important consequences. A lack of understanding of cultural diversity may lead more wealthy and powerful countries to impose inappropriate ideologies and policies on countries where the culture is different (Kalyanpur 1996). So, for example, in countries like Slovakia a failure by external consultants to understand the history (or indeed the meanings) of intellectual disability or to hear the voices of people with intellectual disabilities may lead to inappropriate policies and judgements (Johnson and Nadazdyova 1996).

Sometimes the voices of women with intellectual disabilities from different countries can challenge us to rethink our assumptions or practices and policies in our own countries. Further, if voices of women from around the world are heard we will have more opportunities to work together and identify issues which we have in common as well as those that differentiate us (Driedger, Feika and Batres 1996). Our pictures of women's lives will become both richer and more politicized as a result of the inclusion of this group of women. Our book is a first step to engaging in a wider debate between women from different cultures about their experiences of intellectual disabilities.

Including the contribution of women with intellectual disabilities

Women with intellectual disabilities, perhaps more than other groups of women have been excluded from taking places in either private or public areas of activity in the world. In the past many have been excluded from their families during childhood and have been prohibited from forming adult relationships or families of their own. They have often been excluded from work or community involvement or their participation has been voluntary and unacknowledged. In this kind of situation it is easy to portray these women as victims. Yet, as bell hooks (1996) comments in relation to African American women, such an approach can be disempowering and does not necessarily reflect the lived experience of the women so portrayed. Many women with intellectual disabilities are central figures in their families of origin; others have become lovers and parents; still others have achieved creative and fulfilling careers and many make a contribution to the disability movement and to their own wider communities.

The stories and research in this book reveal how the personal lives of individuals are linked to and shaped by the broader social, economic and political contexts in which they live. They describe the struggle which some women have had to achieve fulfilment in their lives because of discrimination and inequalities. However, they also celebrate the strength and diversity of women with intellectual disabilities.

Writing this book

Writing this book involved a large group of women working together over an extended period of time and across the world. Finding women who wanted to participate in the project depended initially on networks of friends and colleagues in different countries. From these beginnings and the women's enthusiasm for the project, the networks grew and developed. It would have been wonderful if we could have met to discuss and shape the book together. But we were scattered across eight countries, some women spoke no English and some found it difficult to use spoken language at all. So we relied on letters, e-mails, phone conversations and in some instances personal visits to support each other.

Because some of the women with intellectual disabilities who wanted to contribute their stories were not able to do so alone, they worked collaboratively with another woman or as a member of a group. Sometimes the stories were told and then edited and sometimes the women with intellectual disabilities provided documents which then formed parts of the story.

In all instances of collaborative writing, the woman with intellectual disabilities shaped the final story and approved it as well as providing its original words. Where we used translators from another language to English, copies of the chapter were sent back to the original authors for review through an interpreter.

Behind each of the stories in this book are countless others which remain untold in the book. For example, early in December 1997 Kelley went to Prague in the Czech Republic to visit Tamara Kainova and to invite her to contribute some stories to the book. At the time Tamara attended a day centre called the Blue Door in an outlying suburb of Prague. Kelley recalls her visit:

> Tamara and I met in the staff lounge of the day centre. I have almost no Czech and she had very little English. We spent about half an hour

together sharing what we could with smiles and signs until Maria Cerna arrived to interpret for us. On the table beside her, Tamara had two enormous plastic bags filled with stories. Written on scraps of paper, some were in Russian and some in Czech. Some seemed to have been written a long time ago and others very recently. She was extremely excited at the idea of her stories being in a book and spent a lot of time going through her collection to find the ones she wanted to include. At the day centre she spent her time embroidering doilies and making woven mats. She wanted a job with money more than anything else.

This book is concerned with exploring the meanings which a group of women has given to their lives or to the lives of women with whom they have worked or lived. As such, it involves researching women's lives. In undertaking this task the contributors to the book have used a variety of different means and methods.

Autobiography/autobiographical accounts

These have been used to represent a woman and the issues which she has identified as important in her life. Some of these stories were self-initiated and were written by the woman with intellectual disabilities to share particular stories or episodes or her life, for example, Tamara Kainova. Others were initiated through discussion with a feminist researcher, friend, advocate or colleague who then assisted the woman to write an autobiographical account. As Atkinson and Walmsley (1996) describe, there are different kinds of autobiographies and this book contains stories which reflect the 'ordinariness' of women's lives and others that reveal issues where the women are seen as victims of oppression. Some of these stories focus on daily life and relationships, others are imaginative stories or accounts and still others provide an account of an individual woman's increasing politicization. Some stories cross all of these boundaries.

Case studies

Some chapters are case studies of a relationship or of an individual's life. So Rannveig Traustadóttir's account of a friendship between two young women involved her spending many hours with them, observing their relationship and talking with them about it. This participant observation provided a rich account of a friendship and allowed for an interpretation of some of the positive aspects and the difficulties involved in the relationship. Similarly, Kristjana Kristiansen observed workplaces and undertook interviews with women with intellectual disabilities who were employed there and in some instances also with families and co-workers. Both of these chapters and others which fit this category within the book aim to provide interpretations of meaning arising from rich descriptions and conversations.

Group research studies

Some chapters explore issues of importance to women with intellectual disabilities. The identified issues have arisen as concerns voiced by women with intellectual disabilities, or those raised by families, service providers or the researcher herself. The women researchers involved in this project have been motivated by a concern with the dignity and needs of the women who have participated in their study and by a desire to change the structures which have led either to oppression or to difficulties within the women's lives. In all of these chapters researchers have undertaken observations and long interviews (sometimes over an extended period of time) with small groups of participants, placed their responses within a wider context of other research and then sought to recommend changes to social structures, services and policies.

The kind of research involved falls within the ethnographic or qualitative tradition (Hammersley and Atkinson 1994; Taylor and Bogdan 1998) and we believe that the way it has been used in this book reflects how women with intellectual disabilities and women researchers are undertaking work to change social structures and to remove some of the barriers which women with intellectual disabilities have experienced.

Structure of the book

The structure of the book has been carefully developed to reflect key themes in women's lives. Within each part of the book are different styles and kinds of chapters designed to reflect the diversity within each theme. Finally the book has been structured to ensure that it is as accessible as possible to women with intellectual disabilities.

Diverse themes of the book

Our discussions with women with intellectual disabilities and feminists working with them across the world both before and during the development of this book suggest that while there are enormous differences between them there are also some common concerns and themes which run through their lives. These became the core themes of the book. Finding a place in a family (however defined), in relationships, in work and in community involvement were themes that we generated originally as important to us as individuals, but which have been validated as central to women's lives by the enthusiasm with which contributors have sought to write about their involvement in one or more of them. Of course no woman's experience is restricted to participating in one of these areas and so our distinction between them is somewhat artificial and for women particularly the boundaries between such fields remain blurred. For some women, one of these core themes is most dominant in her life while for others, some or all of them may play equally through her story. Even when a woman with intellectual disability was excluded, physically or symbolically from one or more of these ways of finding a place in the world it has often remained important to her as a dream or as a continuing experience of powerlessness and frustration.

Diverse styles in the book

We aimed to reflect the different aspects of women's lives and to do this through the way the chapters were written as well as through their content. Some chapters are personal stories written by women with intellectual disabilities. These involved varying degrees of collaboration with another woman. Other stories describe individual experiences from the 'outside' and are written by friends, family or feminist writers. Each part of the book concludes with a chapter which highlights one key issue in women's lives and reports on feminist research which has sought to increase our understanding of women's experiences. So, for example, in Part I: Finding a Place in Families, Chapter 5 by Christine Bigby explores the lives of women after their parents die. This issue has been one of growing concern to families, service providers and to women with disabilities themselves.

Diverse versions of chapters

When we asked for contributions to the book we requested that all writers use plain English as far as possible in their chapters. We were conscious, however, that many of these would remain inaccessible or difficult for large numbers of women with intellectual disabilities. So we also requested a short plain English version which appears at the beginning of each chapter. Readers can use these shortened versions as their main source of information, as a starting point to then read the longer versions or can dip from the short version into the longer one. We know that many of women with intellectual disabilities will still find the book difficult to negotiate. We hope that they will receive support to read it and that we will find more accessible ways of using the material.

Contested issues

In developing this book we have had to confront a number of challenging and contested issues. This section outlines these issues and briefly explores how we, with the other women contributors, have struggled to find ways through them. We are conscious that we have not always been successful.

Language and labelling

Different cultures use different words to refer to the women who are the focus of the book. Even in countries which use English the labels are different and politically contested (Eayrs, Ellis and Jones 1993). In the UK currently, 'learning difficulties' is the preferred term while in the USA 'developmental disabilities' is commonly used. In earlier days, and sometimes even now, people in the USA use the term 'mental retardation'. In Australia and New Zealand, the most common term is 'intellectual disabilities' and after much deliberation and discussion we have chosen to use that label. First, as far as we could gather, it is the term that is most likely to be understood in both English and non-English speaking countries. As this is an international book, this was an important issue. Second, we found the other terms like 'learning difficulties' and 'developmental disabilities' problematic as they had specific and different meanings in other cultures. Different parts of the disability movement have different ways of referring to their members. Some parts of the movement, like the Independent Living Movement and the people who use the social model of disability use the term 'disabled people' and distinguish between impairment and disability (Barnes and Mercer 1996; Oliver 1996). They see the disability as the result of the societal structures which exclude and discriminate against people who have impairments. Thus they refer to themselves as disabled people to emphasize that the discrimination and the disability come from outside. However, other groups of people with disabilities view the term 'disabled people' as offensive. Some people have fought for a long time to gain recognition of themselves as 'people first' and are resistant to the term 'disabled people'. We have chosen to use 'people first language' as it is consistent with the views of many of our contributors. This certainly does not mean however that we do not support the social model of disability.

Representativeness

We were concerned that this book may be misinterpreted as somehow seeking to represent all women with intellectual disabilities. This has not been the intention of any of the contributors. Rather, the book is based on a view that there is no homogeneous group of women who are labelled as having intellectual disabilities. The lives of the contributors challenge prevailing stereotypes about women with intellectual disabilities and reveal that, like other women, they lead diverse and rich lives and also struggle to achieve fulfilment. The book consists of stories told and written by women who believed they have something important to say to others in their communities.

Othering

We were also concerned that by editing a book about women with intellectual disabilities we were continuing an objectifying approach to their lives; continuing to make them 'the other' by differentiating them as a group. However, women with intellectual disabilities have not had a voice. Their concerns have not been heard. We believe it is important that they are heard and hopefully then they will be included as a visible presence in the work of other women.

Ownership

More difficult to face was the possible accusation of 'colonization': that is, as academics we were taking away the stories of women with intellectual disabilities and they would then lose ownership of them. We anguished for a long time over this issue. This challenge focuses on 'who owns the story?' By placing women's stories in an academically acceptable framework were we serving our own interests and not theirs? Were we precluding them from owning their own publication and doing their own writing by the production of this book? There are no easy answers to this challenge. The women who have contributed to this book have done so because they wanted to. Some of them had prepared their stories long before the book was initiated in the hope that some day there would be a chance to publish them. Other women were paid for their contributions which remained under their control. Women contributors told their stories in the way that suited them, negotiated editing with their collaborator (when necessary) and gave final approval to the form and words of the chapter. They did control the copy although they did not control the development of the book as a whole. For many of these women this book offered an opportunity to begin to talk with other women about their issues. If it also serves as a site for debating how women with intellectual disabilities write, own and share their stories, then we see that as a productive outcome.

Accessibility

We were very concerned that books are not a readily accessible way for women with intellectual disabilities to hear stories. As described earlier, we have sought to increase the book's accessibility by ensuring that there is a plain English version at the beginning of each chapter. However, this problem remains an insoluble one for some women if written media are used. Yet, not to write the book would silence women who wanted to use this forum to raise their voices. We were also conscious that part of the reason for writing the book was to confront and challenge others who had either not considered the issues affecting women with intellectual disabilities or who had constituted their gender as a problem. We believe this is a legitimate and important enterprise and so did the contributors.

We hope that this book challenges, excites and interests you as a reader and that the questions which it has raised for us in its preparation remain with you as you read the chapters.

PART I

Finding a Place in Families

Introduction

Traditionally the family has been seen as the centre of a woman's life, a place of privacy, continuity, stability and refuge where women work to provide warmth and shape future generations (Andersen 1993). Within this traditional view family members are seen as interdependent and having a continuing responsibility for each other. However, for many feminists the family, as an institution, is a contested site. They have challenged the traditional view of family life as one which is beneficial to all its members: 'By demystifying some of the cloaking ideologies which have surrounded the family, feminist approaches to the family have uncovered conflict and violence in the family as potentialities within its structure rather than as individual aberrations from the norm' (Wearing 1996, p.127). They have revealed economic and social oppression of women in families, explored abuse and family violence and examined how the institution of family has restricted women's life opportunities in the public sphere.

Part I of this book, which focuses on women with intellectual disabilities finding a place in families, reflects within its stories and accounts many of the divergent and conflicting views of families contained in the wider literature. It is particularly concerned with relationships within families of origin and so it seemed appropriate as the first part of the book. We also chose the family as the first issue because our discussions with women with intellectual disabilities revealed its continuing centrality in many of their lives. These women also revealed an enormous diversity in their views and experiences of families and family life.

However, the strength of the bonds between family members, whether acknowledged or not and whether positive or negative (or somewhere in between), is a constantly reiterated theme in the chapters in this part of the book.

In Chapter 1 Tamara writes movingly of her parents and her grandparents in the Czech Republic and reveals the important places they hold in her life. However, as a daughter with a disability she also sees it as important to earn the love of others around her by 'being optimistic and happy' and she writes with regret of the effect of her disability on her family members. This chapter contains both the love and interdependence integral to traditional views of family life and the necessity to conform to family values and attributions in order to have a place.

In Chapter 2 Rosemary brings into sharp relief both the power of families to reject members and their ongoing interdependence and responsibility. Verna's early loss of her family did not prevent her from a lifelong yearning for her mother and for a place to 'belong'. Her late life joy in being reunited with family members is deeply moving and her acceptance by them, particularly by her sister, is interwoven with her now unchallenged right to acknowledgement as 'family'.

Chapter 3 documents the lives of a mother and her daughter in Slovakia as they struggle to find a way of being together over time. It brings into sharp focus the problems which people confront when needed supports act to separate family members. The story comes from Janka's mother primarily and her account is one of constant struggle to find services and support. Janka's life dreams also reveal the difficulties which women with intellectual disabilities still confront in finding a place in their communities and acceptance as adult women.

Missy Morton's account of unhappy families (Chapter 4) provides a counterpoint to the positive family experiences of some of the other women in this book. The pain and despair expressed by Louise, both because of her own abuse and its consequences for her own parenting, is a testament not only to the power that can be exercised within the institution of the family against its members but also to the love which many parents feel for their children.

Finally, in Chapter 5 Christine Bigby explores the continuing import-ance of family in the lives of women with intellectual disabilities as they grow older. The ambivalence that many of us feel towards the institution of the family is clearly revealed. For some older women, the death of parents is liberating and an escape into new life and activities. For others (and sometimes for the same women over time) the loss of people who care for and about them leaves them lonely and unsupported.

These chapters reveal the diversity and complexity of family life for women with intellectual disabilities. They emphasize the importance and diversity of relationships at an individual family level. However, they also show how the lives of individuals and of families are shaped by much larger forces. These include attitudes and values about intellectual dis-abilities, women and families, cultural factors, access to appropriate services and the political and economic climate in which a family is sited.

CHAPTER ONE

What is Life Like?

Tamara Kainova with Maria Cerna, Czech Republic

I am 38 years old and live in Prague. I live with my parents and my sister. I go to a day centre but I would like to have a paid job because then I could earn money. I find it hard to walk and sometimes life has been difficult for me. But I try to stay happy. I like to tell stories about my life. I write about myself and my family. I like writing about the country where we go on holidays, the plants and the garden and what life is like for me. There are eight stories in my chapter. I hope you like them.

Who am I?

My name is Tamara Kainova. I am 38. I went to a special school for eight years and I took courses at evening school for four years. I took courses in maths, Czech literature, civics and English language. I learned colors, counting, numbers, days and months. Now my sister and I study at evening school. Every week we look forward to school very much. It makes our friends and us very happy.

I worked in a sheltered workshop for ten years, now I am attending a daily program in the Blue Key [a day program for people with intellectual disabilities] in Prague. I like weaving best, especially making carpets and ceramics. I am on the waiting list for a placement at a sheltered workshop. I would prefer that because I would like to earn money. I speak Czech, Russian and a little bit of English. I would like to speak English well but I don't know how to learn it. I live in a family with my mother and father and my sister Tatjana. We have two dogs: Simona and Vaska. Why did I choose the name Vaska? Vaska is as beautiful as Vasilica Preckcasna [Vasilica is a very beautiful princess in a Russian fairytale]. I like traveling. I have visited many spas in the Czech Republic. I have traveled to Russia (Moscow) several times, to Spain, Switzerland (with my aunt) and to Germany (as part of evening school).

A family film

I think that our family story is like a film about life. I'll tell you about my sister Tatjana our good parents and myself. We've got excellent parents. They help us and they take care of us. Our disaster was caused by a Slovak nuclear factory. There was bad contamination there. My sister and I are ecological victims. In the past we have been badly off. Once we spent half a year in a special boarding school in Jedlicka's institution. They told our parents: 'Your daughters will never read or write or count.' But our parents took us home and sent us to a special school. We finished years eight and nine there. Tatjana studied to be a dressmaker then. She can sew on a sewing machine and she can knit, crochet and cook. She learned all of these things with our mother's help. I can't do as much but I'm fond of studying foreign languages. I try to play the piano and every evening I like to write short stories about my life. I'll tell you one of my stories. It's called 'Chicory'.

Chicory

Next to the road, in the field, on a little hill, there is a nice flower. It stands there in the rain, the sweltering heat and in the hot sun, all night and all day. It's got nice light-blue flowers. It looks like a blue-eyed woman, holding a toddler in her arms and waiting for her husband. They call this flower, 'chicory'. I'm chicory too. I've been waiting all my life for a miracle: like a fairytale prince. Healthy people are busy and not full of trouble. And they are free. But I've been waiting and waiting. I'm chicory forever.

What is life like?

My dear mother was seriously ill this year so I was not able to travel anywhere. I think that you should not hope for anything because then you are not disappointed later. It is better to be always happy and then you are never disappointed. It is better to be a happy person in the world. People round me have to be glad that I am happy like an actress because then they can be fond of me and be happy because of me. I am an optimist who knows that I must keep merry and make people happy. I read something about that in a journal. And I also watched two movies with Irena Pavlaskova [a Czech film director]. Many people say everything is okay but they don't think it is really. I am happy that I came to this conclusion myself although it is so difficult for me. Everything is hard for me and I can do things only slowly. Now I know that life is not easy. I am not giving advice. I am giving only my ideas. Yes it is so.

Fall

'It is already a fall, there is September outside a window…' this is what our Russian granny sang for us. I loved my granny. She had a problem with her flat for a long time. I remember my granny and her beautiful songs. Our father knows many Czech songs, and we were also taught Czech national songs at school. We were healthy and happy. Granny liked it when we invited her to come and see us. She was interested in things here and she watched everything. Granny has one other granddaughter whose name is Natasha. I was her first granddaughter. Our granny was a teacher. My sister Tatjana would like to be a teacher too. But my sister Tatjana is handicapped like me. Granny liked to be with lots of other people.

We like having a good time: at Christmas or somebody's birthday or when somebody comes to see us. It's a wonderful atmosphere and everyone is happy. Our little dogs are merry too although they bark too much because of the kind of dog they are – Spitzes. Spitzes bark too much. Imagine the situation. Simona a-a-a, Vasenka av-av-av. I look out from our balcony and I remember. 'It is already a fall, there is September outside a window…' It reminds me of our granny and her singing. It is a great pity for us that we are handicapped. But what can we do about it? It is our fate. I learned one song to play on the piano. 'That's our Czech song.' I love this song. It is so nice, so nice. I often croon a song, and then I feel happy.

Why do I write?

Once upon a time when I was a small girl I didn't know anything and nobody understood what I said. I was sad when people didn't understand me. I got so upset that I didn't even want to fight and overcome the problem. But now I am an adult, I know that it is important for people to understand me. I so much want this. I would like to be able to communicate with friends. And so I decided to write. Whoever wants to can read my short stories. I'm an adult but I can't write stories for adults. So I decided to write stories for people like me and then I can communicate with them. I have a younger sister, Tatjana. She is also disabled like me. But she can walk and talk better than me. Tatjana helps a lot at home and I write stories.

There are lots of unhappy people all over the world who were born disabled or became disabled later on. But there are also many people who like to moan 'I am ugly, my legs are too short, my nose is too long.' They are always in a bad mood and are awful. I'm not going to write my stories for these people. All our lives Tatjana and I have had to exercise to keep our balance. We have had to exercise, walk and do physiotherapy. We have really had enough of it but what can we do? Once we were patients in Botkin's clinic in Moscow. There were good doctors there and they all wanted to help us. We had lots of different kinds of treatments. Our speech therapist was Larissa. She was very nice and she was not much older than we are. Tatjana and I think that Larissa helped us a lot because we started to talk better and better. Thank God!

Childhood memories

When I was little I knew very little about myself. Now when I look at family films and think about my childhood I am sad and ashamed though I also laugh at how I couldn't do anything. In one of our films Tatjana is trying to walk on her knees in the snow but I am just sitting and sitting on the toboggan. Why was I sitting? Why was I so silly? Why didn't I try to walk like my sister? I am so sorry that I can't go back in time. My mother has told me that everything was much more complicated than I think and that

I shouldn't torture myself by things in the past. We look at old films and we laugh a lot because they seem like a fairytale. In fact my childhood was like a fairytale. When we look at old films we are both happy and unhappy at once.

Our grandpa

All his life he was a merry man. Grandpa always welcomed us warmly when we went to visit him. Grandpa liked to talk to daddy. Our grandpa used to go to a pub where he played cards with his friends but he was always at home by 6 pm. He was very happy when we came to visit him. Once we made a film and in it I was filmed sitting on his lap. At Grandpa's there were always lots of friends. He was a great gardener. He knew every-thing about plants and he gave advice to everyone. At his house there were lots of books in a big bookcase. He liked to read a lot.

My sister Tatjana traveled to see Grandpa when she had school holidays. My grandpa taught me a Czech song: 'Why did the owl hoot so much?' Then we sang it together. I think grandpa followed politics with interest. I was very happy when we went for walks in the park and talked together.

Grandpa was the father of my father. I think he was a shoemaker, but he was a laborer for sure. He liked to watch hockey on TV and he barracked mainly for Pardubice. He liked to do crosswords.

Grandpa was very unhappy that we are disabled. But we exercised every morning from our childhood. We are disabled because we lived in Slovakia in Ziar and Hronow where there was a bad factory where my parents worked. Nobody knew then what caused our disability.

We always came to Grandpa at Christmas. I liked to go there a lot. When my aunt from Russia visited us, we went to see Grandpa. He was surprised that I could translate from Russian. He listened carefully and said I was a champion.

Our Little Rock in spring

We are at our weekend house where it is very beautiful. Lots of plants grow on our Little Rock, which is very ancient and beautiful. There are different kinds of cacti, shrubs and perennials. These are beautiful tiny flowers last-ing many years. Now everything is in bloom.

Our parents are keen gardeners and they like to look at the countryside and at our rock. They admire every flower that comes up. Sometimes I am in a very bad or strange mood. Then I get such a craving to look at our rock with all its spring plants in bloom. There are our favorite lewises showing off their pale pink blooms and the bluebells with their deep blue. There is a lot of bluebells, they look at the sun when it shines and they give off a blue sheen. A lot of the ground is covered by clumps of low pink, white and red flocks. The tulips and the hairy 'koniklec' are now finished. Our whole rock is covered with flowers, cacti and grasses. Soon the opurrcia will surprise us with its gentle flowers. It has big and bad thorns, but it also has gently yellowish translucent flowers. There is a path made out of huge flat stones so it is possible to walk among the flowers. Not far from the rock is a patch of irises. These have awesomely beautiful flowers. But they need lots of work. They call them the 'orchids of gardens'. That's what I call them too. I think that orchids are the queens of flowers and the irises are the kings. Or at least a prince.

CHAPTER TWO

Discovering a Sister

Rosemary West, Australia

Rosemary grew up believing that she was an only child. She became a journalist, writing stories for the newspapers. Her mother grew old and became ill, unable to remember very much at all or to know what was happening around her. Then one day Rosemary received a phone call. It was from a staff member at a large institution for people with intellectual disabilities. The staff member said that Rosemary had a sister, Verna, who had spent all of her life since she was a child in institutions.

Rosemary found that Verna had been born when her mother was very young. Her mother felt unable to care for the baby and she was not married at the time. The baby was given to foster parents. Later a decision was made that she had an intellectual disability and she was placed in an institution. Verna very much wanted to find her family. She especially wanted to meet her mother.

Rosemary and her children met Verna at the institution. They celebrated coming together and Verna's birthday. Rosemary found that Verna was in many ways like other women in her family. It was not always easy for Rosemary. Sometimes she felt anxious about sharing her things with Verna, sometimes she wished that her sister was different. But she also saw lots of good things in her sister, her laughter and joy and her strength. Later Verna met her mother and they spent some wonderful times together although Verna's mother was often unsure who Verna was. Rosemary helped find Verna a place to live in the community. She left the institution and came to the city to live.

Verna and Rosemary see each other on a weekly basis. They have some good times together. Rosemary has become Verna's advocate and helps to make sure that her rights are protected. Sometimes this is hard work and takes a lot of time. Sometimes too, Rosemary is tired or busy with her life and finds it hard to find time for Verna. But she is discovering what it means to be a sister.

September 12 1992. It was late when I got home from work. I pushed aside a list of telephone messages and heated up some baked beans.

'You really should return this message, it sounds interesting,' said my daughter Kate. 'It's from a woman at a Beechworth hospital. She won't tell me what it's about and she says it doesn't matter how late you ring.'

'I'll ring back tomorrow,' I replied. But Kate insisted, 'She said to ring tonight.'

I finished the beans and picked up the phone, just after 11 pm. Nurse Brenda Fitzgerald of Beechworth Hospital answered my call. She said she was ringing on behalf of a client about a family search matter. That did not strike me as unusual. As a journalist I had written many such stories and they never failed to move me. But Brenda went on to ask about my mother: 'Is she living? Where? Does she have Alzheimer's disease?' As I answered her questions, I had the oddest sensation, as if I was about to be hit by a tidal wave. This time Brenda was talking about *my* family's story.

'Has anyone ever told you that you have a sister?' she asked.

'A sister!' It was all I could say. My world, my life, my history was suddenly swept up and whirled around my head, never to be the same again.

I sat down, stunned. I had been raised as an only child, loved, cosseted and indulged. Now there was another. My mother, who had always been so stylish and so proper, had in 1924, aged 18 and single, given birth to a baby girl.

My sister's name, Brenda told me, was Verna Rae West. Brenda steadily ran through the names and dates she had discovered in her 18 months' search through the births, deaths and marriages records, allaying any doubts I might have had about this revelation.

But Beechworth? I recalled it as an asylum for the criminally insane. 'It is now a centre for intellectual disability services,' Brenda told me.

'Does my sister have a disability?'

'Probably not to begin with,' said Brenda, 'but she has spent her life in institutions. She's just a 'dear old lady' of 67,' she said, adding that 'she has her tantrums.' She went on to say that 'her only activities are walking and smoking' and she didn't think she had teeth.

I felt overwhelmed and inadequate. 'My life is chronically overloaded, I fear that I may not have enough to give my sister,' I confided to Brenda. 'You will be surprised how much you have to give,' she said.

As I talked I couldn't help feeling sorry for myself. Other people found sisters with whom they could share interests and experiences. How would I relate to my sister? I had watched those patient good women, out with their disabled sons and daughters, sisters and brothers. I had admired their quiet fortitude and patient strength and I felt that I lacked these qualities.

How could I bridge the difference in our lives and our selves? How could I begin to make up what my sister had lost? 'You can't,' said Brenda. 'And it's not your fault. Besides there is no need to worry, she has a good life now. She is happy and well cared for. But she would love to have a family. If she had someone to send her a card for her birthday and Christmas, that would be wonderful.'

'What can I do next? I'll write her a letter. Can she read and write?'

'No,' said Brenda. 'She's probably never been taught.'

I hung up the phone and wept for a sister who had spent her life in institutions and who never had a family to send her a birthday card. And for my mother, who used to tell me how much she had always wanted a little girl. She had miscarried five pregnancies before me and regarded my birth as a miracle.

'You are my sun, moon and stars,' my mother used to say with her beautiful smile. I would imitate her in babytalk and she would laugh. 'I love you more than all the tea in China,' she would say, tickling me. 'I could eat you all up,' she would say, pretending to bite my toes. I would laugh deliriously.

My mother collected beautiful things and passed them on to me: grandmother's silver teapot, grandfather's cedar bookcase, great-grandmother's cedar balloon-backed chairs. I always seemed to be surrounded by heirlooms.

I was sent to a private school and to university, and every small achievement was heaped with praise. Now I had a sister who had had no family life and who could not read the letter I wanted to write.

I was swept along by the tide of events, with no time to stop and reflect. In a quite uncanny way, this experience tied in with many of the social issues I had covered in my career as a journalist. In some ways it seemed as if my writing life had been a preparation for it. Invisible strands led back to many of the stories and people who had touched me most deeply. Stories I had written about illegitimacy and the tragedy of relinquishment, adoption and adoption reunions, children's rights to know their origins, deinstitutionalisation and disability all now felt like lessons. In some ways I knew so much and yet all my knowledge was not much use to me. What I needed to know was how to be a sister. Many readers of my articles had sent me letters to tell me how the stories I had written or edited had helped them through difficult decisions or situations. Now it was my turn and I would have to do my best to meet my sister's needs and to right the terrible wrong she had suffered.

To this there came a salutary caution from my daughter Mahony. 'To you it may seem she's had a terrible life, but it may not seem like that to her,' she said. 'It's her life and to her it may seem just as valid as yours does to you.'

Mahony had checked Verna's star sign. 'She is a Virgo, quite different from you. She will be solid, earthy.'

I looked around my living room, stacked with the family antiques, each woven into family legend. It occurred to me, first, that half of them belonged to this unknown sister and, second, that I did not want to share them. I felt ashamed of my meanness which was, I suppose, my first taste of sibling rivalry.

Again Mahony offered relief. 'Don't get ahead of yourself,' she said. 'She may not want them.' And so it turned out. Verna liked the bright modern pieces from my mother's kitchen and she liked family photographs, which were easily copied.

Next morning, I was late to work and sent an e-mail message to my editor, apologizing and explaining with a brief run through of the story, ending with the request 'Don't say anything to me in public, I'm a bit volatile.' A few minutes later she came and perched on the edge of my desk. 'How amazing,' she said. 'I suppose it's too soon to suggest this, but if you are prepared to be really honest, it would make a wonderful story.' So for the next fortnight, I was able to indulge myself in the luxury, for a journalist, of discovering all I could about my sister's life. At the same time I was able to cast my mind back to things my mother had said that had not made sense at the time. Gradually, the pieces of the jigsaw puzzle of our family history began to come together in a different, more satisfying way. The first part of this chapter is largely drawn from this story.

Verna was born in a large Melbourne hospital and she spent her first few weeks with our mother in one of the old church refuges where 'unmarried' mothers were sent to conceal their pregnancies and afterwards to breastfeed for six weeks or so until they were ready to return to the community with or (mostly) without their babies. From the refuge, my mother took Verna to a home the nuns found for them. At two months, however, Verna was made a state ward and my mother went back to her home in the country. The reason given on the form for this relinquishment was curtly 'no means', but in those days this was the accepted reason for placing an ex-nuptial child whose family could not keep her. At six months Verna was boarded out with a foster mother. We may never know how long she stayed with this woman or why she was not speaking by the age of five – her records for those years are missing – but in January 1930 she was admitted to an institution for children with intellectual disabilities on the private request of our grandmother. Her diagnosis was CMD (congenital mental deficiency) 'without epilepsy'. The prognosis was 'unfavorable'. The file described her behavior as 'infantile'. Medical notes accompanying the diagnosis were chilling: 'no normal intelligence, can only say a few words, dirty in habits'. I wondered what was then considered normal for a motherless five year old.

Verna's file records began with her admission to the institution for children with intellectual disabilities. There is a photograph of a pretty little girl, with a cropped orphanage haircut and a white pinafore. It is a sad, defiant little face, eyebrows furrowed and lower lip jutting. It reminded me of my granddaughter in a grumpy mood.

In the institution, the tone of the reports became kinder. Verna seemed to be improving. After four months, my sister was said to be 'considerably brighter. Does not speak but attempts to join with others in little games.'

By March 1931, Verna, aged six, was said to be 'much improved. Speaks well and helps with small things in the ward.' That was a month after my mother married my father. At the age of 13 she was transferred to another institution. A few months later she was visited by a Church of England nun at the behest of my grandmother who left her address and the direction that 'no other relatives [were] to be notified at any time'.

According to the file, by the following year, Verna was 'becoming unmanageable' in that she was tending to 'wander' from the ward. She was a 'fair worker in the kitchen but [had] to be watched all the time. She [had] become a big girl and [was] liable to fits of temper.' As I read these file notes, I got the impression that my sister's defiance may have helped her to survive. What 14 year old would not have fits of temper if she were permanently confined to her ward?

In January 1941, a month after my birth, Verna was transferred to Beechworth. She spent the next 51 years of her life there, about an hour's drive from where my mother lived for most of her life. There the tests to which she was subjected told as much about the system as about her.

She was described as a 'healthy, well-grown girl of about 16 years of age' who 'cannot read or write. Cannot give the similarities between an apple and an orange. Has no plan for finding a purse in a circular field.' Then tellingly, 'Takes very little interest in any of the tests. Does not give the impression of trying very hard. Turns her head to one side, drums with fingers of her right hand, remains silent in response to most questions. Appears to be an imbecile.'

My daughter Bronwen suggested that Verna might have been refusing to co-operate with the tests. 'They were the imbeciles,' she said. I thought back to when I was 16, unhappily incarcerated in boarding school. There I subverted the authorities in small ways, but I never dared defy them, as my sister must have done. I was beginning to admire her.

Some of the entries showed how normal behavior could become problematic in an abnormal setting. One, at about the age of 25, read, 'Had a problem with Verna. She is overly fond of men.'

As the years went by the file increasingly dealt with reports of Verna's disruptive behavior and resulting injuries. First, there was the odd scratch, the odd bruise, altercations with other patients. One report records that her left leg was badly scalded when another resident threw boiling water on her. Another says her face was bruised after she attacked one of the kitchen staff.

The file records that Verna enjoyed outings at Easter and Christmas and that her tantrums often happened when others were going out or having visitors. The words 'attention-seeking' appear frequently. The reports are like snapshots. One incident, not so long ago, recorded that she 'threw a tantrum today. Abusive. Rude to other patients. As soon as she was given attention she settled quickly.'

As a result of the Intellectually Disabled Person's Services Act (1986) each resident has a general service plan drawn up covering every aspect of their personal, social and health development and care. Verna's disruptive behavior has made it necessary for her to take major tranquilizers, but the plan was to teach her other techniques for dealing with her emotions and to reduce her medication. The 1989 plan noted that 'Verna would like to know if she has any living relatives' and that the social workers had been asked to help. It was not, however, the social workers who found us, but a nursing aide who, acting on her own initiative and largely in her own time, had found us, along with ten other families.

The weekend after the first phone call, my daughter Bronwen and I drove to Beechworth. Brenda, the nursing aide, came with us. 'I'm not going to give up on this now,' she said. As we swept past the old gatehouse and down the drive, staff members smiled and waved as if we were the royal family. Past a preserved section of the old brick and bluestone wall, past the old asylum building where Verna lived when she first came in 1941 – and there was Verna, sitting in the sunshine on the porch of her home, beaming as if it was her very first Sunday.

We held out our arms to each other and called each other sister. There were warm hugs all around as I introduced her to her niece. I was, however, too ashamed of my reaction to write about her appearance at the time.

In truth, I felt quite shocked and a little appalled. Despite the difference in our lives, I had expected someone who would be like us. And there was Verna, with her toothless smile, her gray hair, her clumsy, shuffling gait and her uneducated country accent. In fact, as Mahony had predicted, almost everything about Verna was different from the way I had been brought up to be.

Brenda and the staff were obviously proud of how she was dressed for that first meeting, in black stirrup pants and a fairisle jumper but I wondered how on earth my mother would cope with a daughter wearing trousers. Even then I always put on a skirt to visit my mother in her dementia hostel.

'How's my mum?' Verna wanted to know. 'Our mother is very old,' I said, to caution her against expecting too much. 'She has lost much of her memory.'

'Poor mumma, poor mumma,' said Verna, distressed. 'I do worry about her.' So this sister was another worrier. We are a family of worriers. My earliest memory of my grandmother was of her closed, worried face. And my mother too had this look at some private moments. I wonder how many of those worried looks were linked to my missing sister.

It was a huge relief to see that my sister's home was quite pleasant and her staff caring and compassionate. With pride she showed us around a large living room with comfortable leather Jason recliners and a TV, and a sleeping ward partitioned into about 40 individual pine-lined cubicles.

On her cupboard she had only a photograph of herself and a plastic icon of the Virgin Mary, mother and child. I gave her a family photo taken on Mother's Day, which I had framed. She kissed it and put it on her cupboard. 'My family,' she said. She had a toy tiger on her bed and I asked if she liked cats.

One of my first impulses had been to give her a cat. 'No woman in our family could live without a cat,' I had said to Kate. But she turned out to have a beautiful cat of her own. It began as the ward cat, but she had made it her own by feeding and loving it. It strolled up and said miaow to us as we talked in the sunshine outside the converted portable school buildings that had been Verna's home for the past seven years. 'Let's go for a drive down the street,' said Verna. So we went and had pies and cream cakes. Verna ate single-mindedly, hunched over her plate, without looking up until she had finished.

As we sat at that little table in the sun outside the Beechworth Bakery, Brenda told me how concerned Verna was about her appearance, how particular in her choice of clothes to wear. It was only a few years since residents at the institution were dressed in drab government-issued institution garb. But since the extension of government pensions to people in institutions and with the advent of government policies of deinstitut-ionalisation and normalisation, Verna had been taken shopping for her clothes in a nearby city. 'You're a beautiful person, Verna West,' said Brenda, affirmatively, and Verna beamed.

I, to my shame, could only wonder how either of them could possibly believe such a thing. But I was also beginning to see through Brenda's eyes, to appreciate that with her insouciant charm and good humor, her fine bone structure and her joyful smile, my sister had her own distinctive but very real beauty which stood out in an institution in which facial disfigurement was common. With teeth, I reckoned, she would have been a beauty in any company. And her gregarious personality, her robust character and her confidence enhanced her appearance. Furthermore, when Verna is at family gatherings her pleasure is infectious and we all have fun, which has not always been the case in our family.

Back at the institution, Verna's unit manager took us all into his office and handed us a four-inch thick file, warning that we might find some of the language distressing and that anyone who used such language today would be thrown out of the service. He and other staff were at pains to reassure me that Verna had had a good life. At this institution, they said, there had been none of the abuses and scandals that bedeviled other institutions.

Walking in the grounds we met a retired nurse, a reassuringly kind, ample and good-humored woman who remembered working with Verna as far back as 1965. From then until about 1985, the nurse recalled, Verna was in a crowded psychiatric ward with 48 of the most aggressive and violent people. 'Not because she was bad herself, but they used to put some of the good ones in to help keep order,' she said. 'Verna was one of the half-a-dozen workers who helped the staff by scrubbing floors, making beds, and helping with the other patients,' she said. 'She was a great help.'

'The beds were so close you could not get between them to make them,' the nurse said. 'What about the nights?' I asked. 'Did the patients attack each other?' 'Yes, but you don't have to worry about Verna. She was a good strong girl and a good fighter. It was survival of the fittest.'

'What about sexual abuse?'

'You don't have to worry about that either,' she said. 'If any dirty old men came to the ward, Verna would take to them with a broom.' She could also remember Verna asking, 'Where's my mummy?' as far back as 1965. 'She was a little bit childish, and when things got tough, she would ask for her mummy. We used to say 'Mummy's gone to Heaven, you will see her one day. And she would accept that.'

That day, as we were leaving, my daughter Bronwen said to her, 'Verna, we're so glad you kept asking for us. We're really proud of you for not giving up hope of finding us. Because if you had, we would never have known you at all.'

I gave Verna some more pictures and for weeks she carried them about with her in a large manila envelope. The unit manager said she was much happier after our visit and her behavior was less disruptive, except that she came to his office about six times a day to ask when she was going to Melbourne to meet her mother.

The following Sunday we had a birthday party for Verna at a country restaurant halfway between Melbourne and the institution. Her spontaneous joy was something most of us leave behind in childhood. She blew out the 68 candles on her cake gustily and led the singing of 'Happy Birthday' to herself twice. She joined in the three cheers and 'For She's a Jolly Good Fellow' and clapped her hands whenever she felt like it. I racked my brains for a clapping rhyme and came up with 'Handy Pandy'. Verna picked it up quickly. She had a way of laughing and throwing her hand up just like our mother did. 'Isn't she marvelous?' said the waitress, who spent 15 minutes placing and lighting the candles. 'I hope I'm as good as that when I'm her age.'

While I dithered over the menu, Verna made up her mind instantly, and would not be persuaded to drink orange juice at the beginning of the meal when she wanted coffee. After the meal she got up and danced in time to the music. Despite her shuffling gait, she danced gracefully with a long step and a sure rhythm. My daughter danced with her and then my son-in-law. 'Mumma, I want my mumma,' she crooned.

Already the pieces of our family history were beginning to fit together better than before. A week after meeting Verna, I found that a dear aunt in another state had known but kept my mother's secret. 'I didn't even tell my husband,' she said. My mother had told my aunt of her 'pretty little baby'.

My mother had declined Verna's father's offer of marriage, though the wardship records show that when Verna became a state ward at two months of age mother was still considering the offer. He paid maintenance for some years, but then came a time, my aunt said, when he 'would not pay maintenance and our mother could not afford to pay'. My aunt said, 'Then they decided the little girl was mentally retarded and they sent her to the institution.' It could have been a convenient diagnosis. Dr Shirley Swain, the Deakin University historian who had chronicled some of the institutions that dealt with ex-nuptial children, said for a child whose family could not pay maintenance and whose foster family did not want to keep her, there would have been pressure for a transfer to the mental health system where there was no obligation to pay.

My aunt was relieved to tell me the story and very glad that Verna was in touch. 'I have often thought about that poor little babe,' she said. It was as if we had all been haunted by that terrible secret and now that it was broken, it was a weight off her shoulders. I could only guess at what it must have been like for my mother. I told her about it without being too direct. 'Mother,' I said, 'there is a special friend who wants to visit you. Her name is Verna, and you knew her when she was a little baby.'

'Oh,' my mother said. 'Was she a firstborn baby?'

'Yes.'

'And is she a little girl now?'

'No, she is grown up now. She is a little bit retarded.'

'Oh,' said my mother, sympathetically, and a shadow passed across her face. 'It's so sad when they turn out like that isn't it?'

The following weekend I stood with two of my daughters in trepidation outside the picket fence of my mother's dementia hostel while Verna and Brenda waited in the car. How would my confused, 86-year-old mother receive this daughter she had denied for so long? It seemed to me that she had structured her life around the need to validate the sacrifice she had made of her own suppressed maternity and of her daughter. We silently hugged each other, then in we went. My mother was waiting, her face bright with anticipation. The hostel staff had been preparing her.

'Are the others in the car?' she asked.

'You have a special visitor,' I told her. 'A special friend called Verna. You haven't seen her since she was a little baby.'

'Fancy that,' said mother. 'Where is she?' So Kate went out and ushered Verna in. 'Hello mumma, hello mumma,' said Verna. We drew in our breaths but my mother was smiling her most beautiful smile and holding out her arms to this long-lost daughter. It was as if she too had been waiting for this moment.

'How wonderful,' she said, embracing Verna. 'You must come up and stay with me some time.'

Brenda and I exchanged looks of disbelief and relief. Verna hugged her back, then gave three little jumps for joy, like the happy child she may never have had the chance to be. Through the day, my mother was vague about who Verna was and how she was related – once she called her 'Grand-baby', another time 'little sister' – but she was in no doubt about her feelings, hugging and kissing her and holding her hand. Several times she asked me who she was and I told her, but she seemed not to hear the answer.

'A dear little girl,' she said as if, perhaps, she was seeing the child she had never known, and taking Verna's hand, so like her own, 'Dear little hand.'

She knew it was a very, very special occasion. 'What a wonderful surprise,' she said, contentedly holding Verna's hand. In the back seat of the car on the way home to dinner at my house, she said, 'I think this is the best surprise of my whole life.' 'You hold on tightly to me so I don't fall out,' said my mother, playfully. Verna needed no encouragement. 'What a lovely day,' said my mother. 'I just feel so...joyful.'

Later on the phone to my daughter, she said, 'It's been a wonderful surprise. The whole family is here now. Isn't it amazing the way we lose track of things, and then find they were there all the time?' As I said to Brenda, 'There is a knowing beyond knowing.'

Verna had no doubts. 'My mum, my mummy, my mumma, my mum,' she said. Her mother was 'really beautiful', 'just gorgeous', and 'so sweet'.

It had been a difficult decision whether and when to arrange for my sister to meet my mother and now, after all, the reunion had been deeply satisfying and a joy for both. For us all. It was a huge relief. I had, after all, done the right thing.

For the four years from Verna's move to Melbourne until my mother's death, I took Verna to visit her as often as possible: weekly or fortnightly while my mother was in Melbourne, once every four or five weeks when she was back in her country town's dementia hostel. We had a little ritual. Verna would hand our mother a bunch of flowers. Mother would admire them and ask, 'Who brought these flowers?' I would tell her 'Verna brought them,' and she would turn, smile and take Verna's hand. 'Well, Verna brought them. Aren't they lovely?' she would say. She was always charming and affectionate to Verna, though confused about her identity.

Occasionally, she would ask me, behind her hand: 'Who is this?' And when I said Verna's name, sometimes she would register and sometimes not.

Once, soon after their initial reunion, my mother suddenly and uncharacteristically became lucid, speaking clearly about the circum-stances of Verna's birth and expressing distress when I said she was living in Beechworth. 'Not in the asylum?' she wanted to know. I reassured her about the quality of Verna's care and told her that she would be coming to Melbourne soon.

Clearly and without a trace of confusion, she told me how she had 'fretted and wept' for the tiny baby she had left. She had been advised that it was better not to see her again. 'I was only 18,' she said. 'There was no way I could have worked to support a child.' She had obviously tried to be philosophical. 'Everyone makes one mistake, don't they?' she said. 'But you have to get over these things and get on with your life.'

On one visit, when she had asked and been told who Verna was, mother said she supposed she should make some plans for Verna. I asked what plans and she said she felt she should make an appointment for her to see the other one. 'The other one, oh what's her name?' She tried to remember. I came to her rescue. 'Do you mean Rosemary?' I said. 'Yes, that's right,' said mother. 'It's okay, Mum,' I reassured. 'I'm Rosemary and I've already met her.'

'Oh, that's good,' said mother, with her beautiful smile. And while I had a momentary stab of sibling rivalry at the thought that she had now remembered Verna and forgotten me, the exchange helped to reassure me that at some level of her mind she had wanted this reunion to take place.

When we met Verna the exodus of residents from Beechworth was well underway and she was one of the last to leave. She was very clear about wanting to come to Melbourne to be near her mother, but it took about a year to arrange for her to move into a pretty near-new house which she shares with three other friends from the institution. The house was bought using residents' funds and, in Verna's case, family money, and is administered by the Department of Human Services.

For the first time in her life Verna is enjoying home-cooked meals and the privacy of her own bedroom. She has a day program involving social activities, swimming, drama, gardening and art with excellent round-the-clock care from skilled and compassionate Department of Human Services staff.

She looks forward to her weekly outings with me, often no more than a meal at my home, and becomes grumpy if for some reason we miss a weekend. She particularly enjoys birthdays and Christmas dinners and visits when my daughters or granddaughters are there. After a few hours, however, she is ready to go home or, as she often puts it, 'back to the ward.'

Moving out of Beechworth has wrought a vast change for the better in Verna's life but she still thinks in institutional terms. Having spent her life in what was in its more benign aspect a hospital, her tendency to address everyone she associates familiarly with as 'nurse' is not surprising. This probably also indicates a rather bad memory, but it has saved her the bother of remembering people's names.

I do not make many demands on my sister, but I do insist she remember my name. From the beginning it grated on me to be called nurse and I would stop her and ask, 'Who am I?' And if she didn't get it right, I would tell her, 'I'm your sister.' Now she rarely has this lapse. The staff in the house feel pretty much this way too, taking pride in the fact that theirs is a healthier and more normal role than the medical model out of which Verna has, it would not be too strong to say, been rescued.

Notwithstanding this, the most burdensome part of my sisterhood with Verna has been the role I have had to assume as her advocate and protector in matters of medical and psychiatric treatment. In her dosette box when she first used to come out with me was a bewildering array of pills. A large triangular one, a little brown one, capsules, rectangular, cream, pink and mauve ones. More pills in a week's supply than I would take in a year. Plus a patch for her angina despite the fact that none of the staff in her house have ever seen her have an attack. This medication runs counter to some quite ludicrously strenuous efforts by staff to prevent medical abuse. If Verna had a headache, which she frequently did when she was upset, they were not allowed to give her an aspirin without a visit to her doctor unless I was there – fortunately family was exempt from these stringencies. This meant that when she became upset or angry she was more likely to be given a PRN (an emergency drug, usually a major tranquilizer).

Eventually I arranged for Verna, whenever possible, to see one par-ticular doctor selected by me from the local practice, instead of a different one each visit, and I made a point of attending her regular medication reviews with this doctor. Still there have been problems despite the fact that her carers are an extremely sensible bunch, dedicated to a policy of non-intervention and drug reduction where possible.

For example my worst experience was when Verna developed severe dermatitis on her arms and legs which became infected. After a bewild-ering array of unsuccessful treatments, and despite my entreaties to have her referred to a good dermatologist, her GPs and staff key worker formed the view that the problem was behavioral rather than medical and caused by her scratching rather than the itch of dermatitis. Her shins and forearms were heavily bandaged and splinted in an effort to stop her scratching.

Meanwhile Verna, driven mad by the itch, was becoming aggressive and abusive and I was afraid that she would lose her place in the community-based house and be re-institutionalized. She was taken to a psychiatrist who prescribed a new and stronger major tranquilizer and referred her to a psychogeriatric hospital for monitoring of her 'self-mutil-ation disorder'.

At this point finally, fearful that admission to a geriatric facility would prove irreversible, I put my foot down and insisted she first see the dermatologist, threatening an appeal to the Guardianship and Administration Board for backing.

Once properly treated by the dermatologist, the dermatitis cleared up within a fortnight. I was left feeling guilty for having failed to protect Verna from ten months of appalling and unnecessary discomfort which had ensued since the first outbreak of dermatitis.

The more fundamental problem, however, lies with a system in which a range of different carers with no particular expertise or experience of the medical system are encouraged to take clients to whichever doctor is on duty for minor ailments that could be treated more cheaply and safely with over-the-counter preparations from the chemist.

This is the third similar instance in which Verna's physical or personal well-being would have been threatened by medical or psychiatric treatment had I not intervened and it leads me to wonder what happens to residents of intellectual disability services who do not have pushy sisters to advocate for their interests.

I see Verna every weekend, unless I am away. Usually she visits my home for a meal, but sometimes we go out for dinner or afternoon tea or, what she likes best, organize a little family gathering.

She also enjoyed visiting our mother every weekend or fortnight before her death. When she died, Verna's grief was pure, direct and quite inspiring to watch. A carer told her on the way, but Verna came into the nursing home needing to check it out for herself.

'Hello mum, talk to me mum,' she said, although our mother had been virtually unable to speak for the previous year and had acknowledged her only by her gaze and by reaching out with her right arm. So it was the lack of these signs of life that convinced Verna that she was dead. 'She can't move her head, poor thing.' She wailed and then walked into the passage crying loudly, 'My mum's dead, my mum's dead.' For the second time she had lost her mother. It was a poignant moment for us all.

While I struggled to find expression for my grief as the practical matters of funeral arrangements pressed in on me, Verna returned to sit and cry beside our mother's bed for quite a while until eventually she asked to go home. At the viewing, she kissed our mother on the forehead and left a rose in her coffin, displaying none of the awkward uncertainty of the rest of us about contemplating this corpse who had once been our mother and grandmother, with her mouth finally sewn into an unnatural smile. 'Poor thing,' she said, 'She's cold.'

Since the funeral, when she speaks of our mother it is with sympathy and pity for her rather than for herself. In fact, Verna's complete lack of self-pity has made it easy for me to be her sister, supporter and friend, for it would have been easy for her to work on my tendency towards guilt had she felt inclined.

Sometimes, when I am tired and overburdened with family or emotional troubles, work or other commitments, her weekend visits and even the Saturday morning phone calls which she so enjoys and likes to prolong feel like too much of a burden, but I remind myself of how much they mean to her and how little they cost me and I persevere. Besides, I could not stand to have a sister and not be involved.

Often Verna rewards me with some small token of comfort and driving her home she will reach out for my hand and laugh infectiously and I will be glad we are together. Sometimes I do not feel up to making conversation and she seems to sense my mood and stays quiet herself.

'I've been good today, haven't I?' she will ask, inspiring a pang in me. 'Will you tell them I've been good for you?' she pleads.

I feel sad that she has to be good and yet the fact is that 'bad' behavior in the human services system is a threat to the pleasant lifestyle that lucky residents like Verna enjoy in the community residential units. When I ask the staff, they reassure me, but other people have even been removed from homes which they partly own for bad behavior and I am not sure just where the tolerance line lies. It will, I know, depend on many contingencies: the personalities and commitment of staff and their loyalty to Verna and to me.

In theory Verna should be able to stay in the comfort of her own home, with varying levels of departmental care, but having supported a mother and an aunt through the horrors of the aged care system, I dread the prospect that she too could be moved into a nursing home or hostel. I am constantly mindful of this in my attempts to balance the need to advocate for her needs with the need to acknowledge the professional role of the staff and to maintain their goodwill and support.

Verna's lifelong incarceration was a terrible human rights atrocity, yet for me, and probably for our mother, she may have appeared at the right time. Mother's dementia protected her from the shame and conflict she probably would have felt had she been in her right mind and I had the time and experience to provide Verna with the support and sisterhood she needs. As it is, little by little, I am discovering what it is to be a sister.

CHAPTER THREE

Coming Home

Janka and Jana Hanková with Sonja Holubková,
Slovakia

When little Janka was born she looked like a big snowflake. Her parents, Jana and Peter, loved her very much. They were students and lived with Jana's parents because they did not have a flat of their own.

When little Janka was 11 months old she got tuberculosis, a very serious illness. The doctors were not sure if she would live. And if she did, she might not be able to walk, or see and she might have an intellectual disability.

After she left the hospital little Janka went to stay in another hospital in the mountains a long way from her mother in order to get treatment. She started to walk although her right hand and leg were stiff. Later she started to see. Her mother was very pleased. But she was also sad. Her husband left her and her daughter was away. She was also very tired. Then the doctors discovered that she, too, had tuberculosis.

She was sent to a hospital near her daughter to get better.

Later they came back to Žilina together. Little Janka grew up quickly. She was very lively and it was hard to control her. When she was three Janka went to special kindergarten. There she met her friend Braňo. Janka says: 'Braňo and me have liked each other since my childhood.'

When she was older, little Janka had to go away to live in a school a long way from her home. She spent 12 years in this institution and learned to become a dressmaker. When she finally came home she had to learn to live a new life. She could not use buses or tell the time. Her mother was afraid of her. She started to go to a day centre where she met Braňo again. He said: 'I love you the way you are.' This made her happy. She said: 'Braňo gives me many presents. I always have a present for him, too. I like to give pleasure to everyone I love. I make presents for people.'

Janka goes to festivals and to a club. The people who run these are not so worried about Janka as her mother is. They help her to learn new things like using the buses, going on trips and meeting friends. Janka says, 'Now I live very well. I get on well with my mum. I like going on trips. I like hiking very much. I am glad that we can be together at the club, young people with and without disabilities. There is always a lot of fun.'

Janka would like to learn many new things: to travel alone, to manage her banking, to visit her doctor alone. And she also has a dream: 'I wish to live as ordinary people do. I want to have my own flat and my postbox with my name on it. I want to be with Braňo every day and be happy with him and love him. We still love each other and if we weren't disabled we would marry. He would go to work and I would too.'

Our story begins in 1978 in Slovakia. It is about two women. The first is Jana from Žilina. At the beginning of our story she was in the final year of her teaching degree at Banska Bystrica. She wanted to teach physical education to children. Peter fell in love with her and used to write her beautiful letters. This great student love ended in marriage. Soon a baby was coming – little Janka who is nowadays a woman – the second woman of the story. Above all else Janka wants to prove that in spite of her disability she is able to live independently and still has dreams to fulfil.

There were big snowflakes falling on New Year of 1978. Jana, who lived only for her husband and the coming baby, was happy and walked to the maternity hospital. She loved winter. She was born in winter too. She felt somehow that when she was born there must have been snowflakes too. When little Janka was born she was like a big snowflake. She was beautiful and Jana seemed to be living her life in wonderland. As she and Peter didn't have their own flat they lived together with Jana's parents. Peter was still studying. Jana was taking care of the daughter they loved so much and preparing for her examinations. It seemed that nothing could destroy their love. Then Jana's grandmother died of an active form of tuberculosis. All adults who had been in touch with her had to be treated. Little Janka didn't get any treatment although Jana took her for regular medical check-ups. Then Jana's university friends told her that Peter was going out with another woman. She couldn't believe it. The wonderland turned into a nightmare. Everything lost sense. She couldn't think about her studies at all. Then a friend said to her, 'You've got a daughter and you must take care of her! You must finish your studies.' Jana recovered and started to prepare for her exams. But in December tragedy fell. Eleven-month-old Janka got tubercular brain fever. The first prognosis was horrible: total paralysis, loss of sight and mental retardation. Now Jana doesn't know how she managed to cope with it. No one was sure if little Janka would live. Peter and Jana went together to the hospital to visit Janka. Christmas was very sad.

Jana thought only about little Janka and believed that she would live. But she couldn't help wondering if she would be able to walk, see or speak. Jana had to do everything alone. She couldn't rely on Peter. They weren't able to manage things together. The doctors recommended that they have another baby.

After her stay in hospital little Janka was transferred for treatment to a sanatorium in the High Tatras, beautiful mountains 180 kms from Žilina. Jana knew them from holidays in the past, but only now did she realize that besides wonderful forests, mountains and holiday chalets the Tatras had many sanatoria. Jana and Peter visited their daughter in one of them.

Little Janka was very affectionate and she started to walk although her right hand and leg remained spastic. Jana saw this as a great victory. Every Thursday she would phone the head doctor at the sanatorium to find out about little Janka's health and progress. One day she was in a hurry to ring after work but the line was busy. She tried again. At the other end of the line there was an anxious voice: 'What's the matter with you? I thought you weren't going to ring. I've got a great piece of news for you. Janka seems to be able to see. She follows the toys with her eyes. Come straight away!'

On the journey Jana was already thinking about where she would take little Janka to get help for her sight. Hradec Králové, where there was a good ophthalmology centre? Or to Moscow? Jana was determined to do everything she could for her daughter. She knew that she couldn't rely on Peter. He was still studying and their relationship was strange. From time to time he went to visit little Janka but he lived his own life. Jana didn't reproach him. After all one can't be made to love someone. She managed to finish her studies, started work, visited her daughter and paid her parents half of the rent from a low salary. Her telephone bill was enormous because of the calls to the sanatorium. She didn't think about herself and wanted above all to help her daughter. Her parents were separating and she couldn't rely on them either. Now she doesn't know how she managed.

Jana felt weaker and more helpless as time went on. Peter disappointed her. Little Janka was still in the sanatorium and she couldn't be with her or look after her. Life seemed to be without meaning to her. She was very exhausted. Then suddenly a spot was found on her lungs. Awful! Tuberculosis! She was sent to a spa in the High Tatras. Although she was ill she was close to her daughter and able to visit her frequently. She slowly recovered.

Between Christmas and New Year Jana and little Janka came home to Žilina together. They enjoyed winter and the happiness of being together. Little Janka developed very quickly at home. She was energetic and inquisitive. She had improved so much that the doctor recommended that she leave the sanatorium early as soon as Jana's treatment was finished.

So they came back to Žilina together. Jana worked and looked after little Janka who at the age of three started to attend a special kindergarten. At first the teachers said that she wasn't 'suitable' to be among the other children but later they came to like her. She was energetic and hard to control and sometimes she had epileptic seizures. Jana's life was like a stretched string. Her relationship with Peter was strange, they neither divorced nor lived together as a married couple. Her parents were getting divorced and Jana, Peter and little Janka lived with them. It was a complicated situation full of problems.

Finally Jana started working as a physical education teacher. She also took care of little Janka. She didn't have a single moment free because her daughter was constantly running around and falling down since her right leg and hand remained stiff. Stress, fears for little Janka and the responsibility overwhelmed Jana sometimes. She was exhausted and now and then she cried and felt she couldn't manage it all any more.

Then Peter filed for divorce because another woman was expecting his child. Little Janka loved him and couldn't understand why her father left her. Finally she decided that he was dead. Jana found it very difficult to explain the situation to her. When her parents divorce was finalized she and little Janka moved into a room in a small apartment which her father rented. Little Janka had her first orthopaedic operation. She didn't stop moving around in spite of the plaster.

Later Jana and little Janka moved to a house where they met a neighbour who had lost her husband. They all helped each other through the hard times. Even now Jana and the neighbour meet every day for coffee. They know everything about each other. Jana started to teach in a new school and she found new friends there. She needed it. Her life started to be a little happier: Janka at home, pupils at school, a few holidays. She and her daughter sang. Little Janka had a beautiful voice and knew many songs they could sing together. She sang to herself in the toilet and the bathroom. It seemed that everything was going well. Little Janka went to a kindergarten together with her friend, Braňo Provazník:

> Braňo and me have liked each other since my childhood. He started to attend ordinary school but didn't do well so he stopped. He was to have gone to a school in Nova Baňa like me but the authorities didn't let him in. I started to go to the school in Nova Baňa and whenever we got our marks I was afraid that I would be blamed for bad marks. But my mum never blamed me even when I got C or D. I was very afraid but she told me that she knew I was doing my best.

Janka had to leave home to go to a special boarding school for students with intellectual and physical disabilities – the only school of its type in Slovakia. It was about 150 kilometres from Žilina and it was hard to get there. Sometimes it was necessary to walk the last 8 kms. Jana didn't want Janka to go to boarding school but she didn't have any other choice. If she hadn't agreed the authorities would have cancelled her daughter's education and labelled her ineducable. Jana didn't want this to happen as she knew Janka and realized that she would learn many new things. Jana didn't know how she could bear to live alone. Her colleague who was to live with her died tragically. Jana nearly broke down. She lived at her neighbour's flat for two weeks until she recovered. She worried about how little Janka would adjust to new things. She sent her parcels and letters and she visited her. She spent all her time with her students. And she kept busy with organising recreational activities and improving her qualifications with more study.

During one visit to the special school Jana couldn't believe her eyes. Janka's plait was cut off. Jana had been taking great care of her hair and everybody admired it. It was short now. She was furious. This was *her* daughter. Who had dared to decide what to do with her hair. She couldn't accept it. She had had similar experiences in the special school before and not just once. The worst incident was with a teacher who slapped Janka when she wasn't able to answer his questions. Janka was so afraid of him that she started to stutter. Jana learned this later and insisted that Janka be moved to another class. But her speech was still affected. Now she is only free of her stutter when she is alone or singing. This was one way she paid for her education in the special school.

Janka had to undergo a second orthopaedic operation. The whole bottom half of her body was put in plaster and the doctor told her to stay home and not go to school. At this time she was in the seventh year of her schooling. While she was at home she started to attend a day care centre for people with intellectual disabilities in Žilina. She liked it there but after her treatment she had to go back to Nova Baňa to finish her basic school. After the eighth and ninth year she continued at the training school. She wanted to become a dressmaker.

> When I came to the training school I tried hard to get high marks. I had a very nice teacher at the basic school so when I learned to make shorts, I wanted to sew a pair for him. So I went to the teachers' room to take his measurements for shorts and everybody laughed. I got mostly C marks at school. When we had the final exam I was very afraid I wouldn't pass it. But I did. I got a certificate too. We celebrated it. We went to Žarnovica for lunch and also for another trip. I'll never forget those celebrations.

Janka came back to Žilina as an adult woman after twelve years away. She had to learn a completely new life. She wasn't able to use buses or watches. Her mother was afraid of her. So the school of real life started. She returned to the day care centre. She met Braňo whom she knew from kindergarten at the centre.

> Braňo's right hand is stiff and he has got problems with talking. However we like each other. He told me he loves me as I am. It made me so happy. He gives me many presents. I always have a present for him too. I gave him a camera for Christmas and he wants to give me a ride in a car for his present. I like to make everyone I love happy. I make presents for people. I embroidered a small tablecloth for Sonja.

Janka met Sonja in the club which she helps to run for people with intellectual disabilities. Joining this inspired her to learn things she was interested in. People at the club weren't as worried about her as her mother. They supported all the members and went for various trips with them. The most special of these was called the *Land of Harmony*. It is a conference for 50 to 100 young people, some of whom have disabilities and some of whom do not. During this trip they find out more about each other, create new things, dance, make theatrical productions and come to understand that everyone is different. In summer they go for a week to stay in the country where they talk about their past, present and future. They call it the *Summer Dialogues*. Students go there too, to support the people with disabilities.

> Now I live very well. I get on well with my mum. I like visiting my aunt and uncle in Mikulov, Moravia. I like going for trips to Bojnice where there is a wonderful castle and to the Tatras where there are high mountains. I like hiking very much. My mum and I like going on holidays. We even went to Italy together. Every Monday I go to the club. When the weather is fine I go there by myself by trolley bus. On Fridays I go to the pottery club. My friends take me there. I am glad that *Summer Dialogues* and *Land of Harmony* happen every year where we are together, young people with and without disabilities. There is always a lot of fun there. Last time I nearly died laughing. I was near to crack. I was laughing with my lungs and my whole chest.

Jana can see her daughter is learning a lot of new things. At home she is able to clean her room, use a vacuum cleaner, change the bedclothes. She can iron flat clothes, clean vegetables in the kitchen, wash the dishes, go shopping and take out the garbage. She can prepare her breakfast, use a microwave and the telephone and she takes her pills herself. Janka likes to prepare coffee and tea.

She is looking for her place in the world and Jana can see she is succeeding. But Jana still cannot imagine her daughter living independently, without support. There are situations that she fears Janka will not be able to manage. She is afraid that someone will deceive her, lie to her, or hurt her. Jana and Janka talk about these things with Sonja. Sonja gives them hope that in spite of the fact that Janka will need support she will be able to stay by herself and fulfil her life dream.

I want to live as ordinary people do, having my own flat and my own postbox with my name, Janka Provazniková on the door as well as on the ring. If it is possible to manage it, even if I am not married, it would make me very happy. The flat could be between Žilina and Banová where Braňo lives. Every day Braňo and I would meet in our little flat and enjoy love and joy. We still love each other and if we were not disabled we would marry and live as other people do. He would go to work and I would go to work too. Braňo would pass his driving test and we would buy a car and drive it.

Janka would like to learn a lot of new things – to travel alone by train, to know where to get off, which train to take and how to use a timetable. She would like to manage in an office, in the bank and to visit the doctor by herself. She would like to travel around Slovakia and the whole world. She would like to learn all the things necessary to live a normal life.

Even people like Braňo and I can live independently. If we only could I would be glad. I wish I had never been ill or had a cold. If only illnesses didn't exist. Who could have invented them? Who invented brain fever?

In the past Jana often woke up at night frightened about Janka. She was afraid that she herself might die or that she would get sick. Who would care about Janka then? 'Perhaps I will go mad? How will I bear all this?' Sometimes she repeated her name or the date of her daughter's birth. She had a head full of questions. These were hard times and she had to manage everything alone. Sometimes her colleagues or neighbours supported her. But Jana never had a partner who would help her with the difficulties of life. Peter let her down. He paid only as much in maintenance as he had to. Then she met another man, he loved her but she couldn't rely on him either.

She gave all her love to Janka. They went on trips together. Jana still doesn't know how she managed to keep Janka's attention for six hours while they went to visit her brother or sister in Moravia.

She often took three younger cousins with them to keep Janka company. She went to summer camps as a cook so that Janka would not miss out. She was always sorry if someone rejected her daughter. Once during the holidays, Janka was at home and a group of girls were playing in the yard. Janka took her toys and ran down to play with them. But when they saw her the other girls packed up their things and ran away. Jana was watching from the window and felt sad. Later on she taught these girls in school but she couldn't talk to them about it.

During a stay in the sanatorium in the High Tatras, Jana met Marián. He has been a close friend ever since. He is witty, kind and attentive. She was always afraid of a possible partner's opinion of Janka. But when her daughter met him, she said 'Uncle you have the same eyes we have. I like you.' And so they became friends. Marián doesn't live in Žilina so Jana and he call each other on the phone each day. It is love by telephone. They share their joys and problems. He has helped Jana several times and supported her a lot when she had health problems. He is sociable and friendly. And he is married. When Jana asks about the future of their relationship he always answers: 'Take your time.'

Jana believes that some day she will have what everybody needs – love and a sincere relationship. It is not easy to accept that Marián has his own job, wife and town. But she is glad the phone was invented! Some day she will have her own husband, her mountains and Janka who will be able to live independently. Then Jana will be able to visit her for coffee. It has always been Jana who has had to solve the problems.

Now she is waiting for a change. She will wait for Marián's solution. She will take her time. She believes that eventually she will have a relationship with a man on whom she can rely. In the meantime she works, swims and supports her daughter to become more independent.

Soon Janka will be going to the annual festival of fantasy and creativity organized by Sonja and her friends. This is a meeting place for young people with and without disabilities from Slovakia and all over Europe who come together creatively and have fun. None of these people believe that it is better for people to live separately because they are different. Janka can show people without disabilities how similar we are with our desires, feelings and dreams. Her sincerity would persuade even the most sceptical. In doing this she is a great artist. For her hard work and achievements she was given the Forest Gump Award at the last festival. She hung it on the wall of her favourite room and is proud of it. By being herself she has made many friends. They have their fingers crossed for her.

The future?

Sometimes Jana, Sonja and Janka meet together to have coffee. They remember how Janka arranged her very own room, how she put her name on the door, how she coped with her first job. Jana will add some nice stories about Marián and Sonja will talk about her work.

At Christmas it will snow heavily. We will go and sing Christmas carols to Janka. She will have decorated her Christmas tree and will have prepared gifts for everybody. She will have baked Christmas cakes, she and Braňo will look wonderful together and they will celebrate this peaceful time. Then she will ring her mother and tell her everything is OK. That she loves her because she helped her to find what she was searching for – herself, love, friends, a job, a flat – her place in the world.

A fairytale? It is not important. The people in this story know that the journey is long. But their goals are clear.

CHAPTER FOUR

Unhappy Families
Violence in the Lives of Girls and Women

Missy Morton, New Zealand

Our families can make us feel safe and loved. Our families can also make us feel hurt and scared. Sometimes we love our families and hate them at the same time.

This is a story about Louise. When Louise was little her father beat her up. Her cousin Ricky hurt her. Here is what Louise told me:

'I hate my fucking real father. I wish he was dead. After what he done to me. He knew that I had spells. And he went ahead and picked on me something terrible. He slapped me in the stomach, in the arm, in the ear. When I was washing my hair in the sink he kicked me in the ass so I hit my head on the faucet. My father even scarred my hand when I was a kid. I was about six or seven years old. One time he grabbed hold of my hand: Now you know what a belt buckle is like. And he hit my hand so hard with it. He hurt me bad and I mean real bad.

Even my cousin Ricky. I was a year old when he started finger fucking me… I thought I was the only one he did this to. But he did it to his own daughter, Rachel. He said, "Let's go get some ice cream or something" and I went to get into the car. And I said "Rachel, what are you doing here? You mean to say he's doing it to you too?" Rachel said "Yes. Yes."'

Louise loves her mother. It was hard for Louise to tell her about Ricky. She was frightened of what Ricky would do to her if she told her mother. One day Louise told Ricky to stop. 'I said, "Ricky, you ever touch me again and I swear to God I'm gonna yell *rape*." Because I was so sick and tired of being molested all my life.'

When Louise grew up she fell in love with John. They had a baby girl named Cassie. At first everything was great. Then John started doing bad things to Louise. She wanted to leave. She and Cassie went to a Battered Women's Shelter where they could be safe from John.

Louise got worried about Cassie. She kept hitting Cassie. She didn't want to but she didn't know what else to do. She asked for help. A parent aide came to help her potty train Cassie.

When Cassie was three years old, Louise made a very hard decision. She sent Cassie to live with a foster family. She visits Cassie and she hopes that if she goes to parenting classes she might get Cassie back. Louise wanted her daughter to be safe, but now she feels as if Cassie has been taken away from her.

Louise misses Cassie. She's glad John is out of her life. She has a new lover Tom and says, 'He's the best lover I ever had.' She feels safer with Tom.

Families are complicated. We like to think of our families as people who will always love us and care for us no matter what. We like to think our families will always act in our best interests. In families the adults are responsible for looking after the children, older siblings look out for younger siblings. We expect that the adults can be trusted to protect children from harm and to teach children how to get on in the world.

At the same time there are systems designed to protect children from abuse by family members and/or to protect the adults from domestic violence and abuse. That we have these systems means that we recognize that families are not always – or, at least, not only – the safe places we might wish them to be. Nevertheless we mostly tend to think of families as at least potentially able to nurture family members. People who have grown up in abusive families often go on to make families of their own, and with every intention that their new family will be loved and cared for in the best possible way. Louise is one woman who grew up in an abusive family and as an adult wanted to create a better family life for herself and for her children.

I first met Louise in New York in 1991. She was part of a Women's Support Group of seven women who were labelled 'intellectually disabled' and had been in violent relationships. The Women's Support Group met specifically for the purpose of allowing the women to tell their stories, to consider their own and each other's experiences of violence, and to look at some of the ways society generally considered violence in women's lives. For example, we looked at and discussed videos prepared by a local Battered Women's Shelter, as well as popular movies such as *The Accused*.

Other women with intellectual disabilities have written about (Williams 1992) or told of (Bogdan and Taylor 1984) violence in their lives as part of telling their life stories. There is now a body of literature examining the incidence of violence and abuse in the lives of people with

intellectual disabilities (Baladerian 1985; Senn 1988), developing theor-
ies and models for explaining the occurrence of violence (Sobsey and Doe
1991), strategies for preventing violence and abuse (Sobsey *et al.* 1991), as
well as feminist analyses of disability, gender, sexuality and violence (Fine
and Asch 1985; Marks 1996; Morton and Munford 1998). In this chapter
I present my understanding of the stories told by Louise; about the
families she grew up in and the families she went on to make.

Growing up

Louise has both happy and horrific memories of her childhood. She spent
at least some time in foster homes or with relatives other than her parents
because of incidences of physical abuse.

> I hate my fucking real father. I wish he were dead. After what he done
> to me. He knew that I had spells. And he went ahead and picked on me
> something terrible. He slapped me in the stomach, in the arm, in the
> ear…washing my hair in the sink, kicked me in the ass so I hit my head
> on the faucet. My father even scarred my hand when I was a kid… I
> was about six or seven years old or something. One time he grabbed
> hold of my hand. Now you know what a belt buckle is like. He
> grabbed hold of my hand and he hit my hand so hard with it… He
> hurt me bad and I mean real bad.

For Louise, moving in with her uncle's family as a toddler was the start of a
long history of sexual abuse by her cousin.

> Even my cousin Ricky. I was a year old when he started finger fucking
> me… Look at the things he did to me. He was in his fucking forties
> when he did this to me… I thought I was the only one he did this to.
> But he did it to his own daughter, Rachel… He said 'Let's go get some
> ice cream or something' and I went to get into the car. And I said
> 'Rachel, what are you doing here? You mean to say he's doing it to
> you too?' 'Yes. Yes.' … One day when I was staying with Rachel, he
> made us play with each other's you know.

Louise eventually escaped this abuse at the age of 13, to live with her sister.
Like many girls and young women, escape was difficult, telling trusted
loved ones was difficult.

> I had to go to the bathroom. My cousin Ricky followed me in the hall.
> I said 'Ricky, you ever touch me again and I swear to God I'm gonna

yell "rape".' Because I was so sick and tired of being molested all my life. My mother said 'Louise, why didn't you tell me?' 'Mamma, how could I?' He threatened me. He'd do worse.

Louise's courage as a young woman enabled her to escape from her abusive cousin. Like many survivors of abuse, Louise wanted a better life for herself as a grown woman, and for her own children. However, she found it very difficult to break out of this pattern of relationships.

Parenting

Louise later met and lived with John and together they had a daughter, Cassie. Louise was frightened of her own anger and violence towards her daughter, and sought help:

> What do you think when she was three years old, I put her in a home? I didn't want to hurt her anymore. When I tried to potty train her, she was a year, eighteen months. She didn't tell me she had to go number two. I took her in the bathroom. And I seen that shit in her pants. I saw red in front of my eyes. I spanked her so hard, but I did not mean it (Louise begins to sob).
>
> I didn't want to do it. But for crying out loud, I didn't know what the hell to do. I couldn't potty train her or anything. So Debra Owens [a worker, maybe a parent aide?] had to help me to potty train my daughter. Why do you think I been going to parent training and stuff like that? Why do you think I been going to all these places? So I can learn to be a mother.

John too was physically and sexually abusive to Louise. She left him, taking herself and Cassie to a Battered Women's Shelter. While in the Shelter, a worker there saw Louise smacking her daughter, and reported her to Child Protective Services:

> They [workers in different social service agencies] keep saying to me 'Louise, if you don't say anything, how do we know how to help you?' The fucking assholes – how in the world do they expect me to talk to them when they're the ones that took my daughter away from me?
>
> Why do you think I been going to parent training and stuff like that? Why do you think I been going to all these places? So I can learn to be a mother. And as I keep on saying 'I paid for it. And I mean I paid for it dearly for the last three years.' But they [Child Protective

Services] took my baby away from me. And they ain't gonna do it again.

Cassie lived with foster parents at the time of this conversation. Louise was able to visit Cassie while supervised and saw her bi-weekly.

Despite ill-health, Louise attends numerous parenting courses run by three or four county and volunteer agencies, and seems to have cycled through some of these courses more than once, in the hope of proving herself a fit mother. She is supported, at least emotionally, in her efforts by her mother and her current lover, Tom.

> But it's because of my daughter that's keeping me alive. And my mother. And now him (she gestures to Tom, and is sniffing back her tears). Straight sex, I don't care. Like for him (points to Tom). He's the best lover I ever had.

Like many women in her situation Louise often finds herself feeling both abandoned and under intense scrutiny, sometimes at the same time. Support services that might have helped her – as a child and as an adult victim of abuse – were not there. She struggled as a parent to find ways to teach and discipline her child. While she did not want Cassie to have the kinds of experiences that she, Louise, had as a child, she had no other models to draw on. The support that was eventually forthcoming seems to have resulted in the loss of the person most dear to her. Louise talks about Cassie being taken away from her, and also about having put her in a home, wanting to do what is best for her daughter. To have her daughter returned, she will probably be caught in the cycle of surveillance that accompanies many such support programmes for people with disabilities (Janko 1992; Morton and Munford 1998). For Louise, even this support would have been worth it to be able to raise her daughter in a life with less violence.

CHAPTER FIVE

Life Without Parents

Experiences of Older Women With Intellectual Disabilities

Christine Bigby, Australia

Parents are often worried about what will happen to their adult child when they die. Many people think that old age will be a difficult time for people with intellectual disabilities. They may not be able to live with their parents and there are few other places for them to go. Also some people think that old people are always sick and just want to sit at home and do nothing all day. So they do not help old people to join in activities and meet friends.

Some people with intellectual disabilities have signs of old age like poor eyesight and poor health at a younger age than other people. But at most ages they are just the same as everyone else. They continue to learn and be active until they are 70 years and over. A few people even think that older people can do things better than when they were younger.

I talked to 27 older women with intellectual disabilities, to find out what life was like for them. All these women had lived with their parents for many years but their parents are now dead. These are some of the things I found out.

For some women old age was a good time. They learned new skills, made new friends and had more choices about their lives. It was often the first time they were treated as adults rather than children. Other people, like neighbours, friends, brothers or sisters, were very important in helping them begin new lives.

For other women old age was a difficult time. Some older women were forced to move quite often. This meant that they lost touch with friends and people in their local area. They lived with large groups of other older people. Very few lived in their own home in the community or in group homes for people with disabilities. The women's families were often unhappy as they thought that where the women lived was not the best place for them because staff did not understand people with disabilities.

My study shows how important it is for older women with intellectual disabilities to have a friend, a sister or a brother who can speak up for them and make sure they get the best possible services. It also showed that it is difficult for people to stay in group homes. And it showed that services for older people don't understand older people with intellectual disabilities very well.

Vera has become more independent. She just does things that she would never have dreamt of doing once upon a time. (Sister of Vera aged 69 who lives in an aged person's hostel)

The next step will be a nursing home and the thing that annoys me so much is I believe there is no need for this. They are showering her and dressing her. Having everything done for her she's just become very very lazy. I can understand the staff. It's a lot easier for them ... She doesn't fit into intellectual disability services. They just said they didn't have much to offer and she's too young for aged services. (Brother of Nora aged 65, who lives in a special accommodation house)

This chapter examines the spectrum of later life experiences of a group of older women who had stayed at home with their parents until mid-life. For this group, ageing coincided with the period in their lives when they no longer had the support of their parents. As the quotes suggest, later life can be a time of increased opportunities and broadened horizons or a time of restriction and vulnerability to inappropriate living situations or service systems. Until the last 30 years people with intellectual disabilities had a much reduced life expectancy. Most did not survive to old age or expect to outlive their parents (Eyman and Borthwick-Duffy 1994). Thus later life and a phase in their lives without parents, for those who remain at home, are relatively new periods in the life course of people with intellectual disabilities.

Parents are apprehensive, sometimes even fearful about their own mortality and the time in their adult child's life when they are no longer around (Card 1983; Richardson and Ritchie 1989). Many authors consider it a time of particular vulnerability for people with intellectual disabilities whom they predict will have poor informal support networks, no significant others and a high level of dependency on formal service provision for their well-being (Gibson, Rabkin and Munson 1992; Hogg, Moss and Cooke 1988; Lakin et al. 1991). The transition from parental care has been portrayed as a time of crisis that may occur unplanned and involve emergency first-time contact with services, inappropriate or multiple residential placements, trauma and loss (Janicki et al. 1985; Kaufman, Adams and Campbell 1991).

Much of the period without parents will coincide with late life, which is also perceived to have particularly negative connotations for people with intellectual disabilities. Perceptions of later life for this group often reflect notions of the classic ageing theory of disengagement that portrays old age as a time of decline, stagnation and withdrawal from social life. Older people with intellectual disabilities are considered to fall into two or more disadvantaged groups and thus be in double or triple jeopardy (Dickerson 1979, cited in Hogg *et al.* 1988) or even decajeopardy (MacDonald and Tyson 1988). In policy documents they are typically characterized as less independent, more frail and less motivated or capable of societal participation or individual achievement (Health and Community Services 1993a, 1993b, 1993c, 1995). A compounding factor is that people with intellectual disabilities are often considered older at a much earlier age than the rest of the community – meaning that these negative perceptions apply to people who are still relatively young. Australian social policy generally regards 60–65 as the age at which people are older. However, 55 is commonly the accepted definition of older for a person with an intellectual disability, although some studies use as young as 40 years (Ashman, Suttie and Bramley 1993; Bigby 1995; Seltzer and Krauss 1987). Most generic aged care policy is targeted at the frail aged who are generally in their eighties. However, half the 'older people' with intellectual disabilities (55 years plus) in Australia are less than 65 years and most are the 'younger older' under 75 years (Ashman *et al.* 1993).

Some evidence suggests, however, that pessimistic conceptions of later life and younger definitions of ageing may not be warranted. Most people with intellectual disabilities without Down's syndrome age in a similar manner to the rest of the population (Anderson 1989). This means, for example, that they continue to develop right up to their sixties, their cognitive abilities do not begin to decline until the mid-sixties and they will not suffer higher rates of disability and chronic illness until into their seventies. As a group older people with intellectual disabilities are also fitter and more able than their younger peers (Strauss and Zigman 1996).

One of the few more optimistic views of later life is found in Edgerton's (1994) longitudinal research that noted positive changes occurring in old age among a cohort of ex-institutional inmates. They experienced a striking improvement in their life satisfaction, social competence and quality of life as they grew older because of increased competencies and the decreased expectations placed by society on older people. Edgerton suggests that 'when they are in their 60s these people are not only more competent in absolute terms than they have ever been before, they are also seen to be relatively more competent than in any prior period of their lives' (Edgerton 1994, p.60).

Most research on older people with intellectual disabilities is derived from large-scale surveys drawn predominantly from service populations. Few studies other than Edgerton's have examined the nature of experiences in later life. This chapter reports some findings from a study that explored the ageing experiences of older people with intellectual disabilities who had spent their earlier adult years at home with parents (Bigby 2000).

The study

Sixty-two adults with intellectual disabilities aged 55 years and over who had left parental care after the age of 40 years were involved in the study. They were recruited through an intensive case finding strategy in 12 municipalities of Melbourne, which ensured that people 'hidden' in the community and unknown to disability services were included (Bigby 1995, 2000). The 27 women in the group are the focus of this chapter.

A detailed description of all aspects of their lives since they had left parental care was obtained using in-depth, semi-structured interviews with various sources. The main source of information was a primary informant for each woman who was someone with whom she had a close long-term relationship. These informants were mainly siblings, but also included friends, nieces, cousins, an aunt and professionals. Additionally the service provider who identified each woman during the case finding process and 22 of the 27 women were interviewed. The five women who declined to be interviewed agreed to the author interviewing others about them.

Much of the data reported here were gained from informants' impressions rather than systematic measurement and comparison pre- and post-parental transition. Some data such as reasons for residential moves could be categorized and quantified but factors such as later life personal development that is relative to each individual's previous life experiences could not so easily be quantified. The qualitative data were analysed for common themes using the constant comparative method (Huberman and

Miles 1994) and with the aid of a 'search and retrieve' computer program 'The Ethnograph'.

Later life experiences

Although each woman had experienced a unique set of circumstances, several common threads had characterized their lives since they left parental care and journeyed into old age. Contrary to expectations, suggested by the literature, most women had a strong informal network with a key informal support person in their life. Change and personal development were central aspects of their lives. Many women had expanded their autonomy and broadened their life's horizons. However, some had also experienced multiple loss and been vulnerable to frequent housing moves and inappropriate living situations.

An overview of the women's characteristics at the time of the study provides a snapshot of one point in time during later life and the period when parents are no longer there. The women's ages ranged from 56 to 87 years with an average of 66 years. They had left parental care between the ages of 40 and 65 years with the average being 51 years. At the time of the study the average time women had been living away from their parents was 14.5 years. Most had experienced several types of primary care and accommodation since they left parental care. Only six had not moved house at all, five had moved twice, eleven had moved three times, four had moved four times and one had moved six times. For most of the women their source of primary care was a formal service, either residential or domiciliary, although five had an informal primary carer. Nine lived in generic aged supported accommodation (mostly aged persons' hostels), seven lived in private homes, alone or with a relative, and only three lived in disability accommodation.

Sixteen women were known to the State Disability Services system, however only nine were using specialist services at the time of the study. The majority had an informal key person who unofficially took responsibility for oversight of their well-being, adopting strong advocacy, service monitoring and liaison roles. Key people also provided affective support and fulfilled a range of instrumental tasks. However, this seldom stretched to the provision of direct day to day primary care. Key people were usually siblings but also included nieces, an aunt and friends/church connections. When women had different sex siblings, sisters were more likely to fulfil this role than brothers. However, when they had only one sibling or siblings of the same sex, brothers were as likely as sisters to take on this role.

The next section presents three broadly representative case studies, one drawn from each of the three types of accommodation in which the women lived. These studies give some insight into the myriad changes that each woman experienced as she aged.[1]

Bronwyn Ferguson

Bronwyn is 63 years old. She has no major health problems and speaks quite fluently. She lived with her mother for 62 years. Her father had left the home when she was a child.

Bronwyn felt her mother had overprotected her and denied her opportunities to build social relationships, a view shared by her brother. After she left a special school, she had not attended any educational or day activity programs. Much of her time had been spent housekeeping and although she made the beds, cleaned the house and cooked, Bronwyn had never been allowed to use the oven. Talking about her mother Bronwyn said, 'She wouldn't let me go out. She didn't think I was as old as I am. She treated me like a little girl and still she didn't think I was grown up. She wouldn't let me be friends with anybody. She wouldn't even let me talk to anybody. There were a lot of people I could have talked to that I liked. I used to go shopping with mum but she wouldn't let me talk to anybody up at the shopping. She didn't used to let me do anything. She was very protective of me.'

In the last few years that they lived together her mother had developed Alzheimer's disease. This significantly increased Bronwyn's caring role and placed further restrictions on her. Bronwyn said, 'I used to look after mum. I couldn't do a thing with her. I couldn't get her to wash her hair and she wouldn't eat. I wasn't getting any rest she was getting me up at half past 12 in the morning so my brother decided to find a place to put her. I didn't go out because I couldn't go out and leave her.'

Since her mother was placed in a nursing home Bronwyn has chosen to live alone in the family home. Her mother had not discussed the future

---

1   The names of all the women in this study have been changed to protect their privacy.

with her or her brother, other than threatening to put Bronwyn in an institution when she herself was first diagnosed with Alzheimer's. Her brother does not fully agree with Bronwyn's decision to remain at home and has suggested she get a flat nearer him and the rest of her family. They live on the other side of town. He is worried that workers from services expect too much of her and may withdraw their support after a while. Bronwyn said, 'When I can't look after myself, I'll get a flat up there [near brother]. I don't want to leave here, it's nice and it's handy to everything.'

While her mother was at home they received support from local government domiciliary services and this service liased and referred Bronwyn to specialist disability services when her mother left home. Bronwyn now receives weekly assistance with budgeting and shopping from a specialist outreach service. A council handyman helps in the garden. She attends various activity programs at both generic and specialist disability services. She is learning literacy skills at a community learning centre and several days a week participates in activities organized at one of the local senior citizens centres.

She said, 'I like what I'm doing now, because I'm never home.' Bronwyn has learnt new skills and made new friends. Her household and cooking skills have improved. She is beginning to understand and manage her money and she has learnt to cook in the oven. She can now find her way around the local neighbourhood but needs help if she wants to go farther afield. She has acquaintances at the senior citizens centre and friendships with several women in her neighbourhood. Bronwyn said, 'I've got a lot of friends, the next door neighbours, the one over the road. Jean down the street and Mrs Mitchell. I'm lucky I've got such good neighbours. I see a lot of nice women down at the centre. It's been real good, I've met nice people, nice women, I've met a couple of chaps that come with us, I do mix with men. You can't help mixing with men. Mum didn't like me mixing with men.'

Two of Bronwyn's brothers have died and she has a close relationship with the surviving one. He is in frequent contact and often takes her shopping and helps to sort out her financial affairs. She phones or sees the family of one of her other brothers; a nephew, a niece, who is her god-daughter and her sister-in-law quite regularly, although they all live some distance away. Bronwyn has a strong relationship with her next door neighbour with whom she now attends exercise classes and on whom she can call if she needs help.

Bronwyn summed up her 'old age' and life since her mother had left by saying, 'I couldn't get out then [when mum was alive] like I do now to different places. I've sort of got more independent to do things for myself.'

Amy Johnson

Amy is 65 years old. She has no major health problems but is not as quick on her feet as she used to be. Her speech is a little difficult to understand for people who don't know her well. She lived with her parents on a farm until she was 45 years old. The isolation of the family meant that Amy had few opportunities to develop friendships or participate in recreational or educational programs. Her niece said that her parents had been very protective and that after she left school she was 'just in the home with domestic chores occupying her time. She did go out and felt comfortable with some people but she didn't really mix with her own friends, they were all family contacts.'

When Amy was 40, her mother died. She and her father remained in the house for five years until his illness forced him to move to a nursing home. During this time Amy and her father depended on each other and were supported by Amy's sister Ginny, who visited regularly. Her niece said that during this time Amy 'had a role to play in the house as far as washing and cleaning. She couldn't cook but she was able to look after herself. She adopted this role of having to look after him [father] and he took on the role of having to look after her, it worked quite well.'

Amy's parents had planned carefully for her future. There had been an implicit agreement that after their death Amy's sister Ginny would care for her. To this end, many years earlier her father had financed the building of an extra room onto Ginny's house. When her father moved to a nursing home, Amy went to live with Ginny and her family. This arrangement worked well for several years until her brother-in-law became terminally ill and Ginny found caring for both him and Amy impossible.

Soon after Amy first moved to her sister's house she began attending a specialist disability day centre, and it was to the hostel attached to this centre that she moved when she had to leave her sister's house. Amy has lived there now for over 17 years. She said that this was the best place she had lived and liked it very much. Beginning to attend the day centre in her mid-forties marked a significant change in Amy's life. Her niece said that since then Amy's quality of life had improved. She said, 'Her life changed dramatically for the better because she was doing things that she had never done in her life before. I can remember mum just being floored the first time Amy came home and said she needed bathers because they were going swimming. I don't think Amy had ever had a pair of bathers in her life, and going to the football and going for counter meals, outings, to the pictures, shopping and things like that. Her life is just wonderful now.'

Amy is part of a supportive family network and involved in all 'special occasion' celebrations. Her closest relative is her sister Ginny whom she sees weekly and with whom she often stays at weekends. She has less contact with her other sister who lives in Adelaide and her brother. When Ginny was ill recently, her daughter Frances acted as her substitute and phoned Amy every week.

Amy has made many new social contacts since she began living at the hostel. She mentioned two special friends but still sees her 'home' as her sister's house and her family as her primary social network.

Beatrice Rowley

Beatrice is 67 years old. She is a petite woman who is quite fit but has eye problems that require an operation. She communicates well and is very aware of her intellectual disability. She lived with her mother for 51 years. Her parents divorced when she was young and her sister, whose marriage only lasted a short time, also lived at home. When she was a teenager Beatrice formed a strong relationship with her sister's child, Jean.

Beatrice's behaviour was very difficult when she was young and, according to Jean her niece, Beatrice's mother had been very jealous and protective of her, shielding her from forming relationships with others. Her life had not been very sociable or active and most of her time was spent at home with her mother. Beatrice helped her mother to run the house, did errands and sometimes performed domestic tasks for neighbours. For a short period, in her early twenties, she attended a specialist day centre.

Specialist disability services became involved with Beatrice shortly before her mother died. They organized for Beatrice to share the house with a woman of similar age with an intellectual disability, but who had spent much of her life in an institution. Beatrice had basic self-care and domestic skills but little idea of household planning, shopping or budgeting. Her housemate had fewer functional skills than Beatrice. Outreach staff visited twice a week and assisted the women to establish routines and run the household. Beatrice was introduced to various social activities such as attendance at a local senior citizens club. Outreach staff helped her to save and arrange holiday trips to Adelaide and Alice Springs. The neighbours were very supportive and monitored the women's well-being. Beatrice's niece, Jean, who was now her only relative, maintained contact with her, liased and advocated with disability services.

According to Jean these arrangements worked well for the first couple of years but then, when the original workers left, the specialist support diminished. It became less intensive, inconsistent and quite haphazard. Without adequate supervision Beatrice and her housemate coped less well, their diet deteriorated, they went out less and their health suffered. Jean regularly received worried calls from the neighbours but got little response to the concerns she raised with disability services. Recalling her experiences she said, 'Every time I rang up the disabled service I found that they had swapped the person who was looking after Beatrice. In three months she had at least three or four different workers assigned to her case. I think it was a cost cutting way of forcing the whole issue back on relatives. That's what it did, it forced it back on me and the neighbours and we had to become the people responsible.'

Despite Jean's concerns, the two women survived together in the community for ten years until the housemate became very ill and died. Beatrice was by then 61 and went to live in a local special accommodation house she had stayed in previously when her housemate was away. Most of the residents are elderly women much older than Beatrice and some tend to mother her. Several afternoons a week Beatrice attends activities at two local senior citizens centres.

Although Jean thinks Beatrice is happy at the special accommodation house she has some concerns about the environment and its ability to provide sufficient exercise, challenge and stimulation for her. She said, 'You know it is still not the best spot for Beatrice. They just sit around in a great semi circle watching television all day. Beatrice is used to doing the housework, doing some washing, you know going down and buying some milk and bread. She's been living a kind of more active life and suddenly she's with elderly people who just manage to get up and dress themselves and sit in front of the television.' Beatrice has no contact with specialist disability services since she moved to the special accommodation house. Jean said, 'They seem to have given her the flick.'

Beatrice's only family are her niece Jean and her husband and son. Jean is in regular contact with Beatrice. She monitors her care, arranges medical appointments and subsidizes the accommodation fees. She said, 'I have a responsibility for her and I feel quite guilty that I don't see enough of her and that I don't go out there. I should take her out and do more things for her. But I believe she's happy there and getting to see a lot more things than when she was living with my grandmother. Her life is a bit fuller than it was.'

A time of opportunity

As these women's stories have illustrated, in later life many women had participated in new activities, acquired new skills and undertaken previously untried tasks. These developments were more connected to the expectations of those around them than particular environments. For some, like Bronwyn, living independently provided opportunities for personal development, but for others it was a more sheltered environment like a specialist day centre or hostel. For example, Vera had moved to an aged persons' hostel following a long period of hospitalization. Her niece said that despite Vera's frailty she had become more independent and 'She just does things that she would never have dreamt of doing once upon a time.'

Many women had developed new relationships with friends, neighbours or co-participants of programs expanding their social network beyond the family system for the first time in their lives. Several had formed close or intimate friendships for the first time. For example, Isabel had married aged 61. She then lived with her husband, supported by several members of the church community, for 22 years until, at the age of 83, her ill health forced them to move her to an aged persons' hostel.

After the death or incapacity of their parents the women's relationships with other family members had changed as someone, usually a sibling, took over some of the parents' previous roles and substituted as the key person in their life. Although key people often had a powerful influence on life decisions, negotiated services and managed their affairs, these relationships appeared less controlling and more egalitarian than those the women had with their parents. Most key people held a different perspective from parents and had higher or different expectations of the women's capabilities, were less protective and often, despite some misgivings, less restrictive. It seemed that for the first time in their lives these women were treated as adults and sisters rather than children and daughters. Key people had often consciously taken definite steps to encourage skill development, seek out opportunities for social contact and broaden the horizons of the woman with intellectual disability. This changed relationship with the dominant person in their lives led to many women having increased life choices and more control over them.

Although most women had always played a significant part in the domestic tasks of the household, the last few years with their parents, in particular, were often characterized by a significant amount of caring and greater interdependence with parents. It was not until their death or their move to a nursing home that most parents relinquished 'care' of their daughter (the approximate average age of parents when they relinquished care was 83 years). Parents had hung on until the last minute and consequently many women became carers for a frail aged parent. This aspect of relationships with parents and women with intellectual disability as carers has been explored by Jan Walmsley (1997; Chapter 14). Women had also shared an aged life style with parents well before their own health or capacity warranted such restrictions. The cessation of interdependence, caring tasks and the restrictions that accompanied them may well have been a contributory factor to the increased freedom and opportunities experienced by women in later life.

Loss and vulnerability

As the figures given earlier and the case studies illustrate women with intellectual disabilities were vulnerable to residential mobility as they aged. This was associated with length of time away from parental care. Mobility frequently resulted from factors such as changes experienced by carers, problems with the quality, inflexibility of services or policy changes rather than the greater care needs of the woman. For several women residential moves were accompanied by the cessation of attendance at the specialist disability day centre which they had attended for many years. Once this occurred it inevitably meant failure to retain contact with long-term, centre-based friends.

Frequent housing moves made the women's support networks vulnerable to loss. A characteristic of the informal networks of older people with intellectual disabilities is the context-specific nature of relationships; people do not see friends out of hours and invariably lose contact if they move out of the particular context (Bigby 1997). Housing moves meant that women not only lost their family home and often moved from the locality they had lived in for many years, but they also lost social contact with neighbours and local friends. In contrast women who stayed on in their family home or moved within the local area retained local friendships and acquaintances. Although people who moved to supported accommodation had contact with other residents, they were seldom part of a neighbourhood. The directions of residential movement were from informal to formal care, but also into and then out of specialist disability accommodation. Decisions to make a move of the latter type were, however, often contentious and disputed as inappropriate by relatives. Thus, as they aged women were more likely to live in larger congregate style accommodation than in private households and more likely to live in generic aged than specialist disability accommodation.

The women seemed vulnerable, as they aged, to living in environments considered by their close associates as inappropriate. No informants raised concerns about the quality of specialist disability accommodation, but concerns were voiced about all three types of aged care accommodation. They were criticized for fostering dependence rather than independence, providing insufficient stimulation and having staff who were not attuned to the women's needs.

This criticism is strengthened when it is noted that, unlike other residents, most of the women with intellectual disabilities in generic aged care required assistance with tasks of everyday living because of their lifelong intellectual disability rather than age-related health or function decline. Like Beatrice, they were all substantially younger than other residents. The women were vulnerable to the loss of specialist disability services as they aged. These included residential, day activity and case management services. At the time of the study only 6 were using such services compared with 14 straight after transition from parental care. Once people had moved to aged-care accommodation contact was rarely maintained by disability services. Generic aged-care providers received no support or consultation from specialist disability services regarding the provision of appropriate care or programs for their clients with intellectual disability. Women living in generic accommodation did not participate in disability-specific day programs or receive case management from the state government's Disability Client Services.

Being older appeared to act as an obstacle to obtaining help for the first time from disability services. The carers of several women who had never used disability services were told, when they enquired about services from the State Disability Services system, that these had little to offer older people and carers were discouraged from submitting formal requests for assessment and services.

As the women aged, they experienced the physiological processes of ageing which, for some, began to mean deterioration of their health and loss of physical and adaptive functions. These losses were particularly marked for one woman with Down's Syndrome who experienced the early onset of Alzheimer's, and for those aged over 65.

Conclusion

Ensuring maximum opportunity and minimising loss

Many changes experienced by women as they aged were unplanned and unexpected, determined by external circumstances and strongly influenced by the expectations of others. This suggests the importance of having a strong informal support network whose members can assist women to negotiate the unpredictable and navigate the service system. The high reliance of these women on formal services for primary care also indicates the importance of informal network members who can act as advocates and monitor the quality of service provision. Assisting parents to ensure the continued involvement of other family members, friends and church associates in the woman's life when parents are no longer around may be more important than making concrete residential plans that are liable to unforeseen change and may not be flexible enough to take account of both positive and negative life changes. Support networks, particularly friendships, are vulnerable in later life and need to be carefully maintained and nurtured. This can be done by both addressing the frequency of residential moves and assisting the maintenance of ties when contexts change.

Women with intellectual disabilities in their fifties and sixties should not be automatically consigned to aged-care services. Various factors indicate they are vulnerable to 'being placed' in aged-care services that are considered inappropriate. Both placement decisions and inappropriate-ness may be accounted for by the differing perceptions of 'older'. The women may be perceived as 'older' by the disability service system but are still relatively youthful in comparison to the frail aged at whom the aged-care residential system is targeted.

This study has provided little evidence to support the notion that people with intellectual disabilities should be considered 'older' at an earlier age than the rest of the community or that their fifties and sixties are marked by decline and withdrawal from social life. A major concern is that attitudes and policies which reflect these views become self-fulfilling. In fact these women's later life experiences suggest that notions of the 'Third Age' as a time when people are 'old' but still healthy, productive and able to pursue new roles and experiences may be applicable to older people with intellectual disability (Laslett 1989). However, if the full potential of this stage of life is to be realized, the disability service system must revise its pessimistic preconceptions of older people and adopt a more positive, optimistic stance towards later life. A climate must be fostered that ensures a full range of primary care, day activity and leisure options is available to women with intellectual disability in later life.

A service gap appears to exist for women with intellectual disabilities who remain healthy and so do not suffer substantial functional decline in their fifties and sixties. They are vulnerable to the loss or denial of access to specialist disability services yet the generic aged-care services to which they are steered are not always appropriate. Greater consideration should be given to the continued role of specialist disability services in providing support for everyday living to this group. An emphasis on domiciliary outreach services to enable women to remain in the community and ensuring a flexible response by specialist disability accommodation ser-vices to the new demands that ageing can impose on the system would address this service gap and the high level of residential mobility and reliance on aged-care services. Generic aged-care service and specialist disability service systems can complement each other. Each has expertise to offer the other to ensure the provision of responsive appropriate services for older women with intellectual disability.

Retirement from specialist day centres is an unresolved issue and in Australia no upper age limit exists for the receipt of disability services. Rather than focusing on retirement, the focus must shift to how existing or alternative new services can provide optimal skill maintenance and development, stimulating leisure, recreational and social opportunities appropriate to each individual's rate of ageing. Such services are likely to utilize and support access to generic aged programs. Optimization of opportunities and minimization of vulnerabilities will inevitably depend on respecting the choices of women with intellectual disabilities, holding high expectations of their potential, maintaining strong informal support networks and on the collaboration and co-operation of aged-care service systems, disability service systems and members of informal support networks.

PART II

Finding a Place in Relationships

Introduction

Relationships are very important in most people's lives. Many writers have pointed out that this is particularly true for women who tend to define themselves in relation to the people in their lives – particularly the people they care most about (Gilligan 1982). When we were thinking about editing this book we thought about the most important areas in our own and other women's lives. One of the most crucial was that of relationships and we wanted to explore what relationships meant for women with intellectual disabilities. Which issues were similar? Are there significant issues of difference? We were aware that for some women with intellectual disabilities the restricted nature of their life experience might have had a profound impact on their relationships. For example, many women with intellectual disabilities have been locked away in institutions (Johnson 1998) or other specialized services preventing contact with people in the wider community. In the past such places have also been segregated by gender.

In Chapter 6 Janice Slattery provides a good example of how we as women construct our lives and tell our stories in terms of our connections with other people. Her story is one of relationships with the people in her life: her family, her husband, her friends and her colleagues at work. Mostly her account of these relationships is happy but not always. The saddest part of Janice's story is the account of a relationship which didn't occur. Janice never had the child she wanted so much. Janice's story is similar to the lives of countless other women. The differences are that because of perceptions of her disability she never had a child; she had difficulties meeting people while she was in segregated services; she felt overprotected by her parents as an adult and she had difficulties finding work.

There is a long tradition of women coming together for 'womanly' things and 'womantalk' (Spender 1985) where they share practical, emotional and social support. These gatherings have usually not been accessible to women with intellectual disabilities. In Chapter 7 Kristjana Kristiansen tells the story of Jenny and how becoming part of a women's community has influenced and enriched her life. But friendships between women with and without disabilities can also be a challenge, especially when one of the women has severe disabilities. In a case study of one such friendship (Chapter 8), Rannveig Traustadóttir challenges us to go beyond the traditional view of friendship as a reciprocal relationship between equals. She urges us to examine these relationships critically and tell stories that accurately reflect the experiences of these relationships. Friendships are important for all women. If we do not create an accurate understanding of these relationships it will be difficult for women to establish connections across differences (Fisher and Galler 1988).

Women with intellectual disabilities have had difficulties in being seen as sexual beings and have often had their sexuality denied by those around them. In the Chapter 9, which concludes the relationship part of the book, Michelle McCarthy presents her research in the area of sexuality and sexual abuse. Her chapter provides an extensive discussion of this very difficult area in the lives of women with intellectual disabilities and shows, among other things, how vulnerable they are to abuse by staff, family members and men with intellectual disabilities.

Relationships are important and rewarding in women's lives. They bring with them pleasures, joys and above all a sense of belonging. They may also be a source of sadness, pain and grief. The chapters in Part II reflect the diversity of relationships in which women are involved and the varied impact they have on their lives.

CHAPTER SIX

Family, Marriage, Friends and Work
This is my Life

Janice Slattery with Kelley Johnson, Australia

My family has always been close. I have one brother and a sister and I am in the middle. We all grew up at home. I went to school when I was 6. I had trouble keeping up with the school work and I had a speech problem. So when I was about 9 mum sent me to a special school. It was a good school. But it was different. We used to play a lot.

I didn't go out much when I lived at home because mum worried about me. I moved out of home when I was 26. That was a big decision. Mum and dad were anxious but they said they were right behind me if I wanted to do it. I moved in with my brother and helped him look after his son. This was when I got all the skills to get more qualified and live independently.

I met John, my husband, at an advocacy organisation. He was there on his own with a broken arm. He kept asking me out. I'd been out with other guys before John but they wanted one thing only. John liked me for what I am. I wanted a guy to love me for what I am. We lived together for about five years before we got married.

Then we decided to get married. We had a great wedding with lots of people. Being married has made me more responsible. Part of being married was about having kids. We got tested and found that we could have them. But then they said to me that because of my age and my disability our child could have a disability. We decided not to have one. I didn't want to have a child with the heartache I went through. I went through agony when I was a child. I kept falling over and I got teased at school. I was called terrible names that I don't like to repeat. I do wish I had a child. I'd love to have one. Sometimes I look at us and think 'What's missing in our life? A baby.' Jason, John's son, comes to visit us often. I feel left out because he's not my son. I feel like I'm not included.

I have lots of friends from school and from work. I like going out with them, just being together and talking. Friends are important. Because without friends you've got no one.

I've done lots of work things. I've been a volunteer in a child care centre. I've worked in factories and on committees. But the best job I had was being a paid self-advocate for People First. It was great but after two years the funding ran out. Now I work as a peer educator teaching women with disabilities about their health and I do some cleaning at my dad's factory.

I feel a strong person. I don't like everyone else just walking all over me and I tell them how I feel. I wasn't always like that. But being with advocacy groups built up my confidence and today I'm a lot stronger.

Family

My family has always been close. And they have been supportive to me over the years. I have helped them too. I have one brother and a sister and I am in the middle. We all grew up at home. Both my parents worked when I was small. Dad owns his own business as a furniture carrier. He and my uncle were both partners in the business and they built it up together. When my uncle retired dad took over the business and he's still running it. Mum worked at a laundromat and once she worked at a liquorice shop. She brought us home liquorice. I remember that!

My brother and sister and I always got on very well when we were kids. Sometimes my brother used to punch us and that. I suppose it's just boys mucking around. We complained to mum. When I was younger I was closer to my brother than my sister but now I'm older I'm sort of closer to my sister and that. She's easier to talk to and I can tell her stuff like having babies and all that and she listens and helps me.

When I was small we lived in a house in Templestowe for a couple of years and that was good. There were ghost houses down the street and we used to go down at all hours of the night playing ghosts and all that. Oh, there was this house down the street. We thought it was haunted and we went down there and went in to find if someone was living there and that. It wasn't haunted but we thought it was. We were so scared.

I went to school when I was 6. It was a state school and I had a problem with my speech and my balance and I had trouble keeping up with the school work. I don't remember much about it except that I had a real bad speech problem and I remember going to speech classes in a taxi. I worked hard at my speech because when I was about 4 or 5 people couldn't understand me because it was very bad and it took years and years for me to get it right. And some of the words I still have trouble with. And that is about all I remember of my state school years.

When I was about 9 mum thought she would find me a school with speech therapy so I went to a different school until I was about 16 years old. It was a special school. It didn't have real education like they have in a normal school. This school was a boarding school and it had day students. I went home every day and the students who didn't have parents stayed at school. It was a good school. I got on with everyone there. But it was different. The classes we had weren't numbered. You know like in other schools they have class 1, 2, 3. We used to play a lot. There used to be a park opposite the school where there was a pond and all that. And I remember one time we went to the pond and I was climbing onto this branch and I fell into the water and my clothes were wet and I cut my foot. This nun took me back and dried my clothes. I was always good at spelling. I remember we did a spelling bee at school and I came first and they presented me with stockings. But someone was very nasty and cut them up. I think it was jealousy. Mum drove me to school each day. My brother and sister went to my nanna's [grandmother's] after school but I waited at the school until mum picked me up.

We loved going to nanna's because we could muck around. We used to go over and spend the night and that. She had a loft outside and when I was a kid I used to fall out of it and that but I never managed to hurt myself. And nanna's house had a big staircase. We used to ride down the banister. It was great fun. And then my brother used to pull us up the staircase by a rope. Every school holidays we used to go over to nanna's place and she used to make the *best* scones, homemade scones and apple pie. I loved her apple pie. She was a good cook.

I did my Holy Communion and my sister came that day and did it with me. After we went to my grandmother's and we had a full celebration. Tea, cakes and that. It was important. I went to church to do confirmation and I picked Mary as my confirmation name because of Mary Mother of God. The funny thing is that when I was a kid I always used to go to church but now I don't seem to go a lot. I don't know why. The only times I go to church is funerals, weddings and Christmas Eve. None of my friends go. We're Catholics but none of us go. John's [Janice's husband] Catholic and he doesn't go. When I was a kid and we went to church, when we came home mum had a roast dinner. She stayed home and cooked it. But now we don't have a roast dinner. I miss it. Mum's roast.

I never used to be able to talk to mum about anything like sex or anything. I don't know why. I s'pose I was embarrassed. It was embarrassing. At school we saw a video about periods once and I didn't know what to expect because mum never told me anything about periods until I got it. So I looked at the video and I said, 'That won't happen to me.' And then five minutes later it did. I thought I was dying. I didn't talk much to dad about this kind of stuff.

I didn't go out much when I lived at home. There was one stage when I went to the pictures on my own because I was sick and tired of being at home every weekend and I just wanted to go out for a change on my own. Mum was overprotective towards me. She didn't want me to go out in case I met creeps and that. She didn't stop me from going out, she just worried about me. So I just stayed at home mostly. I went out a fair bit with my parents. They had a holiday house by the beach and when we were kids we used to go down there. It was right across the road from the beach up the sand dunes and we had great fun when we was down there. But when we were older we stopped going down there so they sold the house and bought another one in Queensland. We don't go there very often because of the money.

I moved out of home when I was 26. That was a big decision. I was getting tired of living at home and sort of frustrated. I wanted to live independently on my own and that. I couldn't do that while I was at home because my parents had to do everything for me and that. And I wanted to learn how to do things on my own. I talked about it with a friend of mine and I said, 'Can you come home with me and talk to mum for me because I don't think I can do it on my own?' I needed back-up. So she came and talked to mum for me. And mum and dad were scared about where I was going to live and that.

And mum said that if I wanted to try it on my own she'd be behind me; her and dad. Dad was happy about my leaving home. But mum. I don't know about mum. I get the feeling mum didn't want me to leave home. Most parents don't want their kids to leave home. I was the last to leave and it was really hard for mum to let me go. Because she thought I wouldn't be able to cope by myself. And that's why it was difficult for her to let me go. I think she thought because of my disability I would have problems coping. I proved them wrong. I did cope.

They said they would help me look for private rental accommodation and we found some but they were dealing in drugs and that and mum didn't want to plug me into the position. So she said, 'No, I'm not putting her into that accommodation.' And then luckily my brother said there was a spare room with him and so I moved in with him, my nephew and another friend called Lenka.

Colin, my brother, was by himself with his small son, David, who was about three at the time. Colin went out a lot and I used to baby-sit David and that. I wasn't anxious about looking after him because while I was living at home I had looked after kids as a volunteer.

I was living there for three years and while I was living there that's when I got all the skills to get more qualified and live independently. We took it in turns to do the cooking but I did most of the cleaning up. At first it was easy to live with Colin because we got on very well, but then later on it got harder because you can't ever live with one of your family. It's difficult. You sort of get on one another's nerves and that. But Colin helped me a lot like with budget and cooking. He helped me a lot with my rent, money, bills and that.

When I did finally leave home I was really happy because I didn't have my parents saying 'What time will you be home? Be home at a certain hour' and that. I was just happy that I was free. Well not free; but I was happy that I was finally standing on my own two feet.

I was born this way. Mum says something happened to me at birth because I have always had balance problems and speech problems. But she couldn't tell me what happened. It was just one of those things that happened at birth. My disability has made it harder for me. I couldn't ride a bike like everybody else could and I couldn't drive a car like everybody else when I got older. And it sort of stopped me doing a lot of things I wanted to do.

Like I have to ride a three-wheeler bike and that and I would've loved to have played netball and that but that's what I can't do. I did get a bit angry about my disability. I never had a good education like my brother and sister. Like they went to primary school. They went to high school. They went to college. I never had any of that. I always have to accept that I won't be normal with my balance as everybody else. From this day on till I die I'll always accept that I can't be normal like everyone else in my balance. But it doesn't stop me living. Sometimes I wish that people can accept the way you are sometimes. When I trip over, people don't help me they walk around me.

Marriage

I met John at a Southern Region Council meeting [a disability advocacy organisation] in 1985. And John was there on his own with a broken arm. And then when I joined AMIDA[1] I met him a second time. And then he kept on asking me out. I thought he was a creep. I said to myself, 'Who is this guy asking me out?' And he kept on asking me for my phone number and I gave in to him. And then he rang me and when we saw each other again he asked me out. I said, 'Oh okay.' He took me home afterwards and then he came round to watch videos and that just as a friend and then we went out together.

But the first thing was that he shouted[2] for me and he took me home all the time and that. So we started out as friends to see if things got serious. And things got serious in the end and that.

I'd been out with other guys before John but mum thought they weren't good for me. And then John came along and mum thought John was right for me. And I said to myself, 'Oh, I've found Mr Right at long last.' The other guys just wanted one thing only. John liked me for what I am. And the other guys just wanted me for my body and that's it really. I wanted a guy to love me for what I am. And that. When I first met John we were going out for a year. My family never thought I would move in with him. But then I couldn't be away from him. I missed him every night and everything. I was over at his place nearly every weekend and that. And after a year I moved in with him. We went out as friends at first and then we just took one day at a time. And then it just happened.

But we didn't want to get married straight away. We wanted to live together first to see how the other person lives and to see their bad habits and that. And we wanted to get a house and sort of get money behind us

---

1   AMIDA is a state-wide self-advocacy organisation for people with intellectual disabilities. In the past it managed community-based accommodation for people with intellectual disabilities.

2   Shouting means paying for someone's meals, drinks or leisure activity.

and all that before we got married and all that. So we were living together for about five years before we decided to get engaged and then married.

After that time we wanted to keep living together for a long time and we wanted to be legal and all that and I keep on saying to John that I didn't want to get married in my forties and that. And so it was funny the way it came about because we were talking about getting married one day and we were up at Southland one day looking in this jeweller's shop. And I said to John, 'Oh look at all the lovely engagement rings' and then I don't know what happened. It just came about. We put a lay-by on an engagement ring and that's how we got engaged. And we told my sister because my parents were up in Queensland. And I asked Tracey how mum and dad would feel about my getting engaged. And she said, 'Oh they'll be happy' and that. So I rang mum up in Queensland and I said, 'Oh mum, guess what, we've got some great news' and she said 'Yes, I know you're engaged' and I said 'How did you know?' and she said 'Oh a little birdie told me.' And mum said she hoped we would be happy. And then John got on the phone and you know how guys talk. 'Oh, I'll look after your daughter and all this. I'll make her happy and everything.' And we *are still* happy.

We got married in 1992. And we had to go to a marriage counselor [to make sure] like whether you are going to bring up the children in the name of God, whether you're going to love each other and if you are going to stay together, are you two committed to each other and that. And we thought John and I had been together for years. By now we're committed.

It was a great wedding. Mum and dad paid for it. I wanted to get involved in that and all John and I organized was the guest list. Mum organized everything else. I wanted to invite this person and that person and mum didn't want this person and that. And I was so angry because I thought whose wedding is it? Mum's or mine? Mum did a great job with the flowers and the dresses and organising the reception and the church and everything. And we picked the church because all my family except my brother got married at St Mary's Catholic Church in St Kilda so we wanted to get married there too. The wedding was at the school where my sister went at the Catholic church. And the reception was in Clayton where John and I made our debut. We had lots of people at the wedding, 50 on my side and 50 on John's side. My sister was matron of honor and John's niece was bridesmaid and we had John's brother-in-law as best man and our friend was groomsman.

For our honeymoon we went to Fiji. We stayed on a little tropical island called Naviti Resort and it had cabins and everything. I want to go back to Fiji for a holiday. But John has been there twice.

After we came back we moved into John's house. He had taken out a loan and bought a house. And over the years we've done a lot to it. We've done the plumbing and the spouting. We've got curtains in the house. I didn't like blinds so we got curtains and that.

Being married means I've got more responsibilities. I've got a house to look after. I've got cats to look after. I've got more responsibilities and I can't go tripping around the world. Leaving my husband alone. I'm not single. I've got more to think about now. It makes you grow up a bit more. I'm happy with my life as it is. Like even though I've got these responsibilities I'm still my own woman. I still go out and that. And John knows that. I always like to be my own woman. And be free. And do my own things. I'm not tied down to the kitchen all day. And just as John's got his work I've got my involvement with AMIDA and Reinforce[3] and doing other things and I enjoy that.

We like going out together. I go out and watch him play his sports, games like basketball, going on holidays. We have the same friends and also I've got friends that I met before John. I don't go out as much now as I used to. I stay at home. When we were younger we used to do silly things like stay out all hours of the night. We don't do that now. He used to bring me home about one in the morning. We don't do that now. We've been together so long and we do love each other but like we aren't like young kids in love all the time.

John is loving. He buys me birthday presents. He buys me presents for our anniversary and he buys me presents for Valentine's day. He's very thoughtful that way even though we do have our arguments. And our moments. But he can be very thoughtful John. Mostly when we fight it's over money.

That's like all couples. When you're not working you're under a lot of pressure. With John when I was working we used to have all this time

3   Reinforce is a state-wide self-advocacy organisation for people with intellectual disabilities.

together to spare. We used to have a lot of money. But now he's working and that and all my money seems to go on bills and shopping and stuff.

But sometimes I do feel second best. Like I feel his friends are more important than me sometimes. He talks nicely to them. And when he comes to me he doesn't even listen to me. It's especially when he's watching cricket. He treats me like I'm not there half the time. And I say, 'Why oh God, why do I bother?' I organize the bills. Because if I don't, they don't get done. I like to pay the bills and get them out of the way and that so we don't have to worry about them. If I leave it up to John it doesn't get done until the next week or the week after and that. We're not really in financial debt because I've got my job with dad's company Mondays and Thursdays and that pays.

Part of getting married was about having kids. We got married at 35 and I didn't want to rush into having kids. Then John and I talked about it and I wanted to find out if our child would be like me when I was a child. So we went to Family Planning and everything. And then eventually we got tested and we found that we had all the chromosomes so we could have a child. But I wanted to go to a genetic counselor. So John and I both went to see one. Mum came and helped me. I was 37 at that time and they said to me that because of my age and because of my disability it would probably be a 50/50 chance it could be a Down's Syndrome child and that.

I found out that you have to have your first child before you get to 36. And John and I went home and we talked about it. It was a very hard decision for us. And we came to the decision that we didn't want to put our child at risk of being teased at school like I was. I was teased about my balance and that and my speech and we didn't want our child to have that. And also we didn't want to put my health at risk because of my age. And if I did have a child with a disability I would have difficulty raising it. Like I wouldn't know what to do. I wouldn't know how to get him speech therapy or where to go to school and that.

We decided against it. And I said to the genetic counselor, 'As long as we've got each other. That's all that counts.' And she said, 'That's a good attitude to have.' And everyone was so proud of us that we went to a genetic counselor and to Family Planning because most couples rush into having kids. But we wanted to find out if we could. And we could. But I wanted to find out whether it would have been like when I was a child or not. And I said to mum, 'What happened to me when I was a child?' And mum said it was just one of those things at birth. The doctors didn't even know what happened.

John and I didn't want to have a child with the heartache I went through. I went through agony. I had very bad balance problems. I kept falling over chairs, tables and everything. Even when I walked I fell over. And I got teased at school. Terrible names that I don't like to repeat. Really awful names.

I like kids. I get so clucky, especially when I go into shops and see kids' clothes and all that. And seeing people walking down the street pushing their babies. Tiny babies; they are so *cute*. And I say, 'Oh I wished I did have a child.' I do regret not having children. But John and I met at a later time, and we got married later. That was the problem. If we'd met earlier and got married earlier I would have had a child. But we didn't. Oh well, we're happy with each other now. Sometimes I feel so left out because all my friends are having children. And that does hurt sometimes. I've got my niece and nephews. And my sister's having another baby. And I told her that I'd love to have a child. But I have got my nieces and nephews. And Tracey laughed and said, 'Yeah you can hand them back afterwards.' I said to Tracey I sort of envied people in a way having a baby and that. And she said, 'Yeah I know, it hurts.' And I said, 'Yeah it does.' Because it could have been me one day. But that's just wishful thinking. And I'm too old anyway now. Sometimes I look at us and think, 'What's missing in our life? A baby.'

If I did have a child I wouldn't be able to manage it when it was really little like bathing and that. And there was a nurse at the community centre I used to go to. And she used to talk to mum. And she said if I did have a child, there was help out there for me. But mum was worried about it. Because she's getting older and if I did have a child she didn't want the responsibility of looking after it.

I really want to put in the chapter about me not having a baby because I think that's really important. Because other women might feel the same way and then they can read about it. I think it is important for other women to read about. At first it was very hard for me to talk about it, but now I have come to the decision that it is not so hard for me to talk about it now.

Jason is John's son. He's part of our family but I see him differently because he's really part of John's family. I feel left out because John always says 'he's my son, he's my son' and when he's with John I feel like I'm not included and that. John only started to see Jason when he was about 6. He lives with foster parents. We have him for the first weekend in the month. We have him for seven days in the Christmas holidays and we have him on Good Friday to Easter Monday, and special occasions like birthdays and that. And we have him all day on Boxing Day [second day of Christmas]. We had him for five days in January then he wanted to go home. We went to the park, we went to the pictures. We didn't do nothing much. It was too hot to do anything during the holidays. So he watched cartoons all the time. That's the hardest thing. John's already got a son and I haven't. That's the hardest thing for me.

I've got three cats. My babies. I don't know what I would do without them. Mitsi, Flossy and Caesar.

Friends

I had plenty of friends at school and nowadays I still meet up with my school friends and that. When we meet we talk about how good school was and the reunion we had. When we left school we always had reunions and it was great to meet our old school friends. But now the school building has gone: sold to monks. I've got heaps and heaps of friends. They go back years and years. I met friends when I lived away from home. When I got involved in AMIDA I made heaps of friends there.

With friends I like going to the pictures with them, going out with them. Just being together and talking together. With friends I can talk about things, like babies. The really important people, the ones that really understand, are the people who have had to go through it themselves. They really understand. Like Amanda she really understands. She has been there. But other people don't.

Amanda is a friend. We met at AMIDA. I was on the staff and Amanda was working for Reinforce and she used to come and have a chat and a gossip session. And then Amanda was on the Committee. And that's how we met. And we've been friends ever since. Sometimes Amanda says things and I don't agree with her and we end up in a row. We think life is too short to be arguing so we make up. Friends are important. Because without friends you've got no one.

Work

After I left school I went to Gawith Villa. It was an activity centre. Back in them days it was called Gawith Villa for Helping Hand for Mentally Retarded Children. It took us years to change the name. We protested at the name and I was involved in that. For a long time they took no notice of us. At that time they treated us like kids and not adults though I was 16. Like you can't do anything without their permission. Put up your hands if you want to go to the toilet. Like school days and that. The staff lived in the old-fashioned years and that's why they treated us like kids. Then over the years it changed. They got new staff and they got workshops where people were treated like adults and not like kids.

In the early days at Gawith Villa we made moccasins and cotton reels. But when it changed I started going to college and doing courses. I did typing and numeracy and literacy and home economics and sewing and electronics. And that was it. It was different doing courses to going to school. When I was at school and living at home I didn't know any skills and that. But when I finally moved out of home that's when I wanted to get more skills for living on my own. So I did all these courses like electronics, typing, home economics so I could learn to cook and that. I did a ten-week typing course, my first typing course, I did like it. After that I did heaps of typing around neighborhood houses as a volunteer and I was really into typing. I felt really good at doing something real. We got a certificate for the courses. But I don't know what I did with my certificate.

I had a break from Gawith Villa for two years. Mum found me a job as a volunteer at a crèche [child care centre]. I did that for two and a half years. And there was this one child and she was too close to me and that and I took her under my wing and I fed her every day and played with her and that. And when she went home she cried because she didn't want to leave me. I love being with kids. That's why I loved working in the childminding centre but when I left there I wanted a change and that. Also I did a lot of voluntary work over the years. I wanted to get some kind of work that pays you. But in crèches people are looking for voluntary people.

I was at Gawith Villa for a long time and then I joined AMIDA's committee and so I left. It was the hardest decision I had to make leaving

Gawith Villa because I knew everyone. I just got sick and tired of seeing the same people day in and day out. And I knew everything we did there. So I decided to leave. I joined AMIDA's committee[4] because I wanted to try myself out. It was fun. I started to do the typing for AMIDA. It was voluntary but I enjoyed it and I met great people. The best thing was going upstairs to the coffee area, sitting down and having a chat and talking to people. That was great. Memories of just sitting around the table. Just talking. Then they sold the building and we all protested. We did a sit-in and a log of protests. But it did no good. When it closed we had a disco and my brother ran it. He did a great job with the disco. We had colored lights and everyone was dancing and that was the closure. And then when we moved out that was the saddest day of everyone's life.

Then I started really working a lot at AMIDA. I had my own office. I was going in doing the minutes, typing the minutes, photocopying them, sending them out. Doing the mail out. All on my own with Annie's help. It was great fun. I enjoyed it. But I couldn't get paid because I was on the committee. But it was good work and I enjoyed doing it. I was secretary too.

Then I had to leave because I got my first full-time job in 1989. It was a lace company. I was packing laces and winding them on cards. I took the job because I thought it would be independence. It would be great getting more money and being off the pension. It was very exciting for me to get my own pay packet and everything. But it didn't last very long. Only a year and a half because the company went down and I was retrenched.

So then I stayed home for a couple of months and then in 1990 there was an article about a self-advocacy worker for People First in Victoria and I thought that would be good and I applied for it. I thought I wouldn't get it but I applied. And I had all my references and got some help with a resumé. I had an interview and the interview wasn't as good as my references because I was nervous and I knew a lot of the people on the interview panel. But they didn't give me the job because they knew me. They gave me the job because my resumé was really good, because of the work I had done with AMIDA over the years. So I was delighted when I got the job.

4   AMIDA is run by a management committee, the majority of whom are people with intellectual disabilities.

I was there for two and a half years until the funding ran out. I was disappointed because it was a great job. I was doing most of the work stuff I had done for AMIDA but I was going to meetings, representing self-advocacy, going into TAFEs [colleges], showing our videos and that. But the difference between People First and AMIDA was that I was getting paid for what I was doing and that was good. It was a great salary. We were lucky because we had just got engaged at that time and we had all our wedding plans made and that. And it was lucky while I was working I managed to save up for our honeymoon. I was really angry about the funding [running out] because it was a great job. That was the only job that I was good at doing. I liked the pay, I liked the work, especially going out to talk. I liked going to conferences.

I think I got involved in AMIDA because I wanted to do something good with my life and that. Also most people asked me to be involved in these things and I just say 'yes'. And when I do get involved I really enjoy it. I just enjoy being around other people, getting to know people and making friendships that's what's really important. I enjoyed doing the things I did.

And now the video tapes that I've done over the years. People come up to me and say 'Can I have your autograph?' and that. I do enjoy making videos. It gives you great things to do in your life. And that's what makes it all wonderful about being in videos. Being amongst friends and making a video together. Getting to know people better. It is hard work. We made *Josie's Story* back in 1989 about people standing up for your rights and I made the *Home of the Brave* about Caloola [an institution]. And we did *Improving Our Lives*. And I'm going to be starring in one about housing and accommodation and rent assistance and everything about renting. And I think that's all the videos I've done.

Now I work part time for my dad, as a cleaner one day a week. And I work at the women's health centre, teaching women with disabilities about health. But that is only sometimes. That's sometimes six months before you have a session. Then I've got a training session once a month and that's an extra 50 dollars. If I didn't have that, if I just had the pension and the mobility allowance I wouldn't get by. I'd be struggling and that.

I feel a strong person. I don't like everyone else just walking all over me and that and I just tell them how I feel sometimes. I wasn't always like that. I used to feel like a weak person and people would just walk all over me and that but ever since I joined AMIDA and that they've helped me to be stronger. I didn't know anything about my rights or anything until I joined and then they helped me. The staff helped me. We would go to meetings and that and would tell people what we wanted and that. And I would say well I can't get up there and talk about myself and they would say 'yes you can'.

And so at a conference ten self-advocates got up and spoke about what they did and where they lived and everything and I was one of them and I was a bit nervous to get up there and talk but I had Annie to help me and that. And then with People First I had a support worker but I did most of it myself. So that's where the strong part of me came into it because I did most of it on my own. Going to conferences on my own. Giving speeches at colleges and that. And it sort of built up my confidence a bit. And today I'm a lot stronger.

CHAPTER SEVEN

Learning From and With Women
The Story of Jenny

Kristjana Kristiansen, Norway

This chapter is about Jenny. She works at a hotel together with many other women who do not have intellectual disabilities. Kristjana talked with Jenny and visited her at her workplace and learned about why work is important in her life.

Jenny says the money she gets for working is not very important. What is important is how much she learns about everything from being with the other women. Jenny learns most at coffee breaks and at lunch time when she talks to and listens to her women co-workers. Here are some things Jenny has learned.

The women talk about their homes; how to fix things and buy things. The other women have not visited Jenny in her home but she has learned a lot about how to run a home from talking to them.

On Fridays the women often talk about their plans for the weekend. Jenny has learned about what other women do on weekends and she has learned about new places to go. On Mondays they often talk about what happened over the weekend and how they feel about it. The women share their happy, funny stories and their sad and scary stories. So Jenny has learned a lot about how women feel about many things that happen in their lives.

Jenny has learned a lot about being with men, and she agrees with one woman at work who says 'Men are weird, aren't they?'

The women discuss clothes and hair and what colours and styles look best. Jenny gets advice from the women. She has learned that she looks good in green clothes and now she has red stripes in her hair.

Jenny has learned to have more faith in herself. And she has learned about politics at work. The women discuss political campaigns, such as whom to vote for and why. Jenny is also active at the trade-union meetings to improve working conditions.

Jenny talks about God with some of the women. Talking about God is very important to Jenny.

Jenny has learned how to do a good job at the hotel but mostly what she has learned at work is about what it means to be a woman. By being together with other women who talk about their lives, Jenny has learned a lot about what women can do and how they feel.

This chapter will describe some ideas about learning, a bit about how it happens and also why it is important. Most specifically this chapter is about a woman named Jenny. In a qualitative study looking at the social meaning of work in the lives of women with intellectual disabilities, Jenny's story emerged as an instructive example of the importance of the workplace *in learning about life in general*. The first part of this chapter is organized into major themes that have emerged to highlight some of what Jenny has learned at her workplace. Most of what follows is based on what I have learned from many hours listening to Jenny, and sharing coffee and lunch breaks with her and her women co-workers.

Jenny is employed in one of the better hotels in a middle-sized city in Norway. She has been there for nearly two years. She works in the hotel service department where she has responsibilities both in the laundry and cleaning supplies sections. Jenny has Down's syndrome and a long history of institutional incarceration, followed by five years in community services including day-center placements. Jenny is 32 years old. About a year ago she moved into her own flat and receives some home support services there. She has not had contact with her family in the past 20 years. She is the only person with an intellectual disability employed at the hotel and the other 18 employees in her department are all women. There is a long tradition at this workplace to meet for coffee most mornings half an hour before the day shift starts, and also to have lunch together. These times have been key in Jenny's life: *learning to be a woman by being together with other women* who share their lives and thoughts with each other.

Living alone for the first time

It is difficult for anyone to live alone for the first time and often more diffi-cult for people with intellectual disabilities who can be dependent on service systems for housing and home support. Historically, many have been abandoned by their families and communities (on the advice of the 'experts' of the time) and very few individuals have had a chance to have a real home. Many (including Jenny) have instead been grouped with strangers in large congregate settings far away from family and community roots and traditions. Many now have their own homes for the first time, with or without assistance from service systems. Help in the home has typ-ically been organized via formalized service system arrangements under names such as individual service plans, goal and treatment regimens,

Activities of Daily Living (ADL) training programs. This assistance is provided by paid helpers who are in a teacher/therapist/trainer role, and it usually has a focus on skill mastery of the person to be taught who is in the recipient/trainee role. Some people receive more help than they need; others may not receive enough help when they do need it, or not the type of help they need. Exactly how this help is provided and by whom will vary, but there are in any case a number of questions we can ask for people who need help learning about 'home'. Is this the best or only way to learn about having and maintaining one's own home? Many home support programs still unnecessarily invade people's privacy and personal autonomy. Doesn't the presence of formalized training programs in the home interfere with the ambience and experience of a cozy home atmosphere? Aren't there other ways to help Jenny become more independent in managing her own home that are less bureaucratized than formal programs, yet relevant and intense; ways that encourage her competency at 'home skills' but also promote her identity in roles as home owner and independent woman?

At Jenny's workplace her women co-workers often discuss practical problems to do with their house and home. Frequent topics are: managing the household budget ('How will I pay all the bills this month?'); new home products ('Have you seen that ridiculous kitchen gadget everyone is buying?'); gardening techniques ('I think I finally won my battle against crabgrass in the lawn this year'); doing or arranging for home repairs ('Anybody know the name of a good plumber?'). Jenny herself mentions going shopping with some of the others from work to buy curtains after work and getting help to write down the length and width of a window. One Saturday several of the women, including Jenny, helped one of the women in this group re-shingle her roof, followed by a picnic where they went through a brochure together on how to build lawn furniture. Jenny also told about getting help with a telephone bill which she thought had some errors. Her home helper told her it was accurate but Jenny did not understand it until 'Rannveig [a co-worker] showed me how they figure it out.'

In these ways the women assist Jenny in learning to better manage her house and home more independently. Jenny's story shows how the women from her workplace supplement (or even replace) much of what has previously been provided by the paid public service system. Perhaps most importantly, both what Jenny is learning and how she is learning are quite different. And these women co-workers are rarely even in Jenny's house! Jenny is not in a service recipient role receiving home training from a service system; she is a co-worker learning home skills alongside other women who share their conversation, problems, questions, and practical lives with her and each other. Additionally, her co-workers provide a sort of informal monitoring of her home situation; about what is going well and not so well, and what can be done differently. And they do this safeguarding in the same ways that they do it for each other.

Friday lunch and Monday morning coffee

Friday lunch and Monday morning coffee are the shared break times that Jenny seems to value most. Conversations at these times seem to revolve around 'What are you thinking about doing this weekend?' on Fridays and 'How did it go?' on Mondays. In one of my first meetings with Jenny to talk about why work was important for her, she said, 'We talk a lot about what to do on weekends, like where to go and what to do.' Jenny's span of interests has been expanded by hearing about what the other women have as hobbies and leisure-time activities. Although the women rarely meet each other socially outside work, they have greatly influenced Jenny's social participation by sharing information. These exchanges happen in typical and natural ways, as woman to woman, not 'a trainer teaching the client Jenny'. Jenny says, for example, 'Birgit told about [...] where I go ice-skating now,' and 'they talk a lot about that coffee house that plays music, where I ate lunch.'

On Monday mornings the talk often centers on successes and failures of weekend plans and expectations, including (from a day I was there) discovery of a good restaurant, a disappointing blind date, a humorous adventure at a car wash and reports of a colorful visiting theater group that still has tickets for coming performances. In short, Jenny learns much on Fridays about what other women do and want to do on weekends and on Mondays she hears much about the joys and struggles of women's real lives outside work.

'I always try to look my best'

Jenny says this often. Many people with intellectual disabilities are helped to learn the basics of dressing and hygiene, but seldom the finer nuances of developing their own fashionable style. One of the very first things Jenny told me about what she had learned at work was 'I look good in green' and 'I bought new green clothes.' I learned that several of the women had attended a session on 'color-season analysis' and then went clothes shopping. Jenny has been supported to experiment and develop a unique style of her own. She is typically elegantly dressed, with a modern eye-catching, red-streaked haircut. One of the women introduced Jenny to a clothes shop which has frequent sales of top quality fashions and accessories. This co-worker told me, 'Jenny was a timid brown mouse with an awful haircut' when she started here, and 'now she moves so differently, so confidently, with that amazing smile of hers and that smashing new hairstyle.'

'Men are weird aren't they?'

Jenny said this to me one day. Talking about men and relationships with them is another common topic of discussion at break times, and certainly something Jenny refers to often. Historically people with intellectual disabilities have not been perceived as adults capable of having intimate relationships. Relationships have been discouraged, often even by such extreme controls as segregation by sex, forced sterilization, forced abortion, and not being allowed to enter into marriage. In more recent years many women have learned to live with abusive relationships, often because they have not been helped or supported to know what to expect or want in a decent, respectful relationship.

At work Jenny has heard women tell of their personal experiences with men. She listens to how people tackle certain situations, how it feels and what it means, and she hears how the other women give support and advice. She has heard about rape, drunken men on the street and obscene telephone calls, but also about giving and receiving flowers, going away for romantic weekends, pregnancy and childbirth, and getting married. She adds, 'I had a boyfriend before who told me what to do, and I did some dumb things for him. I left him. I told him I was better off being alone. Now, I have a new one.' By discussing her relationships with the other women, Jenny may be better able to recognize and avoid abusive relationships, and be more able to seek loving relationships with mutual respect. Specifically she says she has learned 'to decide for myself sometimes' as, for example, 'I can ask him to wash the dishes, even though I am better at doing it.' She also laughs and says that one woman in the group often says that women are easier to understand than men and Jenny agrees.

Re-writing the rules of 'okay' and 'not okay'

This has been an important struggle in Jenny's life and deserves a somewhat lengthier discussion. Jenny's previous world consisted of well-learned rules about what to do and not do, what was allowed and not allowed, in various settings at various times. These 'rules' were probably transmitted to Jenny directly and indirectly, reflecting service system regulations, and mostly via the complicated spoken and unspoken messages from service workers about what was 'okay' and not. Jenny has always been described by phrases such as 'well-behaved', 'eager-to-please', 'compliant', 'good at doing what she was told'.

From early in life and especially at the institution it seems that Jenny had learned two things: first, that the different parts of the world consisted of sets of rules quite simply divided into categories of 'okay' and 'not okay'; second, that she was expected to follow these rules. Since most rules were probably presented without accompanying rationales one can guess that Jenny followed these rules without understanding their purposes, or consciously electing to accept them. In new situations Jenny had used most of her attention to seek out new 'rules' and became extremely uneasy when this was not possible. This became most clear when she moved from the institutional setting into community settings where there were often no rules, or where the rules were inconsistent and complex.

When Jenny started her job at the hotel many of the women were baffled (and sometimes slightly annoyed) that Jenny constantly asked if 'this or that was okay, or wrong' and so on. She had even asked if it was okay for her to go to the toilet each time the first few days. They said to me afterwards that they thought it was very frightening and sad that 'she had been so controlled and regulated'. Their typical responses such as 'you do not have to ask' or 'don't worry about that' not only did not lessen Jenny's anxiety, but actually made her more confused and frightened. We can understand Jenny's anxiety when we remember that she had been taught to believe that all settings had definite rules, that it was her duty to find and obey the rules, and that she had always been 'good' because she had been obedient. 'It took time before we realized that Jenny thought the world was all about rules. She went around with a worry list in her head all the time about what was okay and not okay. And she had ended up with us who love to break rules and make new ones. No wonder she was terrified,' I was told.

Explanations and support for Jenny in this area have been especially important for her, both when she is confronted with 'ruleless' situations, or when she experiences conflict with what she had always believed was okay or not okay and is now beginning to question. She had, for example, a great fear of evening curfew, even though she now has her own flat where the rule remains only in her own mind. Many evening events were anxious ones for Jenny who frequently looked at her wristwatch and incessantly worried about 'going home in time'. As a result, she rarely relaxed or enjoyed herself.

This is the one area where the women tell me they have consciously tried to help Jenny. 'She can now discuss what to think about when you try to decide if you want to go home in the late evening, such as if there is someone who can drive you there, if you must go to work the next day and so on. And hard as it is to believe, one of her new phrases is "oh, that's nothing to worry about".' Co-workers summarize what Jenny is starting to learn this way:

- Not every place in the world has rule lists.
- Sometimes she can think about rules and disagree with them.
- Sometimes she can decide for herself.
- Sometimes she must decide for herself.

They add, 'Jenny has learned how to say "no" a big and important step for her, especially in her relationships with men.'

Higher thoughts

Developing higher thoughts is an opportunity and a challenge available to few people with intellectual disabilities, and women in general in many societies. People with intellectual disabilities have historically been excluded from 'higher order' discussions, in idea realms such as the political, philosophical, ideological and spiritual. The assumption has probably been that people 'like Jenny' would not be able to comprehend such ideas and/or perhaps do not have the need to explore and develop value systems and personal beliefs. The women at Jenny's workplace sometimes talk about things being 'right or wrong' (which is often different from 'okay and not okay'), and this has had a major influence on Jenny's growing sense of values and beliefs. Jenny's story reveals that she grasps the essence of many 'higher order' ideas and that discussing and thinking about such things is important for her. Here are three examples.

Jenny was previously registered to vote, but never had. She had been registered to vote by others but without understanding what voting really was, or much about political issues or campaigns, and what might be important to think about. Politics was a frequent conversation topic at work breaks during a recent political election campaign and Jenny heard about local and national issues. The women talked about what the different political parties might do for women, for hotel workers, for ageing parents, for local collective transportation and health benefits. 'I worry about blind people,' Jenny said. One woman helped her to write a letter to the main political parties asking about proposals concerning people with mobility impairments and the local bus system. The letter was distributed at the hotel to collect supporting signatures and Jenny received much positive attention for this initiative.

Jenny also reports, 'We talk about God sometimes. I used to want to see God. I worried I couldn't find him. He is difficult to see. He doesn't answer questions like other people do. Hard to understand. Lots of questions inside me. I think about God. It is important to talk about God, and also Jesus. Some people don't like that. That is okay for them but not for me. Mari and Lisbet and I talk about God.'

Jenny was encouraged to join the union of hotel workers. She attends most meetings and also the associated social events. She says she has learned how to go to meetings and about what 'they call solidarity' which she explains as, 'We need to help other people.'

A career not just a job

Having a career not just a job, is an articulated goal for most adults in most societies. But many women with little or no education, and most people with intellectual disability are often forced to be content with having any employment at all, with few or no hopes of career advancement. Jenny's co-workers are for the most part not content with staying forever where they are and help each other to apply for salary raises, qualifying courses, better job posts, etc. The result for Jenny is that she is surrounded by a 'work' culture where she is seen and treated as a co-worker. Most of the women are active trade unionists and the general opinion is that employment, work conditions and career advancement are important and to be taken seriously. One of the women said to me, 'I asked the person from the supported employment office who was here to check up on Jenny, if there were plans to get her a better paid position, and they said she was lucky to have this job. I got so angry. The only thing I could say was that she has the best work record of us all – not one day off sick, and the only one here every day before the shift starts!'

Jenny has not learned to do her actual job tasks much better than when she started. But what has she learned? She is surrounded by the meaning and feeling of work and co-workers and the seriousness of doing a good job. She is known as a good worker, although her actual job skills are only slightly improved.

The point of this last section and of this entire chapter is not about 'learning to do a good job' but about learning. Most of what Jenny learns is not about work or the job: *it is about becoming a woman.*

Reflections about learning

We learn to be who we are in many ways. Most of this is usually called the process of socialization, which has been well described elsewhere. Basically, socialization happens through society's major social structures such as membership in families and educational systems, but also in many unspoken, subtle ways that are often more powerful. Much of what steers our socialization has to do with society's expectations and beliefs about who we are and who we 'should' be, which in turn determines what we are encouraged to do. Some of the more important ways in which we learn are rather obvious: we learn to be who we are by where we are (or not), what we do (or not), and often most importantly from and with the people around us (or not). Learning to become who we are then becomes both an ideological question (what is important to learn and from whom are we learning what?) and also an empirical one (how does one learn most powerfully?).

Most societies have had sets of beliefs and expectations about people with intellectual disabilities that have been very different from the ideas held about other members of society. Ideas about 'who these people are and should be' have been the basis for designing and providing responses, including the past century of segregated incarceration. When an individual is grouped together with others whom society says are 'your own kind' and then surrounded with settings, locations, activities, routines, language, images and expertise that strengthen such a devalued perception, it should not be surprising that an individual 'lives down' to the low expectations and learns to be what society expected. This is often called a 'vicious circle' or self-fulfilling prophecy (Merton 1968) and has had disastrous consequences for groups in society that are perceived as having low value (Wolfensberger 1992), including people with intellectual disabilities, and also women in most societies.

As people with intellectual disabilities are now being increasingly supported to participate in valued settings and roles in society, massive changes are also happening in their personal competency development. Many people are becoming more independent and competent. But also, much of this learning is no longer happening through programmed regimes in artificial training situations. Instead, individuals are learning about real life in the real world.

Access to paid employment and the role of worker are important for an individual because of the value attached to being employed in most societies. But also for many people the workplace provides a setting for learning about many things that have nothing directly to do with the job or the workplace itself. Jenny's story illustrates quite vividly that *where* and *how* and especially *with whom* one learns can have powerful results in learning about life and learning to become a woman.

One word of caution, however: Jenny's situation just happened. It was not planned or arranged by services that her co-workers would be so supportive; nor has what I have described even been recognized or appreciated by the local service agency. Also, the meaning of this work situation in Jenny's life has, for the most part, not been consciously thought through by the women co-workers. One can say that Jenny has simply been fortunate. This point is necessary to make since Jenny's story can otherwise invite a naive and romantic belief in 'natural supports' and 'happy stories' that can be a disservice to some people who may need more formalized and arranged supports.

Women throughout the centuries and in most cultures have assisted each other by sharing experiences, reactions, skills and wisdom. This informal and long-standing tradition can now also be more available to women with intellectual disabilities who have often been excluded from this transmission of wisdom. This is the lesson to be learned from Jenny's story.

CHAPTER EIGHT

Friendship

Love or work?[1]

Rannveig Traustadóttir, Iceland

Michelle and Susan are friends. Michelle is 21 years old and Susan is 19 years old. They are both students. They met when Michelle was doing a school assignment. Rannveig spent time with them when they were together and talked to Michelle about their friendship. She also wanted to talk to Susan, but because she is deaf and does not speak or use sign language Rannveig could not understand her. Michelle and Susan have been friends for two years. Many people think Michelle is a very special person to be Susan's friend. When they are together they go to restaurants, they go swimming and shopping and

1   Preparation of this chapter was supported, in part, by the US Department of Education, Office of Special Education and Rehabilitative Services, National Institute on Disability and Rehabilitation Research under Cooperative Agreements no. H133B003–90 and no. H133B980047 awarded to the Center on Human Policy, School of Education, Syracuse University. The opinions expressed herein are those of the author and no endorsement by the US Department of Education should be inferred. Preparation of the chapter was also supported by the Research Fund of the University of Iceland.

they do other similar things. Sometimes Michelle's other friends are also with them. They also visit each other and Susan sometimes sleeps at Michelle's house. They like each other and like being friends. Like many other people, they have also had some difficulties in their relationship. Susan sometimes has difficulties with her behaviour. It is hard for Michelle to understand Susan's behaviour and she is sometimes a little scared of Susan. When this happens, Susan's mother tries to help them.

Because of Susan's disability Michelle has to do most of the work of the friendship such as planning where to go and finding out how to get there.

Sometimes Michelle talks about the love she has for Susan but sometimes she talks about the work she does for the friendship. So their friendship is based on both work and love. Rannveig thinks friendships between women with and without intellectual disabilities are important and that we need to hear the stories of these friendships.

Michelle Bauer and Susan Clark are friends.[2] When I first met them, Michelle was a 21-year-old university student and Susan a 19-year-old high school student. When I met the two young women in 1991 they had been friends for one and a half years. At the time I was doing my PhD

2   These are not their real names. Their names have been changed in order to protect their privacy. I would like to express my deepest gratitude to the two young women for inviting me into their friendship, spending time with me and teaching me about the love and the work of relationships.

dissertation in the USA. I was interested in learning about friendships between people with and without disabilities and was looking for pairs of friends to spend time with and to interview. One of Michelle's professors at the university told me about her and said she had a friend with a disability. Michelle was willing to meet me but said she would have to check with Susan and her mother to see if I could also meet Susan.

Michelle's friend, Susan, is labelled as being profoundly deaf and intellectually disabled and as having challenging behaviour. Susan and her mother gave their permission and I spent some time with Michelle and Susan when they were together and interviewed Michelle a few times. Susan does not express herself verbally and uses a limited number of signs so I was unable to interview her. What follows is therefore mostly based on Michelle's views of their friendship. It is her story about establishing and maintaining a friendship with a person who has significant disabilities. Despite the difficulties in obtaining Susan's view of their relationship, I attempt to draw out her side of the story, based on my observations and Michelle's account. The chapter attempts to outline both the difficulties and the rewards of the friendship for the young women and the last part is a critical examination of their relationship in the light of the traditional ideal of a friendship as a reciprocal relationship between equals.

Becoming friends

Michelle was studying elementary education and planned to graduate with a dual certification in regular and special education. She first met Susan through one of her courses at the university. One of the assignments was to spend time with a person with a disability. Michelle called it a 'volunteer program' and described it in the following way: 'Last year in the beginning of the semester we had to volunteer three hours a week with a person with severe disabilities or autism. I was placed with Susan and her family.'

Michelle said this was a 'wonderful experience' and she became very close to Susan and her family. After the course was over, Susan's parents wanted to hire Michelle to work with her. For a while Michelle accepted money for being with Susan. She needed a job and if she had not taken the money it would have been hard for her to find time to spend with Susan. After a while, though, Michelle felt she could not accept the money 'cause

I love Susan…we are friends and I would not want anyone to pay me to be their friend.'

Being friends

At the outset Michelle always went over to Susan's home and spent time with her there. Most often Susan's parents went out and Michelle sometimes cooked dinner with Susan and her younger sister or they did other things around the house. A few weeks later Susan and Michelle were going out together and Michelle started inviting Susan to her apartment, sometimes to stay overnight. Michelle tried to include Susan in diverse activities with her friends around the university. To facilitate Susan's inclusion in various activities, Michelle often provided her friends with advice and encouragement about how to include Susan and interact with her. She was proud of how accepting her friends were of Susan. One of their favourite activities was to go to the university campus for a pizza. They also went to restaurants outside the university campus and they went shopping or swimming.

For Susan and Michelle to get together Michelle had to do quite a lot of planning and preparation to organize her time with Susan. She needed to come up with an activity and decide whom to involve, when and where to go, how to get there, and so on. Because of Susan's communication difficulties it was difficult for Michelle to consult Susan directly about things. At the beginning of their relationship Susan's mother explained Susan's preferences and what she liked to do. Susan did not need assistance with going to the bathroom or eating, but she needed help with things related to communication, such as ordering food in a restaurant. In addition to giving Michelle advice, Susan's mother also helped them to communicate. Susan could not use a telephone, so Michelle always called her mother and planned things with Susan through her.

Michelle wanted Susan to be accepted by others and became very upset when some of the college students, or other people they encountered in the community, stared at her and did not act in an accepting or welcoming manner. Michelle was not quite sure how to handle this and became frustrated and upset. She said:

> Sometimes it is very hard because people stare at you, and that really bothers me if people stare. Because she is a person and they make her feel uncomfortable. It is not fair to Susan. She has every right to be on

[the university campus] going for a pizza, as anybody else does. I don't know. I don't think they know how to communicate with her, I think they are still learning how to treat her like a so-called 'normal person'.

Sometimes Michelle got very angry when people acted in a negative way toward Susan in public. Once when the two of them were at the mall, Michelle said, 'People were just giving her the worst looks and I knew she could tell.' Michelle said she wanted to say to these people, 'Have you never seen a person before? She is no different than anybody else!' Michelle felt helpless and frustrated when she met what she saw as society's rejection of Susan.

The difficulties

Michelle found it difficult to deal with some aspects of her friendship with Susan. For example, her limited means of communication created some difficulties in their relationship. It was often hard for Michelle to figure out what Susan wanted to do or where she wanted to go, and she was sometimes not sure what to order for Susan at a restaurant. Although the communication was difficult, it was Susan's behaviour that Michelle found most challenging. She referred to Susan's difficult behaviour as 'challenging behaviours', 'temper tantrums', 'outbursts', or 'fits'. Susan and Michelle had been friends for close to a one year before Susan had her first outburst in Michelle's presence. They had been swimming at an outdoor pool when it started raining so they left. Michelle said it was like something happened on the way to the car. Susan suddenly seemed to become very scared. Michelle described what happened:

> All of a sudden she was a completely different person. She was very destructive, she ripped the rear view mirror off the window and made a crack in the window. She was pulling on the steering wheel, the stick shift, and she was throwing everything out of the car: the towel, her shoes – everything. I could not drive like that 'cause if she would grab me we would have been in a car accident. So I called her Mom. I was scared. I was shaking.

People had told Michelle that Susan had challenging behaviour, but she had never seen Susan like this and it really frightened her. 'It is scary, especially when she is so much stronger than I, and she cannot, as far as her feelings, express herself verbally.' Michelle was afraid that Susan's mother would blame her for the outburst. Instead, Susan's mother was angry with

Susan and told her this was unacceptable behaviour. She also explained to Susan that if she wanted to have friends she had to treat them nicely.

Susan's mother was concerned that Michelle would stop seeing Susan because of this incident. But Michelle said that she could not turn her back on Susan. 'Everyone has their bad days,' she said. Michelle feels very supported by Susan's mother and says that she is not sure if she could sustain the friendship with Susan if her mother wasn't there to fall back on when things got rough. Michelle has a great deal of admiration for Susan's mother and feels like she has learned a lot from her. 'She is wonderful. She is like my second Mom.'

The incident at the swimming pool was only the first in a series of outbursts which Susan has had when with Michelle. Susan's difficult behaviour has strained their relationship and has made Michelle insecure and a bit scared of her. A difficult friendship like Michelle and Susan's needs someone to support it and Susan's mother is the one who provides this support. When Michelle does not know how to handle Susan's behaviour she calls her mother for help. Susan's mother is the glue that holds the relationship together. This support is important not only for the person with the disability, but also for the non-disabled person. With Michelle and Susan it is very clear how important this assistance is in keeping their friendship going.

The rewards

Despite the difficulties of the relationship, Michelle finds it rewarding to be Susan's friend. 'If I can,' Michelle says, 'I want to make a difference in this world, and it starts with one person.' Being Susan's friend made Michelle feel as if she was making a difference. She was Susan's only friend and she knew she was the only person who made it possible for Susan to belong to a network of peers and go to places like the restaurants on the university campus. Without Michelle, Susan would not have had these experiences. Michelle found it particularly rewarding when she saw that her efforts made Susan joyful and happy. It made Michelle feel good about herself to know that she had enriched Susan's life by being her friend.

Michelle believes it takes a special person to be with people with disabilities. 'You have to be special,' she said. 'You have to be so kind hearted and willing and accepting of people… Some people are not patient enough.' Because she has a friendship with Susan, Michelle believes she has these qualities; that she is a 'special person', and this makes her feel good about herself.

Michelle also liked the attention, admiration and praise she got for being Susan's friend. She got this kind of praise from many sources. Her professors at the university thought highly of her because of her commitment to people with disabilities and interpreted her involvement with Susan as a sign of her commitment. Susan's mother also gave Michelle a lot of praise for what she was doing, and Michelle's roommates and other college friends said things like 'Oh that's beautiful…you must be a special person' when they talked about Michelle's friendship with Susan. All of this made Michelle feel rewarded and recognized for what she was doing.

Susan's perspective

I could not interview Susan and could not speak with her because of our communication difficulties, although I did spend a lot of time with her and Michelle. So, obviously, I have difficulties knowing how Susan saw their relationship. Although I cannot be sure, I have hunches about her perspective and would like to reflect on them because I think it is important to attempt to understand the views of both young women and the meaning of the friendship to each of them.

At the beginning of the time I spent with Michelle and Susan I felt quite certain that Susan was very happy about their friendship, eager to keep it going and even grateful for Michelle's willingness to be her friend. Susan seemed eager to be with Michelle and appeared to enjoy her company very much. Michelle provided Susan with all kinds of things she would otherwise not have possibilities to take part in, such as spending time with non-disabled peers in Michelle's home, going to restaurants with a group of non-disabled women her own age, going to the mall, swimming, access to the university campus to do various things and more. As time went on, however, I became less certain about how Susan viewed her relationship with Michelle. I began to suspect that Susan might have developed some negative attitudes toward Michelle and their relationship. Below I will share some of my speculations about what might have been Susan's perspective on their relationship.

When a person has a disability we automatically assume that if a non-disabled person offers a friendship the person with the disability will be eager to become that person's friend and will be thankful for the offer.

While this may have been correct for the first period of the friendship between Susan and Michelle, it may not be how Susan came to view her relationship with Michelle.

At the outset Susan seemed to have been very impressed with Michelle and eager for them to spend time together. One of the indicators of this was the fact that Susan did not have any 'behavioural problems' or 'outbursts' in Michelle's presence for the first year of their relationship. Because of her disabilities, Susan has a difficult time communicating her points of view. Her behaviour may be the only way she knows to communicate. Whether it was intentional or not on Susan's behalf, her behaviour has had great significance in their relationship. If we understand Susan's 'outburst' as communication, we can assume that something went wrong in their relationship and Susan expressed her discontent through what others understood as 'behavioural problems', 'fits', or 'outbursts'. Maybe Susan was trying to express something about her friendship with Michelle?

As Susan and Michelle got to know each other better and 'grew closer', as Michelle described it, Michelle also became closer to Susan's mother. One evening when Susan, Michelle and Susan's mother sat around the kitchen table talking, Susan's mother told Michelle that she (Michelle) was the kind of daughter she had always wanted. Despite Susan's label of 'profound deafness', she may have understood the conversation or simply sensed the increasing closeness between her mother and Michelle. Her 'outbursts' in Michelle's presence may have been caused by jealousy of Michelle.

Spending time with Michelle both at home and out and about may also have increased Susan's awareness of her disability and made her frustrated and caused the 'outburst'. It is also possible that Susan did not want to be Michelle's friend and her behaviour was intended to get that point across. Because Susan's mother always made the arrangements with Michelle for their outings together, Susan may not always have had much of a choice whether she went out with Michelle or where she went. Her behaviour may have meant that she did not want to go out with Michelle or that she had some ambivalent feelings about their friendship.

Friendship: Love or work?

Michelle also seemed to have some ambivalence about their friendship and talked about her relationship with Susan in two 'languages'. The first is what I call the 'language of love', which Michelle used to express her love and affection for Susan. This is the language Michelle used when she described how 'Susan grew to be very special to me' and became a close friend. Michelle also used this language when she said that Susan and she were friends 'just like any other friends' and that 'Susan is a person just like any other person.'

The other is the 'language of work'. Michelle used this language when she talked about the work of the friendship. For example, Michelle frequently talked about 'working with Susan'. When she delineated what things were like when she first met Susan, she usually said, 'When I first started working with Susan...' And when she described how things developed she sometimes said, 'Then, eventually Susan and I started going out to the community.' The expression 'taking people out to the community' is how paid service workers usually talk about their work. Friends would rarely describe going out together this way. Michelle also stated: 'I love taking her out', reflecting that Michelle was doing the work around their outings. Similarly, using the language of work, Michelle reported 'we tried having her sleep over' when she talked about having invited Susan to her apartment to stay overnight.

At first, Michelle's two languages – the language of love and the language of work – seem contradictory. On the one hand, Michelle emphasized that she loved Susan and was her friend and insisted that they were just like any other friends. On the other hand, and often in the next sentence, she used the language of working with Susan. Initially it sounded as if Michelle could not make up her mind whether she was Susan's friend or if she was working with her. A closer look, however, reveals that this way of talking made perfect sense to Michelle and very accurately reflected her experiences of being Susan's friend.

Michelle's first language, the language of love, reflected the emotional aspects of the friendship: affection, emotional closeness and intimacy. Through the language of love she attempted to construct their friendship as close as possible to the friendship ideal she had learned about in her university courses, from the literature in the intellectual disability field, from professionals and from Susan's mother.

Michelle's other language, the language of work, reflected the day-to-day reality of their friendship. This reality was different from the ideal in the literature and was characterized by many of the difficulties which Susan's disabilities brought to the friendship. Some of these difficulties required Michelle to perform a considerable amount of work and made her feel insecure, frustrated and even scared. Michelle was recruited to work with Susan as a requirement of a course. Their relationship developed beyond that and they became friends. But as much as Michelle wished them to have a 'beautiful friendship', as she called it, when they were together it somehow felt like she was working. Being with Susan required a lot of work on Michelle's behalf. Michelle's two languages, therefore, reflected their friendship very accurately.

Friendship: The ideals and the reality

The ideal of friendship as a relationship between equals made Michelle and Susan's friendship somewhat problematic. Held up to this classic ideal, their friendship did not fit because people with and without disabilities are not seen as equals by most people. It is widely documented in the general literature that friendships are relationships based on common interests and experiences and that, especially adult friends, are highly homogeneous (Bell 1981; Bulmer 1987; Gouldner and Strong 1987). Friends are alike 'in social and demographic characteristics as well as in attitudes, interests, intelligence, and personality traits' (Bell 1981: 19). In the general population friends are likely to be equals in terms that friends with and without disabilities usually are not. The key concepts in the classic friendship ideal are: autonomy, freedom, choice, equality and reciprocity. The key concepts in the friendship ideal constructed in the literature on friendships between people with and without disabilities are: inclusion, acceptance, social support, informal support and peer support (Amado 1993; Hutchison 1990).

Individuals within the intellectual disability field are actively recruiting people like Michelle to be friends of people with disabilities in order to solicit support and assistance for community participation. But most of the friendships that are being promoted within the disability field do not fit the culturally dominant view of friendships. This is particularly true of friendships with people like Susan, who have significant disabilities and need a great deal of assistance from their friends. Such one-sided continuous dependency is unusual among friends in the general population where friends, as a general rule, only provide a considerable amount of support in crisis situations and for a limited amount of time (Bulmer 1987). In fact, some authors who write about friendships in the general population warn that too much dependency can destroy a friendship (Block 1980). In a study of friendship in the general population Pogrebin (1987) writes:

> We know that friends can occasionally work miracles to cheer and inspire us, but friends cannot compensate for all the financial and structural deficiencies in a person's life. Friends may help us with a loan or a gift when the unemployment insurance runs out, but a friend is not a job... It's too much to ask of private friendships that they fill the gaps created by large social problems, or to suggest that people who are poor and powerless would be happy if only they knew how to run their personal lives. (Pogrebin 1987, pp.11–12)

The misfit between Michelle and Susan's friendship and the culturally dominant friendship ideal also helps account for Michelle's language of work when she talked about her friendship with Susan. Consciously or unconsciously Michelle seemed to compare her friendship with Susan with the dominant ideal of a friendship. In this comparison, her friendship with Susan did not seem like an ordinary friendship. Instead it was, as Michelle called it, a 'special friendship', unlike her other friendships. Compared to her other friendships, it was sometimes more like work than a friendship. We typically think of being with friends as 'leisure', not as 'work', but when Michelle was with Susan she performed a lot of work. However, because their relationship was constructed as a friendship, the work Michelle performed in the context of her relationship with Susan was not acknowledged and not paid for. By definition, a friendship should be 'free' – you cannot buy friends or pay people to be your friends. This serves to hide the work performed by the non-disabled friend and it tends to hide the fact that some people with disabilities are dependent on assistance from their non-disabled friends.

Friendships in the general population are usually reciprocal in the sense that both parties feel that the relationship is balanced in terms of contributions and benefits (Bell 1981; Rubin 1985). Friendships between people with and without disabilities are usually not reciprocal in the same sense. Instead, the non-disabled friend is typically expected to provide social and practical support to the friend with the disability and the friend with the disability is not expected to reciprocate. Michelle found her friendship with Susan rewarding, but these rewards did not make the relationship reciprocal in the conventional sense. Instead, the rewards derived from the satisfaction of making other people happy, the recognition of being seen as a special person and receiving praise from her professors.

The greatest reward, however, came from Susan's mother, who seems to have been the person who took on the role of balancing the relationship on behalf of her daughter. In order to enable her daughter to have a friendship with Michelle, Susan's mother took on a second mothering role. She came like a 'second mother' to Michelle, as Michelle described it.

The friendship ideal promoted in the disability literature and the discourse in the disability field are different from the classic friendship ideal. The disability literature highlights friendships as beneficial and rewarding for both parties. As other authors have noted, there is a tendency to romanticize these relationships (Lutfiyya 1989). It is rarely acknowledged that such friendships may be difficult at times and that it often takes hard work to construct a friendship with a person with a disability. Rather, these relationships are portrayed as 'natural ties' (Knowlton 1989) and the work is interpreted as 'natural support' (Nisbet and Hagner 1988). This language serves to hide the complex work of facilitating and maintaining a friendship with a person with a disability. It was not just Michelle who performed a considerable amount of work to keep her friendship with Susan going. Susan's mother also contributed a lot of physical and emotional labour to sustain it. She provided Michelle with the support she needed to be Susan's friend. She comforted and reassured Michelle during Susan's difficult periods and did her best to manage Susan's behaviour so that it did not escalate to the point of ruining the friendship.

The misfit between the two friendship ideals (the classic ideal of friendship and the ideal in the intellectual disability field), on the one hand, and the day-to-day experiences of the two young women on the other, also accounted for the contradictory manner in which Michelle talked about her friendship. Her two languages resulted from what Smith (1987) describes as women's 'bifurcated consciousness', or the 'line of fault' between women's actual experiences and the concepts available to express these experiences.

The increasing emphasis on the importance of personal relationships and social networks in the lives of people with disabilities has resulted in a growing body of literature on relationships between people with and without disabilities. Much of this literature on friendships is written as inspirational texts intended to promote friendships between people with and without disabilities. It typically falls into two main categories. The first consists of positive stories about friendships between people with and without disabilities, portraying the friendship as beneficial for both parties and emphasizing the good it does, not only to the person with the disability, but also to the community, humanity and the non-disabled person. Aiming and intending to encourage and inspire people to establish a friendship with a person with a disability, these accounts paint a rosy picture of the relationship and highlight the positive aspects and the rewards (Beach Center on Families and Disability 1997; Forest 1989; Perske 1988; Pierpoint 1990; Strully and Strully 1985). The second is represented by upbeat texts describing how to promote, facilitate, encourage, establish, and maintain friendships between people with and without disabilities (Amado, Conklin and Wells 1990; Forest and Lusthaus 1989; Hutchison 1990; King's Fund Centre 1988; O'Connell 1990; Schaffner and Buswell 1992). Some of these texts resemble how-to manuals, are somewhat technical, and focus more on social support than friendship (e.g. Mount, Beeman and Ducharme 1988; Newton 1989). Sometimes the literature combines stories of friendships with advice about how to go about encouraging and facilitating friendship (e.g. Amado *et al.* 1990; Beach Center on Families and Disability 1997; Hutchison 1990; O'Connell 1990).

Compared to the friendship between Michelle and Susan, much of the disability literature falls short of capturing the complex nature of friendships between people with and without disabilities. Moreover, much of this literature presents an over-romanticized picture of these relationships, and many authors shy away from discussing the difficulties. This trend in the disability literature to paint a rosy picture of friendships between people with and without disabilities and over-emphasize the positive sides of such relationships makes life difficult for people like Michelle. Although Michelle worked very hard to make her relationship with Susan a 'beautiful friendship', they still had difficulties. Michelle has not been able to solve the difficulties in their friendship and when she compared her friendship with Susan to the literature she sometimes doubted herself and wondered what she was doing wrong.

Conclusion

Friendships are important to women and most women devote a considerable amount of energy to their women friends. Women's relationships are often characerized by solidarity and mutual support (Bassaro 1990; Raymond 1986). In this context the relationship between Susan and Michelle has a number of characteristics in common with traditional women's friendships. This story about the friendship between Michelle and Susan reveals how complex it can be to maintain a relationship with a person who has significant disabilities. Michelle's self-doubts seem to derive largely from the fact that their friendship has problems that are rarely recognized by those who discuss friendships between people with and without disabilities.

When writing about friendships between people with and without disabilities it is important also to tell stories about the difficulties such friendships may encounter. All friends have problems, tensions and issues that put strains on the relationship. When one of the friends has a significant disability, difficult issues are even more likely to arise. If women with intellectual disabilities are to find a place in friendships with other women it is extremely important to tell stories that accurately reflect the experiences of these relationships.

CHAPTER NINE

Consent, Abuse and Choices
Women With Intellectual Disabilities and Sexuality[1]

Michelle McCarthy, England

Michelle McCarthy does not have an intellectual disability herself. She has worked with about 70 women with intellectual disabilities in England, trying to help them make choices about their sexual lives.

Many things are the same for women, whether they have an intellectual disability or not. But some things are different. This is what Michelle has found from talking with women.

Masturbation (touching your own private parts) is a hard thing for women with intellectual disabilities to talk about. Most say they don't do it.

Having sex with other women, or feeling attracted to other women, is also very hard for women with intellectual disabilities to talk about. Michelle has not

---

1   My thanks go to the women with intellectual disabilities who spoke with me and whose names have been changed to preserve their privacy.

met any women with intellectual disabilities who say they feel like this.

Many women with intellectual disabilities want, and have, sexual relationships with men. These relationships are very important to the women and they want them to carry on. But most of the women have said that the sex part is not very good for them. It doesn't give them good feelings in their bodies. The women think that sex is better for men than it is for women.

Sexual abuse is when someone is made to do sexual things that they don't want to do or when they don't really understand what is going on. This happens a lot to women with intellectual disabilities.

When women are sexually abused, they can feel upset, confused, frightened, angry. Some women get problems with their mental health, like feeling very depressed or panicky. Other women feel like they want to hurt themselves or hurt other people. Not everyone feels like this and some women with intellectual disabilities seem to carry on with their lives as usual. There is no right or wrong way of responding to abuse.

It is hard to talk about sex and hard to talk about sexual abuse. But more women with intellectual disabilities have a chance to do this now and are telling other people what their lives are like.

In considering the major themes of this chapter and indeed of the course of my work with women with intellectual disabilities, it was interesting for me to reflect on how I got involved in this area of work. In the mid-1980s I was closely involved with a small group of women in setting up and running a rape crisis service for women in our area. I was also part of a management committee of the local Women's Aid refuge for women escaping violent relationships. These were voluntary activities that I did in my 'spare' time. During that period I also was working full time with people with intellectual disabilities and then went on to train as a social worker, with a view to returning to the intellectual disability field once qualified. I have to say that at that point in time I considered my work with women on issues of violence and sexual abuse and my work with people with intellectual disabilities to be two completely separate areas of interest. Nobody I knew or anything I read at that time suggested otherwise.

It was not until I came towards the end of my social work training in 1987 that I began to make connections and understand that, certainly in terms of experiencing sexual abuse, women with intellectual disabilities had much in common with other women. In 1989 I joined a specialist team to provide sex education and specifically sexual health information to people with intellectual disabilities. Like my colleagues, at that time I anticipated that the main part of our work would be relatively straight-forward safer sex education (whatever that means). None of us anticipated what the reality would turn out to be: namely that most of our time would be spent with women and men with intellectual disabilities who needed help and support around issues of consent, abuse and choices.

Everything that I have learned about the sexuality and sexual abuse of women with intellectual disabilities over the past ten years has consoli-dated that first important lesson: that women with intellectual disabilities have much in common with other women. I have also learned that there are a number of ways in which the experiences of women with intellectual disabilities are distinct. The rest of this chapter aims to highlight the differences and commonalities.

Since 1989 I have worked on a one-to-one basis with approximately 70 women with intellectual disabilities on sexuality issues. Most of the women have had mild or moderate intellectual disabilities, with a small number having more severe intellectual disabilities. None had profound or multiple disabilities. This is not because more severely disabled people do not need assistance in this area – clearly they do (Downs and Craft 1996), but because the nature of the particular service that was on offer relied on people being able to communicate verbally about their experiences and feelings.

It is important to note that my work with women with intellectual disabilities does not purport to be representative of all women with intellectual disabilities. I am aware that the women I have worked with are not a random sample. On the contrary they are women who have been referred, or in a small number of cases have referred themselves, for assistance with matters related to sex, sexual abuse, sexual health and/or a particular relationship(s). The implication of this is that if there are women with intellectual disabilities who are living sexual lives which they experience as mutual, pleasurable and safe they would not have come to my attention or anyone else's.

Speaking about sexual lives

The vast majority of women I have worked with are white British women and have been aged, for the most part, in their twenties, thirties and forties. I am therefore not well acquainted with the views and experiences of Black and other minority ethnic women, nor of the very young or older women.

The women I have worked with have lived both in institutions and in community settings and one of the aims of my doctoral research was to investigate the differences in women's experiences in these two different contexts (McCarthy 1999b). In fact, I found relatively few differences, which is surprising, shocking and depressing.

In my work with women with intellectual disabilities I have tried to enable them to speak about their sexual lives in broad terms. However, the focus of my input concentrated on helping them identify what they did and did not like sexually and seeking to build on the former, while minimizing or eradicating the latter. Facilitating such explicit discussions of sexual matters was a challenge in both ethical and methodological terms, although space does not permit an exploration of them here (see McCarthy 1999a for a detailed discussion).

Masturbation

None of the many women with intellectual disabilities whom I have met have spoken openly and positively about masturbation. This should come as no surprise as there are definite social taboos for all women in speaking openly about the sexual pleasure they can give themselves (McNeil 1992). What is different, however, is that even after support and encouragement from me (i.e. telling the women that I think masturbation is a normal, positive activity that most women, including myself, do at some point(s) or throughout their lives), still only about one-third of the women with intellectual disabilities have said that they do masturbate or have done so. This is quite different from other research evidence with non-disabled women where much higher proportions say they masturbate, for example, 82 per cent (Hite 1976), 81 per cent (Quilliam 1994).

Whether women with intellectual disabilities really do masturbate much less than other women or whether they simply feel less able to say they do (particularly to people in positions of authority such as staff members) is impossible to know. Probably both factors are true. Until women with intellectual disabilities receive messages which enable them to understand that masturbation is not shameful or harmful, then we are unlikely to get a better insight into this. It is quite clear from my work that most women with intellectual disabilities have picked up very negative messages about masturbation. The following comments were typical:

> I think it's rude, disgusting and vulgar. (Annette)

> It's wrong because women can injure themselves. (Sylvia)

> A man might see you…he'd have the shock of his life. (Liz)

One woman gave a much longer response which revealed what she felt was appropriate and 'normal' sexual behaviour for women and men:

Helen: I don't think it's a good thing to masturbate, I wouldn't do it. I don't know if there's any harm in it or not, but I don't think it's a good thing.

MM: Well, there's no harm in it and most people do it, women and men. What do you think is wrong with it?

Helen: It's a funny way of showing that you feel attracted to a man, wanting to masturbate. I think it's a totally unreliable, unreality sort of behaviour.

MM: Are you saying it's not real sex?

Helen: It's no good trying to attract a man like that, men would think it was funny, it would put them off, it might give them bad ideas.

MM: Most women don't masturbate in front of a man to attract him, but they do it for themselves, because they like it, for their own feelings. Would it be all right to do it if it was in private?

Helen: I still don't think it's a good idea, because men do it a lot if they feel sexually inclined towards a woman and they can't get one, but for women it's not a good idea, even if they're in bed, because it doesn't prove anything and it's wrong to do it.

MM: Is it wrong for men to masturbate?

Helen: No, because they'd like a woman to be in their life and they haven't got one. Masturbating is a good sign that they get those feelings, that they get urges.

MM: So men get sexual urges?

Helen: Yes.

MM: Do you think women get sexual urges?

Helen: No.

MM: Why not?

Helen: The only sexual urges a woman can have is if a fella takes her to have sex. Otherwise they haven't got any.

In view of attitudes like these, the content of sex education needs to change to give much more positive emphasis to masturbation, both as an activity in its own right and as a way in which women can learn about their bodies, their desires and their pleasure; information which may also prove useful in sexual relations with a partner (McCarthy 1999b; Thompson 1990).

Sexual activity with other women

None of the women with intellectual disabilities with whom I have worked has spoken about having had sexual contact with another woman. One woman had allegations of sexual abuse made against her by other women, an unusual occurrence according to the literature and anecdotal evidence (McCarthy and Thompson 1997).

Once again, it would be wrong to draw the simple conclusion that sex between women does not occur, or only does so at a very low level. Social taboos and prejudices about same-sex relationships have clearly been picked up by many women with intellectual disabilities:

It's dirty and wrong. (Jane)

If you're hard-up for a man, why go with a woman? (Sylvia)

With reference to her sister, who was lesbian, another woman said, 'My mum didn't like it very much ... my mum thought it was terrible actually.' (Susan)

None of the women had received any positive messages about sexual attraction or relationships between women, so it is not surprising that they only felt able to express negative views of their own. Whether this would inhibit them from having sex with other women if they wanted to is again impossible to know. However, it is possible to observe that men with intellectual disabilities, who also receive many negative messages about same-sex relationships, do nevertheless engage in high levels of same-sex activity, although like many other men they do not necessarily label themselves as gay or homosexual (Thompson 1994). Even allowing for some under-reporting, it is generally accepted that sex between women is probably the least common form of sexual expression for people with intellectual disabilities (McCarthy and Thompson, 1998). It is not possible to know exactly why this is, but elsewhere (McCarthy 1999b) I have speculated that the following factors contribute to the under-representation of same-sex activity among women with intellectual disabilities, compared to their male peers:

- Women are not socialized or accustomed to taking the initiative sexually.

- Women are more likely to want sex in the context of an established relationship and with no role models or support for lesbian relationships these are unlikely to develop.

- Attraction to a particular individual is more likely to encourage a woman to have sex, so if a woman is not sexually attracted to another woman she is unlikely to have sex with her (whereas men will have sex anyway regardless of whether they 'fancy' someone or not).

- Many women learn what sex is through abuse by men, but as they are rarely abused by women they do not learn what sex between women is.

- Most sex between men and women in institutions involves an exchange of sex for money. There is no history of women paying anyone for sex; therefore no incentive or motivation for women to engage in this. (McCarthy 1999b, p.204)

To counter some of these factors, sex education for women needs to give the information that sexual relationships with other women are a positive life choice for many women (for a rare but excellent example of this, see the *Four Stories* video).

Sexual pleasure

The vast majority of women with intellectual disabilities with whom I have worked spoke of lives which are largely devoid of sexual pleasure. This is not to say that their sexual relationships more broadly do not give them various kinds of pleasures and satisfactions, but the bodily experience of sexual pleasure and specifically of orgasm is not among them. Most of the women have spoken of sexual experiences which are exclusively or predominantly penetrative; vaginal penetration for all women and also anal penetration for over half. Only one woman appeared to know what a clitoris was and what it was for. None of the women appeared to know what I was talking about when I tried to describe strong feelings of sexual pleasure, particularly orgasm. These findings support those of other similar research studies (Andron 1983; Andron and Ventura 1987). Few of the women gave any indication that sexual attraction or sexual arousal were reasons for them engaging in sexual contact with men (I appreciate these are difficult things for anyone to discuss). Indeed, it was often very difficult for the women to give any reasons why they had sex with men. When they did say, however, most gave as reasons the fact that they liked or, occasionally, loved the man. Most women gave a very strong impression that their relationships with men were extremely important to them and they understood that in order to develop and maintain a relationship, very often, they felt they had to engage in sex, even if the kind of sex they were having did not afford them much personal pleasure. In other words, it was seen by many women (though not all) as a means to an end.

Finding relationships with men and retaining a sense of self within them

Although most of the women with intellectual disabilities I have spoken to valued their relationships with men very highly, just like other women they were aware of difficulties and conflicts which had to be managed. For example, one woman who said she liked sex within certain limits nevertheless felt it was a cause of some conflict with the various men with whom she had been in relationships (usually without intellectual disabilities themselves):

Mary: I don't mind it, but not all the time, not all the time, like every night, because you get fed up. When I go out with someone, I don't mind sex sometimes, but I don't like doing it a lot. But when I went out with T he wanted it morning, afternoon, tea time, every night.

MM: Well, that is a lot, isn't it?

Mary: I don't mind it once, like just of nighttime, but not all the time.

MM: Well, yes … from what you've said it does seem a bit much.

Mary: Yes, I was glad to get out to college.

MM: Right, to get away from it you mean? [*both laugh a bit*]

Mary: Yeah, like when me and B do live together, I don't mind him once, but not more than once.

MM: But do you think the men like it at other times?

Mary: Yeah, they always like it, anytime, morning, afternoon… [*with emphasis*] Yes, I know that very well.

Another woman cared about her boyfriend, also a man with intellectual disabilities, but was very concerned about the fact that he told other people what she considered to be their private business. In this she has much in common with others, especially young women who resent the fact their boyfriends often 'brag' about their sexual activity, with the result that the women can develop what many people consider to be bad reputations (Lees 1993):

Lorraine: He keeps telling everyone that I've got a baby in my stomach and I haven't. My mum told me off because he keeps saying that.

MM: And you don't like him saying that?

Lorraine: Yeah, what he says to other people, broadcasts it to everyone … he even tells the people at work as well.

MM: How does it make you feel, that he talks to people about having sex with you?

Lorraine: It makes me feel upset… I don't like him telling other people that, broadcasting it.

Like other women, women with intellectual disabilities have to face dilemmas about which men to trust and which to avoid. Two of the women living in institutions whom I spoke to reacted very differently to advice they had been given about going with men who did not have intellectual disabilities (whom they refer to as 'outside' men). One woman was very cautious:

MM: What about going with men from outside?

Fiona: No, I know better than to do that, it's dangerous.

The other woman was not so cautious, relying more on her own judgement:

Karen: I've been with outside men.

MM: How do you know they're outside men?

Karen: 'Cos they come in by car.

MM: They come into the hospital looking for someone to have sex with?

Karen: I don't go with all the men who come in cars, but I did think a lot of one of them. But the trouble was he promised me money, but didn't give it to me afterwards. I mentioned condoms, but I don't know if he loved me or not.

MM: Did he use condoms?

Karen: He didn't. You can't trust all men in cars, I won't go in their cars unless I can trust them.

MM: How do you decide if you can trust them or not?

Karen: Well I look at them and by the way they come along and all this and that and the way they look.

MM: What is it about the way they look that makes you trust them?

Karen: I can tell by their eyes if they're a murderer or a raper.

Other women simply found it hard to come to terms with the fact that they could not get or sustain the kind of relationships with men which they wanted. Some found it hard to extricate themselves from relationships they wished to end; others found it difficult to keep a relationship going:

Lynne: I haven't really got anybody that sticks with me long term.

MM: Long term…is that what you would like?

Lynne: They never do stick with me.

MM: Do you know why?

Lynne: They might not fancy me. Nobody's really interested in what I could say long term. I'm never going to get a long-term partner, because I know there's not many people interested in having it with me.

MM: Why do you think that is?

Lynne: Because nobody can be bothered. God knows why. I think to get somebody really interested in you is difficult enough. OK I'd like somebody to be very, very interested, but I can't find anybody.

MM: Yes, I think a lot of people find that really hard, it's not just you.

Lynne: I'm sure your fellas have been with you a lot longer than I've had any men.

MM: That might be true, but I don't know how long your relationships have been.

Lynne: A week, maybe two weeks, not very long, then they sling me in. I have really nobody I can turn to.

Other women also expressed the view that the men made the decisions about whether a relationship would become sexual or indeed whether it would be a relationship rather than a one-off sexual encounter. First, Maureen, gives her view on whether decisions about sex are usually made jointly by men and women:

> They might talk about it together, but sometimes men don't, they just say 'come on, I need you' and they just pull you down and before you know where you are, they're at it… They cover your mouth up somehow, they get a bit brutal and when it's over, you're left there … sort of thing…that's not very nice, is it? … But sometimes the man might ask a woman.

Next, Karen speaks from her experience of how things have transpired for her:

> A man looks at you, then if he likes you, he says he wants to go with you and do something with you. Then he says 'lay down, I want to interfere with you', or 'I want your body', because he likes you. Then he lays down on top of you, puts his arms around you and kisses you, then he puts his thing up you, then he gets off you and says he'll see you again and thank you and all that, for giving me your body and maybe he says he loves you, then he says he gotta to go now.

Although much of what the women with intellectual disabilities have had to say about their sexual lives has been negative, there have also been women (albeit the small minority) who have spoken very positively about the sexual relationships they enjoy with their boyfriends. Catherine, for instance, was a young woman who was very positive about her relationship in a broad sense and also the sexual side of it. Catherine's boyfriend was a man with intellectual disabilities of roughly the same ability level as her and they were well matched in other ways; they lived very similar lives, in group homes, going to college, sharing similar interests. In short, he did not have many of the advantages over her which other men often have in relation to their female partners (see below). The result was that Catherine felt, for example, that she had control over whether sex took place: 'If I don't want to do it, I don't do it.'

She felt she could communicate with her boyfriend: 'If there's any problems, we always talk about it. We kiss and make up.' Her own positive experiences may have contributed to the fact that she held more positive views about sex generally than many of the other women. She thought masturbation was acceptable and of all the women she had the most accepting views on same-sex relationships.

Sexual abuse

As I indicated in the introduction, issues of sexual abuse came to dominate the work of a team which was actually set up to address sexual health issues. First I want to outline what is known about the nature and extent of sexual abuse against women with intellectual disabilities. Then I will discuss what impact the abuse seems to have on women and how they struggle to make sense of it.

Nature and extent of sexual abuse

Awareness of the nature and extent of sexual abuse is still developing and has come about partly from an increased willingness in recent years to listen to what people with intellectual disabilities have to say about their lives. The development of both sex education groups and individual work, as well as more general self-advocacy networks, has enabled many people with intellectual disabilities to speak out about abuse they have experienced.

But although knowledge is developing, it is still incomplete. What really happens in terms of what, where, who, how and why cannot be completely known because sexual abuse by its very nature is a secretive and hidden activity. On top of this is the shame and guilt that both victims and perpetrators may experience, which inhibit them from speaking out about their experiences. What is known from mainstream research on sexual abuse is that most sexual abuse is never reported to the authorities (see Kelly 1988; London Rape Crisis Centre 1988). There is no reason to think that things would be any different regarding reports of sexual abuse by people with intellectual disabilities and, indeed, there are reasons to be more pessimistic about the proportion of abuse which is disclosed, given that many people with intellectual disabilities have additional communication and sensory impairments.

However, the fact that we do not know everything does not mean that we do not already have a good picture of sexual abuse as it affects people with intellectual disabilities from a growing body of evidence. There have been several prevalence studies and a smaller number of incidence studies. For reasons of space, these cannot be reviewed in detail here, but interested readers could look at the following research studies: Chamberlain *et al.* (1984) carried out a retrospective study of case notes of 87 young women with intellectual disabilities who attended an adolescent clinic. They found a sexual abuse prevalence rate of 25%; Elkins *et al.* (1986) conducted a very similar prevalence study at another US specialist clinic and found a prevalence rate of 27%; Hard and Plumb (1986) conducted a prevalence study in which they directly asked people with intellectual disabilities about their experiences of abuse. The study looked at a whole population of people with intellectual disabilities, namely those attending a day centre, and prevalence rates of 83% for women and 32% for men were reported; Buchanan and Wilkins (1991) surveyed a small group of staff (total of 37) who reported knowledge of 67 cases of sexual abuse among the population of 847 people with intellectual disabilities they worked with – a prevalence rate of 8 per cent; the largest and most recent British prevalence study was carried out by a colleague and myself (McCarthy and Thompson 1997). We conducted a study looking at all the 185 people with intellectual disabilities who had been referred to us for sex education over a five-year period. We found a prevalence rate of 61% for women and 25 per cent for men.

Dunne and Power (1990) carried out a small incidence study in Ireland, looking at the 13 cases of confirmed sexual abuse that had been brought to the attention of a community intellectual disability team over a three-year period at a particular service (serving a total population of 1500). The data were collected from staff only and gave an incidence rate of 2.88 per thousand per annum; the largest and most influential of the British studies are the incidence studies of Brown and Turk (1992), and Brown, Stein and Turk (1995). They surveyed statutory intellectual disability services in the South East Thames region through written questionnaires to senior managers within health and social services: the resultant incidence rate in 1992 was 0.5 per cent per thousand per annum. This works out at approximately 940 cases in the UK, although this figure was revised upwards as a result of the second survey (Brown *et al.* 1995).

It is apparent from these studies that both the prevalence and incidence rates vary widely. The reason for these variations is due in part to the differences in definitions of abuse, the different populations sampled and, crucially, to differences in research methods including whether abuse rates for women and men are calculated separately or together. Also important to note is the fact that reported instances of sexual abuse decrease the further away from the individuals is the focus of the study. Therefore the highest rates of sexual abuse are reported when the individuals themselves are questioned, for example, Hard and Plumb (1986) and McCarthy and Thompson (1997). When staff are questioned they can only report those cases which they know about and which they believe to be true. As there are high levels of disbelief when people with intellectual disabilities disclose sexual abuse, it is not surprising that these figures are much lower. When senior managers are questioned they are likely only to report those instances of abuse which were formally recognized and responded to, producing yet again a much smaller number of cases (Brown and Turk 1992). See also Brown (1994) for further discussion of these issues.

Although estimates of incidence and prevalence rates have been made using very different methodologies, clear patterns still emerge that paint a picture of the sexual abuse of adults with intellectual disabilities which has similar characteristics to the sexual abuse both of adult women and of children (see, for example, McCarthy and Thompson 1997; Turk and Brown 1993). Both women and men are victims of sexual abuse, with studies varying in their reported figures from about 75 per cent women to almost equal numbers of men and women (see Brown *et al.* 1995). While a number of studies do not investigate any differences in the abuse experiences of men and women, those that do find gender differences: specifically that women are abused more than men and are less likely to be believed (Hard and Plumb 1986; McCarthy and Thompson 1997). Hard and Plumb (1986) found that while 100% of men with intellectual disabilities were believed when they disclosed abuse, the same was only true for 45 per cent of the women. In my recent study, in 32% of cases the abuse of women with intellectual disabilities was not even taken seriously enough to be reported to service managers, whereas this was only the case for 7 per cent of the men. My analysis of this is that there are different thresholds for belief and intervention, based on the perceived 'normality' of heterosexual contact (even abusive contact) compared to any homosexual contact (almost all perpetrators of women and men are male). There are still strong beliefs that women should tolerate abuse from men and these are found among service providers, the judiciary and among men and women with intellectual disabilities themselves (McCarthy and Thompson 1997).

Perpetrators

As stated above, perpetrators are overwhelmingly men. They are usually known rather than strangers: They are often in positions of trust and authority and have often abused others. It is assumed (based on extrapolations from known multiple abusers) that they will go on to abuse other adults with intellectual disabilities through their connections with services. Perpetrators come from four main groups: present or past service users with intellectual disabilities; family members; staff and volunteers;

trusted adults within the community such as family friends, neighbours, tradesmen and so on.

From the McCarthy and Thompson prevalence study (1997, p.112), Table 9.1 shows perpetrators by their relationship, if any, to the women they abused.

Table 9.1. Perpetrators' relationship to the women they abused	
Perpetrators	Of women (n = 59*)
Men with intellectual disabilities	25 (42.4%)
Family members	16 (27.1%)
Staff	4 (6.8%)
Strangers	6 (10.2%)
Other	7 (11.9%)
Not known	1 (1.7%)

* Of the 59 perpetrators of women with learning disabilities, 58 (98.4%) were male and 1 was female.

From this study and others (e.g. Brown *et al.* 1995) we can see that men with intellectual disabilities often from the same service, make up the biggest single perpetrator group. Over-reporting is often suggested as a reason why men with intellectual disabilities feature so highly in abuse statistics of this kind, as these men are considered more likely to be caught and reported than others who may be more skilled at covering their tracks (Turk and Brown 1993). That may be a partial explanation for those studies which rely upon asking staff about clients' abusive experiences. But when people with intellectual disabilities are asked, as they were in this study, the reports of abuse by men with intellectual disabilities may well be underestimates. It is well recognized that non-disabled women still in ongoing relationships with men may find it hard to acknowledge abuse in the first place (Kelly and Radford 1996; Wyatt, Newcomb and Riederle 1993). They may be very reluctant to report it because they do not want to get their boyfriends into trouble and/or because they fear the consequences if they tell anyone. There is no reason to think this would be any different for women with intellectual disabilities. Evidence of it can be seen by the fact that although many women with intellectual disabilities felt negatively about the actual sex that had taken place, the majority who expressed their feelings about the perpetrators had positive or mixed feelings towards them. Also, many women with intellectual disabilities did not want any action taken against the men they cared about (McCarthy and Thompson 1997).

The second biggest category of perpetrators against women was their fathers and stepfathers. Much of this abuse takes place during the woman's childhood, but also during adulthood. Unlike some other women who can move away when they grow up, many women with intellectual disabilities remain in the parental home for prolonged periods of adulthood. Even when they do leave home, perhaps to live in a group home or other supported accommodation, some women find that their fathers continue to sexually abuse them during visits home.

In this study, relatively low levels of abuse by staff were reported by both women and men with intellectual disabilities and this is very likely an underestimation. As the researchers were also staff members, in effect people with intellectual disabilities were being expected to report one member of staff to another – a potentially very frightening thing to do, especially if they had been threatened by the perpetrator not to tell.

Dynamics of abuse

In order to understand quite what was happening to people when they were abused, the study distinguished between those instances where the victim clearly did not consent, those instances where it was unclear and those instances where the victim did consent, but this was not free and informed consent. In fact, little of the abuse reported by women involved the use or threat of force. Therefore we were interested to explore the dynamics of the interaction, whereby one person is able to get the other to comply with them to the point where they can have penetrative sex (as happened in most cases).

In many cases the victims did consent to sex, either explicitly or implicitly, in the sense that they went along with it. We therefore looked at what barriers to consent may have been operating either at the time of the actual abuse or in the relationship more generally.

A significant difference in ability levels was a common feature. It is a very common pattern for a man without intellectual disabilities to take sexual advantage of a woman with intellectual disabilities. One of the struggles for women with intellectual disabilities in forming partnerships with men is that they rarely get the opportunity to be the most able partner, or even to be of equal ability. More able men seeking out less able partners is a pattern long since recognized in long-term relationships and marriages involving people who do and do not have intellectual disabilities (Craft and Craft 1979; Mattinson 1970). It is also very common for men with mild or borderline intellectual disability (or sometimes with no discernible intellectual disability at all in the usually accepted sense of the term, but who nevertheless receive intellectual disability services) to seek out sexual partners who are less able than themselves. Indeed, in many cases it would be difficult for these men to find sexual partners of similar ability to themselves even if they wanted to, as they are more often than not the most able people in the whole service. As they are also the most likely to be sexually active, service providers need to recognize the inevitable outcome of placing such men in intellectual disability services (McCarthy and Thompson 1996).

The women themselves clearly recognized that sex often took place between more able men and less able women. They had a strong sense that it was inherently unfair; that the less able person was by definition at a disadvantage and that therefore it was wrong:

Jane: Some of the men do it, if they can't get a high-grade patient, they get a low grade.

MM: What do you think about that? Is it all right?

Jane: No, I've talked to people about that, I don't think it is right.

It's not fair on the more handicapped ones, because they wouldn't know what's going on. (Alice)

I think it's terrible, I really do, especially if they're not right upstairs [points to head] and somebody cleverer pushes themselves on them, it's terrible. (Kay)

The above conversations all related to other people or hypothetical situations. What was interesting was that the women very frequently had sex with men more able than they were; in effect they were the less intellectually able people in the encounters or relationships. But they did not construct their own experiences as being unfair on those grounds.

It was common for women to be afraid of the perpetrator, whoever he was, and therefore to acquiesce for that reason. Clearly where the perpetrator is their father or a member of staff, the power dynamics are easy to understand. However, there was also considerable fear between service users. The most common reason women with intellectual disabilities have given for why they comply with the sexual demands of male service users is fear (sometimes based on their direct experience) of physical violence (McCarthy 1998). There are a number of service users who have reputations for physical violence and/or verbally aggressive behaviour. Sometimes they enter an intellectual disability service for precisely these reasons. Other service users are often acutely aware of this and if approached sexually by these individuals behave in a reasonable and rational manner by giving in to them. The following conversation about one woman's difficulties in trying to assert herself with fellow service users demonstrates this:

MM: So what do you do when it hurts?

Clare: There's not a lot you can do.

MM: So what do you do?

Clare: Nothing.

MM: Do you ever say that it hurts or say 'ouch'?

Clare: I cry.

MM: Do you cry while they're doing it or after it's finished?

Clare: Whilst they're doing it, because it's very, very painful.

MM: And what do they do when you cry?

Clare: Nothing they just carry on. They say, 'What's the matter with you, cry-baby?' They tell you to shut up and go rougher.

MM: What would you like them to do?

Clare: I'd like them to stop there and then, but they don't.

MM: Well, you don't have to put up with that.

Clare: No. But I'm afraid of R.

MM: What do you think he'll do?

Clare: Beat me up.

MM: Yes, I know lots of people are afraid of him.

Clare: He's a great bloody tall bleeder and most of the girls here are frightened of him. He's bigger than I am.

The importance of gender as a source of power for the men clearly cannot be overstated. Many of the women were afraid of the men because they were men and therefore seen as having the potential to hurt them. A number of the women also believed the myths and stereotypes about men needing sex and it being a woman's role to give it to them and therefore they had sex when they did not want it themselves. In a separate research study I conducted some years ago I documented the actual words that women with intellectual disabilities use to describe their sexual encounters with men which illustrate this (McCarthy 1991).

Women were also afraid that relationships, including high status ones such as engagements, would be called off if they did not comply with what the men wanted sexually.

Bribery and financial incentives played a significant role for women. This relates to the institutional practice whereby men pay women regardless of whether the sex is consenting, abusive or unclear. This sub-cultural practice is well established and is clearly gendered in its operation (McCarthy 1993).

Impact of sexual abuse on other sexual experiences

Experiencing such high levels of sexual abuse would probably have made it difficult for the women to experience other sexual encounters positively and/or to frame them as such. Other research concerning non-disabled women (Orlando and Koss 1983; Wyatt *et al.* 1993) and women with intellectual disabilities (Kiehlbauch Cruz, Price-Williams and Andron 1988) suggests that abusive sexual experiences can have a negative impact on women's subsequent consented sexual experiences. This is illustrated by Pauline's account. In the following conversation she tells me what happened to her and the lasting effect it has had on her sexual life:

Pauline: It was grown up men done it. I nearly was pregnant when that man touched me, that's why my mum took me to the doctors, stop me having a baby.

MM: That something you were worried about then, was it?

Pauline: Yes, my mum didn't like babies…well, she liked babies, her… I don't want a baby on my own. I was 14 or 15 I was, when he done it, a long time, that's why I take tablets about it, stop me having periods.

MM: So you were taking a tablet to stop you from getting pregnant?

Pauline: Yes, 'cos any man do it with a woman. That's why I went to the doctor, stop me getting pregnant.

MM: Do you still take that pill?

Pauline: Not now, I stopped it, I'm old now, I don't have periods any more. If a man wants to get in bed with me, I'd say 'No way!'

MM: You wouldn't want to?

Pauline: No, I don't want sex, not after what that man did.

What is consent? What is abuse?

When women with intellectual disabilities experience a large quantity of sexual abuse and a low quality of consented sex, this combination contributes to their generally negative view of sex. Indeed, as an outsider hearing their experiences secondhand, it was often difficult to distinguish between what was abusive and what was not. This must also have been difficult for the women themselves. Many women felt under pressure from men and had sex they neither liked nor wanted to stop the pressure. Other women, as I indicated earlier, said they sometimes let men continue to have sex with them, even though it was painful, because of fears that they would be hit if they told them to stop. Other women were quite sure that their relationships would end if they refused to have sex with their boyfriends.

In many cases the women's ability to give free and informed consent to sex has been compromised by some particular factors which have to do with their intellectual disability, but, importantly, also some particular factors which have to do with their being women. Many feminist theorists (see, for example, MacKinnon 1987; Pateman 1980) have drawn attention to the problematic notion of consent, when women and men are in fundamentally unequal relationships. Pateman suggests:

> Consent as an ideology cannot be distinguished from habitual acquiescence, assent, silent dissent, submission, or even enforced submission. Unless refusal of consent or withdrawal of consent are real possibilities, we can no longer speak of 'consent' in any genuine sense. (Pateman 1980, p.150)

Many of the women I have worked with and indeed many non-disabled women (e.g. Gavey 1992; Holland *et al.* 1991a, 1991b), have shown that being able to refuse sex is far from straightforward.

It is not possible to unravel the different strands of oppression which women with intellectual disabilities face to know whether the high levels of sexual abuse and the lack of response to it by intellectual disability services or the law are primarily because they are women or because they have intellectual disabilities. However, what we can do is observe that many women with intellectual disabilities often decide not to report sexual abuse when it happens because they know, instinctively or from past experience, that they would not be believed (Brown 1996; Hard and Plumb 1986) and feel they may be blamed. In this respect they have much in common with other women who have experienced sexual abuse (Kelly 1988).

The findings in the research study reported here and other related work (Thompson 1997) indicate that there are rarely any negative sanctions for the perpetrators of sexual abuse against women with intellectual disabilities. When the women do report abuse they are rarely offered specialist support, legal justice or compensation (Brown 1996). These facts also make it difficult for women with intellectual disabilities (and others) to see what 'counts' as sexual abuse and what does not.

Women's struggle to come to terms with abusive experiences

From the women I worked with, it seems to be the case that sexual abuse by fathers has caused the most lasting damage for a number of women. One woman, after the onset of anal rape by her father when she was 16, developed severe mental health problems which sometimes involved her losing touch with reality, resulting in the prescription of long-term medication and involuntary periods of institutionalization for the next 15 years.

Another woman had been raped by her father and given birth to his child when she was 17. Some 31 years later she still had mental health problems and the experience with her father still loomed large in her mind: 'I think that business with my dad is what put me off sex and I get frightened. I try not to, but I do' (Susan).

Another woman believed that it was because of sexual abuse by her father (when she was 12) that she had (and at the age of 52 continued to have) a large number of sexual partners: 'My dad had my body when I was 12... I learned from him about sex, he used to teach me about sex and that's another reason why I'm like I am sometimes' (Penny).

Although I have highlighted how some women felt about sexual abuse by their fathers, I do not want to imply that sexual abuse by other men is necessarily less traumatic. Obviously, there are individual variations in responses which must be respected. However, for the women I spoke to, those who experienced sexual abuse from boyfriends or in a few cases husbands, seemed to cope with the abuse somewhat differently. Those women with such relationships valued them very highly and wanted them to continue. This is very important to note because, although the sex was largely unsatisfactory for the women and indeed often abusive, sex is only one part of a relationship. Moreover, actually having sex does not usually take up a great deal of time. Sex, including abusive sex, can therefore be relatively unimportant within the overall context of a relationship and this did indeed seem to be the case for many of the women with intellectual disabilities in my experience. The women seemed to cope with abusive experiences with partners by not according the sexual side of the relationship much importance in their lives. It seemed that the development and maintenance of relationships with men were more important to them. Coping strategies have been defined as 'any thought or action which succeeds in eliminating or ameliorating threat to the self ... whether it is consciously recognised as intentional or not' (Breakwell 1986, p.79). Therefore it seems that coping with a negative feature of one's life by relegating it to the realms of the unimportant could be seen as part of the women's resistance to and survival of their various negative sexual experiences.

The resistance to and recovery from sexual abuse by women with intellectual disabilities has been noted elsewhere in the literature (see Millard 1994). I am not implying that the women with whom I have worked were not damaged by their abuse at all. On the contrary, some had mental health problems, including depression and panic attacks, others had self-injurious and challenging behaviour. But nevertheless, without the benefit of much if any therapeutic help, very few of the women were incapacitated by what had happened to them and all were trying to make the best of their lives. This is all the more noteworthy because other research evidence indicates that women with the least internal or external resources to draw on, such as older women, poor women, women who had experienced a major life stress before the abuse, generally have more difficulty coping than others (Kelly 1988).

Conclusion

Speaking out, being heard and working together

Due to a traditional lack of respect towards people with intellectual disabilities and an underestimation of their capabilities, they have not usually been given a chance to speak up for themselves, to say what is happening in their lives and what they think about it. Thankfully this is changing: there is a developing self-advocacy movement in many countries and individuals are working together locally and even globally to have their say – indeed this book is a reflection of that.

With reference to sexual abuse, some women with intellectual disabilities in Britain have produced personal safety packs (Walsall Women's Group 1994) and advised other women of their rights to be safe and happy in their sexual relationships (*Between Ourselves* video 1988; People First undated). Others have gone much further and worked alongside women without disabilities to campaign for and set up a refuge for women with intellectual disabilities escaping from violence. They aim to meet their special needs and empower them to take some control back over their lives (Powerhouse 1996a, 1996b).

Now that women with intellectual disabilities are speaking out about their lives and what they want to happen, it is incumbent upon those of us who research and work in intellectual disability services to listen to what they have to say. This does not mean that we will always agree about the nature of the problem and the way forward: for example, I am troubled by the fact that some women with intellectual disabilities are uncomfortable with discussions which focus on perpetrators as being men with intellectual disabilities. They believe this reflects badly on people with intellectual disabilities as a whole and moreover deflects attention from other non-disabled men who also abuse them (personal communications). I understand their concerns and recognize the dangers of men with intellectual disabilities becoming targets for disproportionate attention, as has happened with other groups of men, most obviously black men (Davies 1978). Nevertheless it seems important to me that the real abusive experiences of women with intellectual disabilities are recognized, including those from men with intellectual disabilities. This is just one example of something that will need further exploration and discussion.

Women with and without intellectual disabilities, working together to address issues such as those highlighted in this book has got to be the way forward. It may not always be a smooth path to follow and we will undoubtedly need to disagree and challenge each other along the way. Progress will only be made if all concerned are prepared to work together in a spirit of solidarity and respect – in fact in a spirit of 'sisterhood' – a term which now sounds so old fashioned but as a concept has a lot going for it.

PART III

Finding a Place in Work

Introduction

Historically, women have had less access to the paid labour market than men and their participation in the workforce continues to be characterized by gender segregation, occupational inequalities and wage discrimination (Anderson 1993). Women across the world are more likely to be unemployed than men. When they do have jobs they tend to be concentrated in low-paid 'women's work'. If these are the realities facing non-disabled women across the world (United Nations 1991), what is the situation concerning women with disabilities?

A number of studies have shown that women with disabilities fare significantly worse than non-disabled women (and disabled men) when it comes to employment (Bowe 1984; Hanna and Rogovsky 1991; Trupin *et al.* 1997). However, this research is largely based on information about women with physical or sensory impairments. Only a handful of studies provide information about the employment of women with intellectual disabilities. These indicate that women with intellectual disabilities are subject to the same, if not worse, employment barriers as women with other disabilities (Traustadóttir 1999).

Part III of this book focuses on women with intellectual disabilities and work. As this is an area where they face considerable discrimination, we suspected this would be the most difficult part of the book in terms of finding the great variety of experiences and expressions we anticipated in the other parts. To our joy and surprise, this was the first section of the book to be filled with chapters reflecting a wide range of work experiences documenting both the difficulties in this sphere of life and the creative, meaningful and fulfilling work performed by women with intellectual disabilities.

We start with a short account by Tamara Kainova (Chapter 10) about her work in a sheltered workshop. She loved her job and was devastated when she had to stop working after the workshop was closed. Many western countries consider sheltered workshops an outdated way of providing employment for people with intellectual disabilities and are trying to close them down and create more acceptable work in regular workplaces. Tamara's story provides a view of a different culture where sheltered workshops are seen much more positively as the only hope of employment for people with intellectual disabilities.

Some women with intellectual disabilities are very creative and resourceful in finding their places in work. Sonia Teuben, an actor and playwright, is one. Sonia has written a powerful monologue, 'Gina's Story', based on her experiences before she left home (Chapter 11). The play has been performed by the Back to Back Theatre company where Sonia works. The self-advocacy movement has been a great influence in the lives of many of the women with intellectual disabilities who contribute to this book. Nancy Ward is one of them. She describes her involvement in the self-advocacy movement and how it has led to leadership roles in the national self-advocacy organization in the USA, as well as paid employment as a self-advocacy co-ordinator (Chapter 12).

Supported employment is a new initiative in many countries, created to help people with intellectual disabilities find work in the regular labour market. In Chapter 13 Kristjana Kristjansen describes the experiences of three women who have found work through a supported employment programme. Based on these three women's experiences, Kristjana also reflects on the social meaning of work in their lives.

The concluding chapter in Part III is by Jan Walmsley. She focuses on the issue of 'caring' which has been a stereotypical and much debated area of women's work. Jan's chapter challenges the myths that women with intellectual disabilities are always on the receiving end when it comes to caring. Instead, Jan demonstrates that women with intellectual disabilities, like other women, perform a considerable amount of caring work. Like other women, they affirm their place in the world through caring.

CHAPTER TEN

We Like Working

Tamara Kainova with Maria Cerna, Czech Republic

After I finished special school I went to work in a sheltered workshop in Prague. I began there when I was 18. Two years later my sister Tatjana started work there too. We worked there for almost 20 years. It was good there. We produced small things like yoghurt covers for a milk company and small pillboxes.

Then later Tatjana and I went to another sheltered workshop. It was a beautiful place because it had just been built. There were workshop leaders there and we liked them. Our work was good. But in 1993 they moved the workshop and everything changed. The workshop leaders changed several times and problems arose. We had to leave. We stopped working in 1996. It was a pity.

We like working but we are not able to do anything. We would like to work like other people do. We also need to make some money to support ourselves.

After I finished at special school I went to Druteva to work. Druteva is a sheltered workshop in Prague. I began to work there when I was 18. Two years after, my sister Tatjana started work there too. Before that, Tatjana had taken a course in needlework and she knows how to use a sewing machine. She also helps my parents at home and helps me in my work placement. She is my best friend.

We worked at Druteva for almost 20 years. It was good there. In the beginning Mrs L was our forewoman. She always tried to organize things so that we were not tired and were happy and content. Sometimes we sang songs or she read stories to us but only when we had time. We produced small things like yogurt covers for a milk company and small pillboxes. We stacked invoices, receipts and other papers. Sometimes we had to work fast to get the jobs done. Altogether there were 15 workers. We all did our best. All the workers were good people. There was always a nice St Nicholas Eve at work. It was fun with Mrs L! Then later, Tatjana and I went to another sheltered workshop. It was a beautiful place because it had just been built. There were two big rooms with big windows. There was a cloakroom and a dining room on the first floor. We had lunch there and it was nice. There were also workshop leaders there and we liked them. Our work was good.

But in 1993 they moved us to Holešovice, in the main building of the Druteva [a large institution for people with disabilities]. After moving there, we lost everything. The workshop leaders changed several times and problems arose. We had to leave Druteva. We also left because our parents became ill and could no longer drive us to work every day. We stopped working in 1996. It was a pity.

We like working but we are not able to do anything. We would like to work like other people do. We also need to make some money to support ourselves. Nowadays our invalid pension is not enough and we cannot live properly without work. We are still young!

CHAPTER ELEVEN

Gina's Story[1]

Sonia Teuben with Maude Davey, Australia

This chapter is a play Sonia wrote about her life. When she was little her mother told her to mind the baby. The baby started crying and Sonia didn't know what to do, so she held her so tightly that the baby almost died. After that her mother never let her hold the baby again. Her family called Sonia a spastic and a retard, and she was sent to a special school.

The kids at school used to play Kiss Chasey and one day two boys took her under the bridge. They told her they were going to play a game called Touchy, and they took her clothes off and started touching her all over. A teacher came down and saw them. Sonia's mother blamed her. She said that Sonia

---

[1] Sonia Teuben is an actor with the Back to Back Theatre Company, a professional theatre company based in Australia. In Sonia's first show with the company, *Voices of Desire*, directed by Barry Kay with dramaturgy by Rosemary Fitzgerald, she developed the first version of *Gina's Story*, a monologue about her life before she left home. In 1995, as a part of *Back to Back in Shorts*, Sonia and director Maude Davey with Sue-Ann Post developed that initial monologue into a half-hour script for performance. All performance and copying rights are reserved. Enquiries should be directed to Back to Back Theatre Company, PO Box 1257, Geelong 3220, Victoria, Australia.

only went to school to have sex with the boys. So she kept her at home and wouldn't let her out of the house. Sonia began to do crazy things and her mother would lock her in her bedroom. When her mother's friends came over Sonia would be let out, so she could entertain the guests by acting crazy, and they would laugh at her like it was a joke. Then she would be locked in her room again.

Sonia hated being locked up in her bedroom, but every time she got up she got punished, so she lay in her bed all day being unhappy.

Sonia's mother took her to a doctor who did tests on her and then they gave her some pills to calm her down. They made her tired and weak. She hated taking them.

Sonia got locked in a caravan because she called her mother a slut. When she was in there her sister's husband came in and raped her. Sonia tried to tell her family but no one believed her.

Eventually Sonia got so sick of everything that she ran away from home. An old couple found her and took her to the police. The police took Sonia to a safe house, went to her mother's house and took all of Sonia's things. She found out that her mother had been getting money for Sonia without telling her. So now she had money. But Sonia didn't know anything about the world. She didn't know what money was. She was taken to a shop and told she could buy anything she liked. She bought a packet of cigarettes.

Sonia started getting crushes on girls. One of her support workers took her to a young lesbian group. Sonia didn't know what lesbians were. Sonia became an actor. She earns money and has relationships with women. She dreams about being an actor and singer like Melissa Etheridge, and living with a woman she loves.

She talks to her mother sometimes but they don't see each other often. Sonia feels like she was in prison and now she is free.

[*There is a chair in the centre of the space towards the back of the stage. On the chair is a large soft doll. Gina enters. She is wearing leather jacket and black jeans with a studded belt. Her hair is short and spiky. She has tattoos and a ring through her nose. She stands centre stage and looks directly out at the audience, sizing them up. She chooses one person*].

Hey Bea! You think you're top dog. You think you run this place, but you don't. It runs by my rules now, so piss off. Don't think you can run to the warden 'cause she won't help you, and the screws aren't going to help you either. [*She winks*].

That was Rita, the bikie chick from *Prisoner.*[2] She was my hero. I wanted to be just like her. She was tough, you know. Like me. Looked at people straight in the eye. *That* look you know? She didn't give a shit. Like me.

My name's Gina. I'll tell you a story. I'll tell you my story.

[*She begins to pace up and down the space.*]

When I was young I did weird things. Things like jump on my bum and hit myself. Roly polys over and over again. I'd run around the house and never get tired. I was a wild child.

2   A popular Australian soap opera of the 1980s set in a women's prison.

[*She stops pacing.*]

When I was seven Mum wanted to take a bath. So she told me to mind my baby sister while she had a bath.

[*Gina mimes her mother giving her the baby. Gina doesn't know how to hold her.*]

I was holding her.

She kept on crying so I sing to her.

[*Gina sings a simple lullaby*] Baloo. Baloo. Baloo.

She kept on crying so I talk to her.

'Come on Sis. When you get old you can get tattoos and a ring in your nose like me.'

She kept on crying.

Maybe if she can feel my heartbeat she might stop crying.

[*Gina holds the baby close to her heart, arms crossed over her chest.*]

She kept on crying. I held her closer to me. [*Gina holds the baby tighter.*]

She kept on crying. I held her closer to me. [*Gina holds the baby tighter.*]

She kept on crying. I held her closer to me. [*Gina holds the baby tighter.*]

She kept on crying. I held her closer to me. [*Gina holds the baby even tighter.*]

[*There is silence. Gina breathes a sigh of relief.*]

She's stopped crying.

[*Gina looks at the baby. Something is wrong.*]

She's stopped breathing. She's gone blue! I freaked it and called 'Mum! Mum! The baby's stopped breathing!' Mum rushes in and grabs the baby off me. They rushed the baby to the hospital. Got her breathing again. Then mum came in and she hit me. I tried to explain to her it wasn't my fault but she wouldn't listen to me. She said, 'I never want to see you near your baby sister again. You go near your sister again and I'll chuck you out.'

I tried to explain to her it wasn't my fault.

She got my brother to squeeze me really hard. Like this. [*Gina squeezes herself tightly.*]

She said, 'That's what your little sister was going through when you were squeezing her to death.'

It wasn't my fault. You're the one who told me to mind her. I didn't know what to do.

It wasn't my fault! It wasn't my fault! It wasn't my fault!

But she wouldn't listen to me. Nobody listened.

They wouldn't let me near the baby any more. They wouldn't let me touch her.

I wasn't even allowed out of the house 'cause Mum said she couldn't trust me 'cos of what I'd done. It was like I was in a prison.

They said I was a spastic and a retard. They said I should go to a spastic school where the spastic kids go.

So I went to a spastic school.

In breaks we would play this game called Kiss Chasey. First of all you find out who's it. Whoever's it would have to chase the rest and kiss them.

Eeny meeny miney mo

Catch a nicky by the toe

If she swallows let her go.

Eeny meeny miny mo.

Paul's it! Everybody has to run and hide. Gina runs and hides.

I hide near the sandpit.

Paul found me. He kissed me. [She grimaces.] Yuk! I hated kisses.

He took me under the bridge.

Mark's there waiting. They say, 'We're going to play another game called Touchy.'

They start touching me.

[She runs her hands over her body, demonstrating what the boys did.]

Don't! I don't like it!

They say they're my friends. If I wanted to be their friend I had to let them do it. But I don't like it, you know?

[Suddenly Gina hides her body with her arms.]

Shit! The teacher caught us. She says, 'It's filthy and disgusting. What would our parents think?'

[She speaks to the audience again.]

Mum says I can't go to school no more. She says I only go there to have sex with the boys. She kept me at home and wouldn't let me out of the house. I stayed at home, cleaned the house, watched TV and did nothing.

[She plays a two-person clapping game by herself. She sings.]

Down by the banks of the Hanky Pank

Where the bullfrogs leap from bank to bank

With a lp – lpe – Ope – Oop

It's papadilly and a plip plop.

Next verse

Same as the first

A little bit faster and a whole lot worse.

Down by the banks of the Hanky Pank

Where the bullfrogs leap from bank to bank

With a lp – lpe – Ope – Oop

It's papadilly and a plip plop.

[She goes to the chair and picks up the soft doll.]

This is little Gina. I'm Big Gina. Little Gina's inside me. She is what I was before what I am now. She's very little isn't she? And she breaks easily.

[She talks to the doll, with a touch of menace in her voice.]

Little Gina's cold. Little Gina's scared. Little Gina's scared of being alone. Little Gina's scared of everything.

[She drops the doll.]

Oh poor Gina fall down!

[She punches the doll.]

Oh poor Gina hurt her arm.

[She punches the doll again.]

Oh poor Gina got a bruise.

[She punches the doll again.]

Poor Gina, how'd you get that mark on your arm? I warned you about playing on those swings.

[She punches the doll again.]

Oh booja booja booja![3] Poor malenka.[4]

[She speaks to the audience.]

When little Gina came out mum thought I was crazy. So she used to lock me in my bedroom. As a punishment. When mum had friends over she used to let me out and I'd entertain them. I used to do things like 'The Claw'.

[Gina grabs her throat and struggles with herself as if being strangled.]

Or 'Frozen Moments.' I could hold a moment for twenty minutes sometimes.

[She strikes a pose and remains completely motionless. She breaks the pose.]

Really pissed people off. Then my mother would lock me in my room again.

[Gina mimes locking a door.]

She would zip-lock the door and put powder on the floor.

[She sits down on the chair. The lights dim.]

It was like I was in a hole and I couldn't do anything. My heart would beat fast and I'd go all hot and cold. I couldn't stand laying on the bed anymore. But if I got up I got punished. So I just laid there. Doing nothing.

Down by the banks of the Hanky Pank

Where the bullfrogs leap from bank to bank

With a lp – lpe – Ope – Oop

It's papadilly and a plip plop.

Next verse

Same as the first

A little bit faster and a whole lot worse.

---

3   This could be one of two Polish words: Buzia, meaning face in babytalk; or bozia meaning God, again in babytalk.

4   Malenka means tiny in Polish and is used by a mother to her female child.

[She speaks to the audience.]

Mum used to get these psychiatrists to come to the house. They said I had a 'mental disorder.' They took me to the Royal Children's Hospital and they put me in a ward with other people with bad anger and a temper. Like me. They put me in a room, in a dark room, and they tied my hands to the chair. *[Gina demonstrates these actions.]* They asked me all these questions like: 'Why do you do these things?' and 'Do you know what you're doing?' They gave me this little green pill. They said it was a lolly, and they said 'Repeat after me. Red. Yellow. Green. Orange. Purple.' *[Her voice gets slower and sleepier.]* I was scared. They reckon if I don't calm, don't calm down mum should put me away.

They gave mum a bottle of the little green pills. She gave me one each night. They used to make me tired and weak. All I wanted to do was sleep all the time. I hated them. They hurt Little Gina. It was a pain like Little Gina's heart was being ripped out.

[She rocks back and forward, arms crossed over her chest.]

It's not over yet Little Gina. It's not over yet. You've still got to get punished.

I got locked in the caravan. 'Cause I called my Mum a slut. My sister's husband came in to punish me. He started touching me and that. He raped me. I didn't try to stop him. I was too scared. I had to be nice to him else I'd get kicked out of the family. I didn't tell anyone. No one would believe me anyway after what I did to my baby sister.

[She leaps out of the chair.]

I got sick of it all and I ran away. I was sick of getting punished.

[She runs around the space.]

I jumped the fence, jumped these rocks, cut myself on prickles and ran and ran and ran. I ran in any direction where there was no one around. I ended up in a park on the other side of town. This old couple found me the next morning and took me to the police.

The police took me to this house. They went home and got my stuff in a box. I found out I had $200 in a bank account. I didn't know anything. I didn't know what money was. The lady takes me down the shop and she says 'Buy whatever you want.' I bought a packet of Winfield Blue.

[She picks up the doll.]

Well Little Gina, you're safe with me now. No one's gonna punish you anymore.

Here's a little piece of my heart

It's a strong heart, a little bit dented

But it beats all the time, never misses

I'll just stick it on for now

And sew it properly on later

So I'll always be with you.

But geez Little Gina. You have to start growing up. You gotta start getting out there and doing stuff for yourself. It's serious shit out there!

[She speaks to the audience.]

I started getting crushes on girls. One of my support workers took me to a young lesbian group. I didn't know what lesbians were. Mum never talked about that stuff at home. She only ever talked about normal sex. Men and women. I had a picture of Rita, the bikie chick from *Prisoner*, on my wall. My mother ripped it down. She said, 'Why haven't you got pictures of boys on your wall?' I cried. She was my hero. My whole family used to watch *Prisoner*. Whenever something weird was on mum would say, 'Change the channel! Change the channel!' I never knew why she would say change the channel. Once when I asked her she said, 'Rita was one of *those* women.' Later on she said, 'Sleeping with a woman is like sleeping with the devil.' But I think it's like sleeping with Melissa Etheridge. Not that I know, but I sure have pretty good dreams about her.

[She speaks to the doll.]

OK, Little Gina. Time to move on now.

I'm going to get on that bike

and ride and ride and ride

for thousands of miles

and I won't need petrol

won't see any stop signs

or traffic lights

and no one's going to say

'Go back! You're going the wrong way!'

I'm just going to ride and ride...

[She throws the doll offstage.]

Fly Little Gina, fly. Have fun, be careful and hey! Watch out for those married women. They can be trouble!

As for me, I've got my own life. I can party. I can get a job. I can earn money. I can buy a black Harley Davidson and be the butchest dyke in Geelong. I want to be an actor and a singer like Melissa Etheridge. I want to meet Melissa Etheridge! I want to fall in love with a woman that loves me and I want to live with her. I want to have showers with her and wash her back down with soap and wrap her up in a big towel ... sorry. Got a bit carried away there.

Mum rings me sometimes. I know she loves me, but she just can't live with me. Now I'm free. Yeah, free. That's my story. So far. My name's Gina.

[The lights go out.]

CHAPTER TWELVE

My Leadership Career

Nancy Ward with Bonnie Shoultz, USA

Nancy Ward was the first Chairperson of Self Advocates Becoming Empowered (SABE), the national self-advocacy organization in the USA. She was Chairperson from 1992 to 1996.

In the chapter, Nancy discusses her leadership career. She was raised in Lincoln, Nebraska, and lived there until 1997. She was in special education classes from seventh grade until she left high school with a special education certificate.

Nancy discovered self-advocacy in the late 1970s. It was like a lightbulb going on in her head. It took years in the self-advocacy group for her to become confident that she could speak in public or be a leader. Self-advocacy groups were formed in several Nebraska towns and cities. In the early 1980s, Nancy and others worked to bring the groups together as People First of Nebraska.

People First of Nebraska received a grant and hired Nancy as Self-Advocacy Organizer. She was the only staff person. She worked 20 hours a week and her home was her office. She did this until 1997, when she moved to Oklahoma (about 500 miles away) to become the Self-Advocacy Coordinator of Oklahoma People First.

Nancy cares very much about self-advocacy because she has had problems with people who can't accept her disability and because she has had many friends who have been mistreated because of their disabilities.

After much hard work, she has gained skills she thinks are very important: seeing herself as a person, not as her disability; speaking out for herself; learning about the rights and responsibilities all citizens have; giving testimony to lawmakers; public speaking; working with people in a team; being a leader; letting go so that others can become leaders too; and asking questions when she doesn't understand.

She was Chairperson of SABE during a time when it was just beginning to be known. SABE had many important tasks during this period and now it is recognized as the only national organization run by people with intellectual disabilities.

Nancy decided on her own not to run for a second term, after her first term was up in 1996. She thought it was important for other board members to have a chance to lead SABE.

In the chapter Nancy tells many stories that are examples of things she has learned and done. Her chapter is easy to read because it has words that she uses when she speaks instead of big professional words. The stories she tells help the reader to understand the points she is making.

Learning about my disability

I am the oldest of five children, but my sisters and brothers learned faster than I did. They had to teach me things like tying shoes and riding a bicycle, rather than the other way around. That was really hard for me, because I thought the oldest should be the first to learn everything.

It was also hard for me to keep up in school. In grade school I got special help but when I was about 12 years old the school principal told me I would be in special education classes, and that's where I stayed for the rest of my school years. I didn't understand why I needed to go to a different school than my friends and brothers and sisters were going to go to. I felt angry and hurt, because I thought that because my parents didn't tell me about it, that meant that my parents couldn't accept the fact of me being different than my brothers and sisters.

In junior high things went pretty well because there was an expectation that we would learn. What was hard about it was that even though it was part of the school district and in a regular junior high building, it was segregated. We knew we were seen as different, and we were teased in cruel ways – like being called 'dummy' and 'retarded'. I didn't understand why the other kids called us these names, because the teachers never did. Then one day I overheard my favorite teacher telling someone that we were retarded.

I didn't understand it then, but now I feel that either we shouldn't be labeled at all, or if we have to be labeled we should be helped to understand and deal with it. To me, the label 'mentally retarded' was just a bad name I had been called. When I heard my teacher say that, I felt like she was saying I had something bad, and that there was something wrong with me. If I had understood that I learn differently than other people, then I could have educated people rather than getting mad and hurt when people called me names. When you don't understand what's going on, how are you going to be able to explain it to somebody else? Now I believe that being different is just fine, and that the differences in life are what makes it interesting. I think all children should be taught this.

Visions of my future over the years

My vision for myself was that I would work with people in some way. I wanted this from the time I first started out, but I didn't know where that would take me or what I would do. My first jobs were in food service and nursing homes, and these were not the kinds of jobs I had in mind. I did these jobs from 1968 to about 1980. After 1980, I was at Goodwill Industries for a while. Goodwill is a kind of sheltered workshop. I worked at Goodwill because I could not get into the other service system. My IQ scores were too high. I did not understand why people were judged by their IQ, and it made me angry because I thought that services should be according to what people needed, and that they should have gotten to know me instead of just having me take a test.

During these years, I decided to go to the local community college. I wanted to take courses so I could become a nurse. When I left high school, I thought I had graduated because we went through the graduation ceremony and were given a certificate. I didn't understand that it was different than the other students' graduation; that it was a certificate from special ed. I wasn't allowed to enter the nursing program right away, because I needed many science and math courses. I took those kinds of courses for several years, and then they told me that I would have to take classes for two more years just to get a regular high school diploma, before I could take any of the nursing courses. I didn't understand why they hadn't told me that before, and it was very frustrating, but I did get my high school diploma. I had to take my classes along with working to support myself.

Even though I always knew my family loved and cared about me, accomplishing this changed my relationship with them. They were really proud of me, and they told me so. From the time I was young, I could tell that my family thought I was very slow and couldn't learn much. The expectation for me was different. For example, when I decided to move away from home, I had to go to a boarding home rather than getting my own place like my brothers and sister did. This was a place where dozens of people with disabilities lived together, six to an apartment, and were watched over by the owners of the home. But later I got my own apartment and learned how to live on my own. I could see my family's view of me changing as I changed and grew, but it has always been hard for them.

Discovery of self-advocacy: A lightbulb going on in my head

My friends told me about Advocacy First of Lincoln, the self-advocacy group in the city where I grew up, and I joined in 1978. It was like a lightbulb going on in my head. It took me five years to learn how to have the confidence in myself to be able to do public speaking, because there were no role models then. Nebraska was one of the first states to have self-advocacy (the others were Washington and Oregon, which were not close by) so we had to be role models for each other.

One of the things that People First of Nebraska is very proud about is that the members plan and put on their own convention. It took four years for us to do that, though. In the early days, before we had a statewide organization, there was an advisor who did most of the convention organizing. Then, in the fourth year (1981) she and a member went to Australia for a month and we had no convention. When we realized we weren't having a convention and why, we got mad and decided that we were going to start doing the work ourselves – planning it and putting it on. Some of the work is things like getting the hotel, getting a disc jockey for the dance, planning the meals, deciding who we want for the keynote speaker and inviting that person, and many other details like getting out the registration forms and so on.

I spearheaded the takeover, and the advisor was happy and relieved, even though we had been afraid she would be upset with us and take it as a criticism. We had to learn, by not having a convention, that we all had to be responsible, rather than just relying on one person. We probably wouldn't have done that if we had not missed having a convention in 1981. Most people just accepted that we weren't going to have one, but I realized we could do it ourselves and convinced other people that we could. We asked the advisor what steps to take, and we also knew how it should go because we had been to three before. That made it much easier for us.

This whole experience helped me realize that I could be a leader. Even now, I feel like I am boasting when I talk about being a leader. I always held leaders up on a pedestal, and I never imagined that I would become one. But this taught me that people would listen to me and go along with what I suggested, and that felt really good.

Becoming a leader

How relationships helped

One of the things that went with becoming a leader is that I started to have to think about my relationships with people who didn't have disabilities. Because I was becoming a leader, I was having more contact with people without disabilities who were also leaders. I had more and more questions about my relationships with them.

For example, people with disabilities often get used as tokens, just to make people without disabilities look good or feel like they are doing a good thing. We are like everyone else – we want to be liked and respected for who we are, not just because we have disabilities. When someone asked me to be on their board, or if someone who never used to notice me started being friendly toward me, I had to ask myself whether it was because they thought it would make them look good or if they really liked me and respected my opinions. This was hard for me for a long time, because it was hard to accept that people thought well of me.

After I became clear on how I was feeling about that, I started being able to ask people for support to be on a board. When I was successful with that, I then was able to risk asking people about their feelings of friendship toward me – did they like me because I had a disability, or for myself? I would test it out with some people – I would tell them I didn't understand certain things and would ask for support, in the case of a board; in the case of friendship, I would test it by asking people to go to lunch or other small things that had nothing to do with the work we were doing together.

Finally, in the case of one person I cared a lot about, I talked with several friends about whether that friendship was real, and then asked the person. I felt really good about the answer, but I wish the person had not joked about it. It was hard for me to ask, and I guess the answer came as a joke because it was hard for them too. Maybe they didn't realize it was even an issue, and didn't know how to respond to me at first.

This thinking and testing out of relationships made a big difference. The support and encouragement I got from people – to understand things, and to ask the questions when I didn't understand – was really important. I wouldn't have asked if I hadn't been encouraged to do so, and if I hadn't asked, I never would have understood things or been able to participate in things. By asking when I didn't understand, I learned many things, and that in itself made me grow. I also think it helped me to understand that my opinion was valued, and that people really cared about what I thought.

Self-advocacy jobs and positions

Being chosen to be a leader

Our local self-advocacy groups grew and we formed People First of Nebraska early in the 1980s. All of us, the members and the advisors, were involved as volunteers. None of us were paid. Then we got some grant money from Nebraska Advocacy Services, enough to hire a staff person. The People First of Nebraska Board of Directors hired me as their Self-Advocacy Organizer, and I worked 20 hours a week with them until January of 1997. I was the only staff person, and our office was my bedroom. Becoming a staff person was very much like being an advisor, except that I still had my disability and was still seen as a self-advocate.

I didn't have any role models because we were one of the first self-advocacy organizations in the country, and I was (I think) the first person with a disability to be the only staff person for a self-advocacy organization. I had to learn a lot of skills to be able to do that job. I had a community advisory committee that advised me on different issues, but the buck stopped with me. For example, People First of Nebraska used to have 15 chapters, but it was frustrating because that was too many to support and some of them needed a lot more support than I could give. My advisory committee worked with me to develop a chapter description that included all of the things a chapter needed to do in order to be seen as a chapter. After that, the number of chapters dropped to 11, and it was much easier to support them because they were strong and did most things themselves. The members gave each other the support they needed to do what they wanted to do.

I also had a mentor who supported me by letting me bounce things off of her; she also helped me figure out how to bring up issues that I had or how to present my side of an issue. At the beginning of my People First of Nebraska job, my mentor and our state advisor helped me to learn how to be organized. I had to learn how to keep a calendar, for example, and to be on time for meetings. With the calendar, I wouldn't double-book things.

Another part was to write things down so that I remember them. I still have problems with that. These are some examples of just a few of the skills I learned as a staff person for People First of Nebraska. If I listed them all it would take a book.

Since the time I started that job, I have had many chances to go around the country and help other people learn how to do public speaking and other leadership things. It was hard sometimes, because I saw other states grow much faster and have more than People First of Nebraska had – more chapters, more staff, more development, more money. I got jealous sometimes, and I didn't always see the connection between the work I did to encourage and teach others and the fast growth that happened in other states. I would have liked to have People First of Nebraska be able to develop that fast, also, but there wasn't as much money there for self-advocacy as some of the other states have.

I am now the Self-Advocacy Coordinator for Tulsa ARC,[1] and my job is to work with Oklahoma People First. I support the People First members who are the chairpersons for the regional meetings that bring local chapters together within the regions. I also help to start new chapters around the Tulsa area, and I am the support person or advisor for Tulsa People First. I also work with the Best Buddy Program[2] here, which is a program where a college student and a person with a disability are matched. They become friends and do things together in the community. It is another way that people with disabilities can become part of their community. I started this job at the end of January 1997. One of the things that was real difficult for me when I started this job was that I couldn't just start doing the job right away, and this was because there is a big difference between how things are done here and what I was used to.

Self Advocates Becoming Empowered (SABE)

I was chairperson of Self Advocates Becoming Empowered (SABE), the national self-advocacy organization, from 1992 when it was founded until August of 1996. Our board of directors is made up of people who are

1   Tulsa ARC is the Tulsa chapter of Arc-US (see note 3).
2   Best Buddies is a national program that matches college students with people with disabilities, one on one, so that they can become friends and enjoy the community together.

elected as representatives of their region of the country. We have broken it down to nine regions, and each has two representatives. Our last election was over Labor Day weekend of 1996.

During the summer of that year, I saw that what I needed to do as a leader was to give other people a chance to be the chairperson of the organization. I could have run for another four-year term, and I wanted to because I felt I had done a good job, but I decided not to run for that office. This was real hard for me, because I had told people that I was planning to run, and I didn't know if people would see it as a copout because of how close I am with Tia Nelis, who was also planning to run. I thought they might think I was doing it because I was afraid it would damage our friendship, but it was really because of my feelings about the importance of risk and of letting someone else take the risk of being the chairperson.

It was also because I feel very strongly about leaders being willing to let go. Part of what I mean by that is that even though I know it is important to have officers in an organization, I also feel that the idea of officers can get in the way of the idea of working as a team. The members can feel that they are not as important as the officers, especially if the officers don't change, but they are important. One of the ways to help them see that is to give other people the chance to be an officer. It took a long time for me to understand this, because I thought if I let go that meant that I wouldn't be able to be involved or continue as a leader. I thought I wouldn't be able to be a part of the SABE board any more, and SABE means a lot to me. I am one of the people who had the dream of a national organization and one who helped it become a reality.

Tia won the election at our national convention in Tulsa on 30 August 1996. I was elected as secretary, but I had to give up that position when I moved into a different region to take the job in Oklahoma. Now I am on the Advisory Panel, which is made up of former representatives to the SABE Board. My role with SABE has changed some because of that. I still go to meetings, but I cannot vote. The Tulsa ARC pays my way to meetings now, not SABE. I am very active on one of the committees, and I can give my opinion during the board meetings even though I don't vote. I am very proud of Self Advocates Becoming Empowered.

Conclusion

I care very much about self-advocacy because I have seen people being treated badly. To be able to help them learn to speak out for themselves is really cool. I hope that the examples I have given will help other women with disabilities to become leaders without having to make some of the mistakes I have made. At the same time, I think it is important that people with disabilities are given the chance to make mistakes, because that is the one of the best ways anyone is going to learn. Making mistakes and learning from them is how the learning 'sticks'. You grow more than if you are not allowed to take the risks and make the mistakes you need to make.

Looking ahead, I have three things to say. One of my dreams would be for Self Advocates Becoming Empowered to be able to hire an executive director who has an intellectual disability. Ideally, I would like this person to be a woman. That would help us to have a larger influence nationally, and it would show that a woman with an intellectual disability could have a national job. It would help with our acceptance – and that would lead to my next dream, which would be to put ourselves out of business. In that dream, we wouldn't need organizations like Self Advocates Becoming Empowered and The Arc-US,[3] because people would be accepted for who they are. We can help that to happen by educating the public more and by being around people more. As we do that, people will learn to see us as we really are, as people who can be part of the community, who can have jobs and pay taxes, who have feelings and want to have fun, just like anybody else.

The one last thing that I would like to see happen is this: that the 49 million people who have disabilities in the USA would work together as a team. If we would really do that, we would be in the majority, and we could elect people who believe in us. I feel as though that is what I have worked for all my life, to be a role model for other people and to encourage all of us to work together.

3   Arc-US is a national organization on mental retardation, begun by parents in the 1950s.

CHAPTER THIRTEEN

The Social Meaning of Work

Listening to Women's Own Experiences

Kristjana Kristiansen, Norway

Kristjana has spent the last few years with women with intellectual disabilities in their workplaces in order to find out how work is important in their lives.

This chapter is about three women: Kristina, Gudrun and Aslaug. All of them have ordinary jobs in Norway. Here are some things the women have said about why they like their jobs.

Kristina works at a kiosk in the middle of town and likes all the people coming and going. She says, 'People who know me see me here.' She prefers having a real job instead of being at the day-activity centre where she says she did not learn much.

Aslaug sets the tables in a very elegant restaurant and helps at special events such as banquets and weddings. She used to live in an ugly institution and says she only saw beautiful places like the restaurant on television. She says she likes her job because 'it is the prettiest place I have ever seen. With so many beautiful things.'

Gudrun works at a garden centre. She cannot speak but smiles proudly when she knows she does a good job. Kristjana spent a long time with her at her workplace to understand Gudrun's work. She also talked to Gudrun's to co-workers and others who know her well, to find out what works means for Gudrun. One man who works at the garden centre said, 'She is stronger than most of the men and gets real pleasure lifting those heavy soil sacks that the men complain about.' When Gudrun's mother saw her daughter working she said she realized her daughter was not a little girl anymore, 'She's an adult.'

For these three women, being supported to be in ordinary workplaces doing ordinary jobs feels very important to them. The women feel better about themselves because of their jobs. They know they are respected and trusted. Sometimes other people also have better ideas about what is possible for women with intellectual disabilities when they see them included and working in real jobs.

This chapter summarizes some of the emergent findings from a long-term qualitative study on the social meaning of work in the lives of women with intellectual disabilities in Norway. I have spent many hours and days in the last few years being with women who are employed in integrated, paid work settings, and have tried to understand the importance of work from their perspectives. Sometimes these women can talk about their work and their lives directly, and help us to understand what work means for them. It is important to be with them at their workplaces, so that we can better understand what work means in their lives. Often the research can document these voices and also interpret and explain such experiences at other levels, and maybe contribute to more theory and better practice. Our hope then is to help other women with disabilities and also the people who try to understand and support them to change their expectations and ambitions. Sometimes these women cannot communicate directly themselves. Then it is even more important to observe and participate in their work world, try to understand what it means for them, and interpret this to the outside world.

This chapter presents the work situations and experiences of three women. I have chosen these three women as examples from a larger study because their experiences have some easy to understand central messages that may be of interest to others. One main message is that income appears to be relatively unimportant, and the main positive experiences may be summarized as symbolic and social in nature.

'People I know see me here'

Kristina works in a kiosk in the centre of a large town. The kiosk sells things such as cards, magazines and candy. There is also a fast-food counter which is very popular with teenagers and college students, with two tables inside and several more outside in the summertime. Most of the people who work at the kiosk are in their twenties and most of them work part time. Kristina works at the kiosk five days a week, in the late afternoons and early evenings, including Saturday which is the busiest day. When I first met her she had been employed there for nearly three years.

Kristina is 28 years old. She spent most of her childhood years living with various relatives out in the surrounding countryside, and with her parents for short periods of time. Most of her teenage years she lived at a small institution with 11 other young adults with intellectual and physical disabilities. She now shares a flat with one other woman and receives home support services several times a week. At the kiosk Kristina has three main tasks. She helps to clean the food preparation areas and clears tables, she helps make some of the grill food, and also helps to stack the shelves at the end of her work day. She told me that she hopes some day to be able to wait on customers, but she has trouble understanding money. She also explains that some people have trouble understanding her and adds, 'That's a problem if you wait on people.'

On my first visit Kristina was expecting me and we began with a short tour where she showed me the place, introduced me to co-workers, and explained what she did there. It was an unusually hectic day so we had little time to talk together. I sat instead at one of the outside tables just to watch what was going on. This became my regular observation spot. I visited the kiosk several times before Kristina had enough free time to have a longer interview with me, and I was able to see a lot of what was going on there. I usually greeted Kristina and others I met there, bought a newspaper and a cup of tea, and settled down for an hour or so. Kristina told the others that I was someone she talked to because I was writing a book and she was helping me.

In summertime the place seems to be a sort of 'hang-out' for a large group of teenage friends. Many people appear to be regular customers and they often chat with the people who work there. Several people know Kristina and address her by name, and she is clearly pleased about this. She told me she especially likes to clear the outside tables, and greets all the young people she knows.

When Kristina and I spoke together, she told me the best thing about her job is that, 'People who know me see me here. You know, like neighbours. And my aunt came here once. She didn't know I worked here. She told everybody!' Kristina told me she used to work at a day centre, and didn't like that. Here are some things she told me: 'I didn't learn anything there. It wasn't real work. I got bored. Didn't like being with the others there, you know. Meet lots of people here. Much better here, people coming and going. And people see me here, in this place.'

'My daughter is an adult'

Gudrun is 31 years old and shares a flat with two other women with full-time support staff. She had previously lived with her family, but also had long respite stays at various institutions. I met Gudrun at her workplace, a garden centre which grows and sells a variety of flowers, bulbs and shrubs, as well as garden tools and equipment. Some of what is sold is seasonal, such as Christmas trees and garden furniture. At certain times of the year the area is so crowded with customers that there is a queue at the parking lot.

Gudrun's job at the garden centre is her third job placement through the supported employment agency. The first two jobs did not work out well. In both cases it was obvious that Gudrun did not like her work, nor did she do a satisfactory job, so the decision that she should not continue can be seen as mutual.

Initially, Gudrun was offered a temporary position at the garden centre two mornings a week for six months. At the end of this trial period it was agreed that Gudrun's work performance would be assessed, as well as her future plans and wishes, and the possibility of extending her employment would be decided. After the first two weeks it was already clear that Gudrun enjoyed working outdoors and was also capable of doing very strenuous work. When the six-month period was over Gudrun was offered a more permanent position, and for the past year she has worked six mornings a week for four hours a day.

Gudrun is a very active person, and she is also very large and strong. Gudrun does not speak and has some trouble understanding, but listens very intently when spoken to. She learns each new task by imitation, working alongside someone who demonstrates what is to be done, and then she does the same. I started my first visit by asking Gudrun to show me around the place and what she did there. It seemed as if she was involved in everything, since wherever we went she pointed at everything. Since much of the work at the garden centre is seasonal, it was difficult to get an overall picture during the few weeks I was there, so her supervisor gave me a description of how Gudrun's work tasks vary throughout the year. During the summer months she works outside with the small trees and bushes, and also helps to arrange the garden furniture exhibits. She is one of the main workers involved in unloading and unpacking newly arrived equipment and supplies. Most of the rest of the year she works in the large greenhouses. My visits occurred during the months of March and April. During most of my visits Gudrun was moving trays of seedlings and plants from one area to another, using a large cart that was very difficult and heavy to push.

Gudrun is unable to tell me directly about why work is important in her life, so it was important to spend time alongside her, and also listen to others who knew her and worked alongside her. Here are some things some of her co-workers told me:

> She is stronger than most of the men, and gets real pleasure being able to lift those heavy soil sacks that most of the men complain about. She likes to help customers with them, when they are struggling to get them moved into their cars.

> Gudrun seems to like the competitive thing, working alongside someone else. We have made this into sort of a game, sort of a race, of who can do most, or do it the fastest. But we have talked about being careful, not to take advantage of her, because she seems so tireless once she gets going. Everything seems to be a competition for her, and although she usually wins, she also feels bad when she isn't the best or fastest, if you see what I mean?

> Her biggest problem is break time. She can't seem to relax and take a real break. She gulps down her coffee or lunch or whatever, and wants to start working again right away. She doesn't seem to like that the rest of us sit around, eating slowly and sometimes just sitting and chatting afterwards for the whole half-hour. I don't think she knows breaks are something we need and deserve, like we are just there to work, you know? She usually wanders around impatiently until we start again. If she knows who she is working with after the break, she sometimes pulls at their arm to get them going.

What can we learn from these descriptions of Gudrun? It is obvious that she enjoys her work and is pleased with her accomplishments. She seems to be able to compare her work performance with others and to feel that she is a good worker, and often better (at least stronger and faster) than the others. She also takes her work very seriously and seems to believe the only thing people should do there is work, without breaks.

I also visited Gudrun twice at her flat, once with her mother who was visiting at the same time. It was not planned that we would be there at the same time, but the support staff seemed to limit visiting times. What is interesting for this chapter are some things her mother told me:

> I never believed it when they told me Gudrun was going to leave us and get her own flat. It'll never work, I thought. She can never live in her own place. She's always been very difficult, you know. Strong and often aggressive, and people are afraid of her. Lots of staff complain

about her, and many said they won't work with her. She's too handicapped to move out, I told them, no matter how much help she gets. Surrounded by strangers, who don't know what she needs! It isn't right. I know. I love her. I am her mother. She is our only child. I had a difficult pregnancy, and afterwards wasn't able to have more children. I need to say this because we wanted lots of children. Maybe that's why we love her so much. We wanted more, not because she was born handicapped, but because I think it is natural for women to want and love children. When we found out that Gudrun would be our only child, we loved her even more. But I don't think we tried to hold her back, you know, like keep her as a child her whole life. Even though lots of people told us she would never really grow up. But I have always thought of her as my little girl. I think most parents feel this way. I didn't want her to move out of our house.

Then there was all that disastrous work stuff. You know, the first two placements were awful, and I knew they would be. I was surprised the flat thing has worked out so well. I remember being worried all the time, and alarmed at small things, and wanted to visit all the time. But I was very proud when she got a key to her own flat – you know, my little girl! But what really turned my head around was when I visited her at the garden centre and saw her working. You know her, she's really very handicapped. Can't talk, doesn't really like being with other people, and often is very difficult and angry and aggressive, you know. They asked me not to come the first month, so she was no beginner when I was finally allowed to come. I will never forget, never, never, when I first arrived there and saw her working. I stood at a distance and watched her for a long time. She was really working, and gosh, could she work! I almost started crying, you know, lump in my throat. Look at her, doing a real job, alongside regular people, and some very tough men! And she was smiling that little proud smile of hers. That was when I thought, my daughter has grown up, she's an adult.

What is Gudrun's mother helping us understand? Gudrun likes her job and does it well. Being supported to have her own flat was an important step out of the family home, but we can hear that what really changed her mother's perception of Gudrun as an adult (and not a little girl anymore) was when she observed her daughter performing well in a work role and setting. The meaning of work in Gudrun's life includes changing her mother's perception of who her daughter is: a grown-up woman in an adult world. One can predict this will influence how her mother views her and interacts with her in the years to come.

'Being in a pretty place'

Aslaug works in a restaurant in a hotel in a small city. The restaurant has two sections: an informal café where breakfast, lunch and simple evening meals are served, and a large, elegant restaurant open only in the evenings or for special occasions such as banquets and private parties. Aslaug is 44 years old and spent most of her life in an institution until 12 years ago when she moved into her own flat with two others from the same institution. She now works six afternoons at the restaurant, primarily helping in the kitchen to clean up. Sometimes she helps make sandwiches if the café is very busy. Her main responsibility is to set the tables for the evening meals in the larger restaurant before it opens, and occasionally at other times when there are specially reserved dinner parties and events.

Aslaug is a very small woman who speaks slowly and quietly. She is a bit shy and very polite. When I asked her to show me around, she rushed me through the café and the kitchen areas, and urged me on into the restaurant where she was about to start her daily tasks. She said she would show me what she does, and she showed me the list she uses with pictures, to remember what she should do and in what order. First, she covers the tables with a plastic cover and then a linen tablecloth. Then comes cutlery and, as she adds, 'They use lots of forks and knives and spoons in this place, not only one!' Next, she places a candlestick on each table, and then a vase with fresh flowers that arrive each day and are prepared by someone else. Lastly come two crystal glasses per place and specially folded serviettes. 'I can't do the serviettes. That's difficult. They twist them special. John does that,' she explains.

When asked what she likes best about her job, Aslaug says loud and clear, 'I love being in this beautiful room. Most pretty place I have seen. So many beautiful things. It's why I love my job. Being in this room.' Aslaug has spent most of her life in a rather barren institution and told me, 'I never saw nice things. Not like this room. Only on television. Now I am here, in this room.' She adds, 'A wedding here one time! Here in this room. I met the bride! She was so beautiful. I met her friends! Beautiful dresses! I talked to her! They, John told her I did the tables! She sent me a photo of the wedding after! She was so beautiful! She wrote thank you to me!'

Aslaug works very slowly, and handles each item with great care and respect. She moves cautiously with every single thing, sometimes gazing a long time at each finished task. 'I like the candles and the glasses best,' she says. Being in a beautiful place is important to Aslaug. She told me this again and again, and all of her actions confirmed this when we were together.

Conclusion

The central theme from these three examples is that where these women are is important for them. Kristina likes to be seen working at the kiosk. Perhaps by being seen in an ordinary work role in a place visited by many young people who know her, and away from the day centre, she is able to feel better about herself, and show the world that she is now included and accepted. For Gudrun, working in a place with heavy physical work is enjoyable and she is respected by her co-workers. Her mother's reaction to seeing Gudrun in a work role is very interesting. It was not Gudrun's getting her own flat and door key that altered her mother's perceptions and expectations, but rather Gudrun's performing well in a real job. In a few minutes of being observed by her mother at the workplace, Gudrun stopped being a little girl and became an adult woman in her mother's eyes. For Aslaug, being in a beautiful place, surrounded by nice things and elegant events is very important. Perhaps she feels better about herself because she can now be included in a life which she had only seen on television, a life she thought only other people had.

The meaning of work in the lives of these three women has both a symbolic dimension and a social one. From these three women and their work worlds we can learn that where people are supported to be, who they are with and what they do are important to them. Their ideas about themselves seem to change, and also the ideas others have about them.

CHAPTER FOURTEEN

Caring

A Place in the World?

Jan Walmsley, England

Caring gives women a place in the world. As mothers, daughters, workers and friends women do a lot of caring. But most people believe that women with intellectual disabilities do not care for others. Instead, they need to be cared for. This chapter asks:

1. Is it true that women with intellectual disabilities need to be cared for?

2. Do some women with intellectual disabilities care for others?

3. Does caring give women with intellectual disabilities a place in the world?

To answer these questions I describe the stories of three women: Alice, Beryl and Alanna.

Alice was born in 1894. She spent her life in institutions until she was over 50. But she found a place in the world as a carer in the home of Mrs P who employed Alice to look after her house, her mother and later her children. Alice really enjoyed working as a carer in Mrs P's house, but she ended her life in her own home, which she moved into when she was 65.

Beryl was born in 1935. She lived at home with her parents and cared for her sick mother after her dad died. When her mum died she had to leave her home and got a little flat of her own. She went to a training centre where she helped staff care for people who were more dependent. She also looked after her friends Eileen and Jane who lived nearby. She cooked for them and helped Jane keep her flat clean and tidy.

Alanna was born during the 1960s. She has a teenage son. She brought him up and although she found it hard work she did it.

These life stories show that women with intellectual disabilities do care for others and can find a place in the world through caring. But other people didn't recognize them as carers and they did not get paid for their work.

The question of the relationship between women with intellectual disabilities and caring is an important one. Western feminists have argued that women gain an identity and a place in the world through caring; at the same time pointing out that the duties of caring have burdened women, and prevented their exercise of full citizenship rights. Disabled women have countered with the argument that some women are denied the opportunity to care, and are assigned to the role of dependent people. Where women with intellectual disabilities fit in these arguments is the theme of this chapter, and the question is explored through examining the life histories of three women.

In an important article, Hilary Graham (1983) described caring as the way women find a place in the social world. She went on to chart how caring gives women their place within the private world of the family. Caring is women's route to a place in the public world, in jobs such as nursing, cleaning, teaching and social work.

If caring is the way women find a place in the world, where does that leave women with intellectual disabilities? They are often defined by other people not as carers, but as people who need the care of other people. At first sight this suggests that they are denied the place in the world that caring offers other women. To some extent, this is true. However, in this chapter I propose to show that the relationship which women with intellectual disabilities have with caring is far more complicated than just being at the receiving end of other people's care.

To begin with, though, it is important to show how in extensive debates on women and caring, women with intellectual impairments have been left out, part of the 'other' – the mass of people who do not actually do the caring but are cared for, the objects of other people's care.

Women and caring

The public debate

Caring has become a subject of major interest to researchers and policy-makers in the last quarter of the twentieth century. Since Graham (1983) developed the ideas with which this chapter opened, many thousands more words have been written on the topic of caring. Graham argued for all women. Her point was that as mothers, daughters, lovers and friends women gained an identity through caring for others. She described caring as both labour and love; women expressing their affection for important people in their lives through doing things for them. Caring, said Graham, is associated with the private world of the family, with women's dependency within the family. But it also gives them access to roles outside the family, in jobs which demand emotional labour; jobs which require the worker to help people feel good about themselves.

Graham made a significant contribution to understanding women's place in the world. But as 1980s welfare policies began to emphasize the importance of families and communities taking on more responsibility for caring for people who were unable to fend for themselves (called in Britain 'community care'), the focus narrowed from 'all women' and the significance caring has in their lives to more specific situations where women caring in families, it was argued, took on some of the work that in a more generously funded welfare system, would be fulfilled by paid workers. A number of research studies in Britain took as their focus women's caring. They asked what happens to women where there are greater dependency needs, such as in families where there is a frail older person, a child or an adult with intellectual disabilities. They found that in such situations caring becomes more than an everyday expression of women's identity. It is more akin to burdensome labour. A good example is a British study by Lewis and Meredith (1988), *Daughters Who Care*. The focus was exclusively on the people they termed the 'carers', daughters of elderly frail mothers. They concluded:

> It would be hard to overestimate the emotional and material costs of caring revealed by the caring biographies of our respondents. The investment in caring as both labour and love has a profound impact on the whole fabric of the carer's life. (Lewis and Meredith 1988, p.152)

The authors suggested that many of the women did find an important identity through caring: 'the great majority of our carers wanted to care, and would do so over again' (p.152). They gained a sense of personal satisfaction at having done the right thing. At the same time many found it burdensome and stressful, and some experienced a lot of pressure from others to care, and to do more.

Through such studies the powerful image of burdened and exploited 'informal carers' was born. These empirical studies, and there were many of them, were backed up by statistically based research. The answers to two questions in the 1985 UK General Household Survey were subsequently analysed to discover the extent of unpaid care:

> Is there anyone living with you who is sick, handicapped or elderly whom you look after or give special help to?

> Do you provide some regular service or help for any sick, handicapped or elderly relative, friend or neighbour not living with you? (Green 1988, quoted in Bytheway and Johnson 1997)

Over six million people answered 'yes' to one or both of these questions, and on the basis of this, the idea that out of a UK population of around 55 million, over one in ten is a carer came to gain popular currency.

One of the assumptions behind this body of work and the 'discovery' of the unpaid carer was that the carer is always able bodied. The carers studied by feminists in the 1980s were mainly middle aged, mainly white, mainly heterosexual, mainly women and never women with intellectual disabilities or women who identified themselves as disabled.

The statistics upon which the construction of 6 million plus carers are based are similarly prone to excluding women with intellectual disabilities. It is indeed hard to imagine a woman with intellectual disabilities getting the opportunity to answer the sort of questions asked in the 1985 General Household Survey. If they were asked at all, they might have been unable to read, so would need assistance from others to answer the questions. If others assisted them, did they recognize that a woman usually viewed by them as a dependant was also giving 'special help' to others. It seems unlikely. In any case, if there really are 6 million people in the UK giving special help or regular service to others, then there are a lot of people who need that special help or regular service and women with intellectual disabilities, because they are seen through the ideological spectacles of 'dependency', are in an ideal position to be at the receiving end of care, not giving it.

Hence, the way 'caring' was studied by feminists and the statistical evidence upon which the idea of a carer was constructed excluded the possibility that women with intellectual disabilities were carers. If caring is women's identity, as Graham (1983) argued, and if caring is women's passport to a place in the world, then women with intellectual disabilities are left out, with no place in the world except to be serviced by others. Women with intellectual disabilities are in this public view of caring part of a mass of dependants, the 'sick, handicapped or elderly', the other.

Critiques of the feminist position

During the 1990s criticisms began to be made of the way in which the debate on caring had been conducted by feminist researchers. The main criticisms were from a disability perspective. Briefly summarized they were as follows:

- The research artificially polarized carers and cared for, whereas often in a caring relationship there was reciprocity and inter-dependence (Morris 1995; Walmsley 1993).

- The research focused almost exclusively on the views of those identified as carers to the exclusion of the subjective reality of those they cared for (Keith 1992; Morris 1991).

- Caring was seen as a women's issue, but ignored the fact that many of those who were cared for were also women (Morris 1995).

- Many carers did not identify themselves as such, rather seeing what they did as a part of their roles as family members, partners or friends (Pitkeathly, quoted in Burke and Signo 1996).

- Caring was seen as burdensome – as Lloyd (1992, p.215) put it 'the force of the feminist argument has been provided through the construction of the disabled person as a burden'.

The significance of these debates is well illustrated through examining arguments over the category 'young carers'. Young carers were discovered as a group with particular issues in the late 1980s. Champions of young carers, such as Aldridge and Becker (1993), argued that there were many hitherto unnoticed young people taking on significant caring responsibilities for adult relatives, more often than not lone parents with a disabling condition, and that services must be alerted to their needs. The counter-argument, put especially forcefully by two disabled women, Jenny Morris and Lois Keith, was that the young carers lobby equated disability with inability to parent; whereas in fact it was not the physical impairment that rendered disabled adults dependent upon the services of young carers, but the failure to supply them with suitable housing and support to enable them to be effective parents (Keith and Morris 1995).

The debate on caring outlined above continues to rage at the time of writing. Lined up on one side is the carers' lobby, demanding support for the supporters and care for the carers. On the other side stands the disability movement, demanding recognition that to be disabled does not mean that someone needs the services of a carer. Rather, they argue that the focus of interventions should be to enable the disabled adult to live independently, able to make choices and determine goals with the assistance they need. There are a few voices in the middle pleading for a recognition that both carers and those they care for share common interests, and that any agenda for action should take account of both, but theirs is a small voice compared to the vociferous claims and counter-claims in the long running debate on caring.

Looking at the lives of women with intellectual disabilities

What does caring mean?

The public debates around women's caring and women as carers have largely excluded women with intellectual disabilities. Their voices and experiences have rarely been heeded. Yet many of the issues raised in the debate are pertinent to them too:

- Do women with intellectual disabilities find a place in the world though caring?
- If the world is divided into those who give care and those who receive it, where do women with intellectual disabilities fit?
- How do women with intellectual disabilities view themselves in relation to caring? Do they regard themselves as needing care from others or do they view themselves as carers?

These are difficult questions and in order to supply some answers we turn to life history research. Life history research enables people to be witnesses of their own lives. When people with intellectual disabilities are asked about their own lives, rather than having their experiences mediated by others, often their 'carers', a more complicated picture emerges than an equation of intellectual disability equals being cared for.

Some published studies of people with intellectual disabilities touch on questions relevant to caring. Booth and Booth (1994) explored the experiences of parents with intellectual disabilities through in-depth interviews with respondents about their lives.

Their findings tended to support the view that parents with intellectual disabilities struggle with the role, but that their problems are as much caused by disabling services and environments as they are by individual limitations. Some contributions to *Know Me As I am: An Anthology of Prose, Poetry and Art by People with Learning Difficulties* (Atkinson and Williams 1990) showed that some women, and men, view caring for others as important elements of their lives. Contributors talk about relationships with friends, families and loved ones in terms of give and take, caring and being cared for in turn.

In order to tease out the complexities of women with intellectual disabilities and caring, the rest of the chapter is devoted to an examination of the lives of three women with intellectual disabilities in relation to caring. They have been chosen because they are from three different generations; because they occupy the roles of paid carer, unpaid carer and a mother respectively; and because caring is or has been, in various ways, important in their lives.

Alice

Alice's life history has been researched by Sheena Rolph, a postgraduate student who is tracing the history of community care through the eyes of those who experienced it, including women and men with intellectual disabilities. Alice is now dead. Her story was reconstructed with the help of Mrs P, her employer for many years, and through references to her in official sources, minutes, medical and social services reports. It is included in this chapter because it shows well how caring of various kinds was central to Alice's life.

Alice was born in 1894 and died in 1969. The first information we have about her life is that as a child she was in receipt of care in a public institution. Mrs P told Sheena that Alice was in an orphanage, the Girls' Home in Norwich, until the age of 15. During her time in the orphanage she was boxed on the ears so hard that she became deaf, and for the rest of her life needed to use hearing aids. Possibly as a result of her deafness, she was sent from the orphanage in Norwich, in the east of England, to another type of care institution, a mental deficiency hospital in the west – Stoke Park, near Bristol.

There she remained for 19 years. Alice's reported memory of her time at Stoke Park was that she hated it and spent most of her time scrubbing. In 1930, aged 34, she returned to Norwich to live in a newly opened hostel for mentally defective women, as women with intellectual disabilities were then known in the UK. The policy of the hostel was:

- to find work for the women, either within the hostel itself 'house work, much sewing at first, some kitchen or garden work', or in the local area as domestics

- to prevent the women from meeting men and having children: 'If the hostel cannot cure, may it be the means of preventing more mental defectives from being brought into the world,' said the Lord Mayor in a speech at the opening ceremony

- to provide care: 'A large number of people would be far better cared for, and it would be far better for themselves and the community if they were looked after in an institution such as a hostel,' said one member of the Mental Deficiency Committee when discussing the setting up of the hostel (quoted in Rolph 1997).

We can see from these different motivations that care was central to the purpose of the hostel:

- care as protection for women who need it
- care to prevent the women defectives from bearing children
- and, possibly, care work for the hostel residents.

Though the word care was not used for the type of occupation envisaged, with hindsight it might be argued that the sort of work visualized for the hostel residents was associated with caring for others. As Alice's later story shows, this was the sort of work she obtained.

Alice soon settled in to life at the hostel. The matron described her as 'a well behaved and clean woman, a willing worker'. She was one of the first women there to go out to daily work in the home of a local woman where she did so well that she was soon permitted to live in the woman's home, rather than return to the hostel each night. As she gradually established her worth as a worker who was sufficiently trustworthy not to need daily supervision from the hostel, so she gained a passport to the world beyond a care institution for the first time in her life. Was caring the means by which she made her escape? Officially it was not. One of the rules of the hostel was that defectives going out to work in local homes were not to be left in charge of children. But the details of Alice's story tell a different tale. Here is Mrs P's account:

> When Mrs M [Alice's employer] died, and my mother, I think, was widowed then, and I think matron said, 'Well probably Alice would be a good one to come to you for company'… so she came and lived with

my mother … She became quite a good cook. Used to make a lovely stew! Yes, they used to work together just to keep the house going.

Here is a transition for Alice, from being a domestic who did needlework or housework to being a live-in companion and helper for an elderly widow, a classic caring role. The caring role became more pronounced when Mrs P's mother had her leg amputated. Mrs P recalled:

> She [mother] moved in with me and Alice came too. She took it for granted. For a year we all looked after my mother. Alice was a great help… she used to look after the children too… And Olive [a friend of Alice's from the hostel] came in and gave us a hand too.

This family became Alice's family. She had a caring role within it, although it is noticeable that Mrs P used the words 'looked after' or 'helped' to describe Alice and Olive's contribution to the household. 'Caring' is a word of the late twentieth century, not in common usage at the time in question, the mid-twentieth century.

In her written account of Alice's story, Sheena Rolph considers the role caring had in Alice's life:

> She became a carer herself, looking after the disabled grandmother, the house, the children, the cooking. But her relationship with the family was more complex than that. The family, according to the legislation on licence in the community were her carers and in loco parentis.

Alice remained with Mrs P's family until she retired. During most of that time, until 1956, she remained subject to the legislation governing mental defectives, a person who needed care. Representatives of the Norwich Mental Deficiency Committee still monitored her position and paid regular visits to the family to check on Alice's situation. Mrs P was responsible for ensuring that she avoided contact with males. According to Mrs P this did not trouble Alice. She 'never seemed to think about it'. However, it is a reminder that despite her caring work, Alice was not free to pursue the goals other women might take for granted. Carer she might be, but this did not accord her full adult status. She got her own home only at the age of 65, in an almshouse for poor men and women.

Alice's story is a good example of the complex ways in which care and caring intersect with the lives of women with intellectual disabilities. Herself, in official eyes, the subject of care for the greater part of her life, she nevertheless gained a place in the world through caring. It was her route out of residential care and into a more ordinary life with a family, a situation in which there was apparently reciprocity, mutual affection and respect. Did caring give Alice an identity too? We do not know Alice's views directly because she is now dead, but cards and notes she wrote, which Mrs P has preserved in a memorial album of Alice's life, suggest that it did. There are many examples of cards to and from Mrs P's sons, her 'boys', the family pets, and Mrs P herself.

Beryl[1]

Beryl's is the second life story selected to illustrate the part caring plays in the life of women with intellectual disabilities. Beryl's story is featured because, like many women I have interviewed, Beryl lived at home with her family until the death of her parents. These daughters living at home are ideally placed to become the primary carer as their parents age and become infirm. Beryl's story is a good illustration of the way a woman who has been seen as the subject of her parents' care gradually adopts the role of carer.

Beryl was born in 1932. Her story is constructed from a series of interviews and conversations between her and the author over several years. It is told, as far as possible, in her own words. She was born in Luton, a large manufacturing town in south east England. Her father worked in the dye works and her mother was 'a stay at home'. As Beryl said, 'That's how it was in them days.' She contrasted this with the way she was brought up:

> I been brought up with a mind of my own...when me dad were alive he let me handle my allowance. I always had to draw it myself. He said I ain't doing it for you. It's yours, so you collect it.

Of her childhood she recalled:

> Learnt meself to walk walking along the furniture, all that, yeh. I learnt to walk didn't really do anything till I were 7 year old... I had trouble, bottom of my back, it stopped me walking. I had lessons at home. Didn't used to go out, there weren't no centres then.

---

1   Beryl's story was first published in my unpublished PhD thesis 'Gender, Caring and Learning Disability' (1995).

Chronologically the next events she mentioned followed the death of her father (in 1961) when she was 29 years old:

> Ooh, me dad died five years afore. It was after me dad died me mum got rheumatoid arthritis. I had to do housework, cooking, she couldn't get out see, we lived on a hill, top of a hill, she got rheumatoid arthritis in her knees…except when me brother fetched her, fetched her in the car she never got out…I mean she was 'ousebound…my mum was very ill, cancer… I knew it were coming.

From this, it sounds very much as if she had taken on the role of carer, one she shared with her brother. She lost this role when her mother died and became, once more, someone who needed care:

> Yeah, yeah, then me brother said he were trying to fit me in, I didn't know where I were going at that time. This Centre that opened he heard about it so he got me in there…see my brother who lived in Shefford he kept an eye on me. I used to live in a house on me own, after me mum died he keep an eye on me… He married to his first wife then. She wouldn't accept me sort of thing, so he helped me along then he got me back in me own house that were me mum's house, he got me to live up there he used to keep an eye on me, see I was all right …the Centre, it were opened in March that year, I didn't go till after Easter…her [mum] died in January…when I were going to B [Adult Training Centre] he let me go back home…he only had me a short time, he wanted to have me permanently till I got over.

Characteristically, Beryl referred to any care she needed as 'keeping an eye on me'. Her brother ('He were a good brother,' said Beryl), died aged 54, and at that point she left her old family house and moved into a flat in a large block in a publicly owned housing estate:

> Then I sold that, see before my brother died they wouldn't even think about me getting a flat. They said it wasn't unsuitable, me brother said it was, they wouldn't do nothing till me brother died, then they do something for me.

According to this account family played the key role in Beryl's life until the death of her brother. Caring as give and take is intimately intertwined. The way she told it, it was natural that she would stay with her parents, and take on the job of looking after her mother. She 'didn't want to go out'. She talks of her brother 'keeping an eye on her' when she lived alone in the family house. Although her brother briefly gave her a home when her mother died, she said that it was never intended to be permanent, and she linked the opening of the Adult Training Centre within months with her brother agreeing to her going home. Looking after her mother in her last years seems to have been a source of satisfaction. After the brother died in 1985, family faded in importance:

> He [brother] got some nephews by his first wife, don't see the youngest one hardly at all. Oldest one sends me cards on me birthday. Youngest one got a boy of his own now, a year old, never seed it... I got some cousins down Devon way. I learnt all the telephones since me brother died. His second wife, she remarried, don't see her at all.

Close relationships with men, other than her father and brother, were non-existent as far as Beryl's account went. Like Alice, she dismissed sexual relationships as unimportant:

Jan: What about you, Beryl, have you had any boyfriends?

Beryl: No, don't want one.

No more was said on the subject. But in her later life Beryl still did some caring for others through her relationship with two close women friends, Jane and Eileen. Both were in their forties, considerably younger than Beryl. I joined the three of them at Beryl's flat on several occasions. Beryl was very much in charge, doing all the cooking and shopping and organizing Jane and Eileen to lay the table, pass the sandwiches and pour the tea.

Beryl's importance in this trio is best illustrated through her relationship with Jane (43), her neighbour. Beryl had known Jane through the Training Centre before Jane went into hospital in 1974, and resumed friendly and neighbourly contact when Jane moved into a flat three doors away, quite by chance.

Beryl made sure I knew that Jane needed help in keeping her flat in good order. Jane corroborated this. She told me:

> Yes she does help me, sometimes she comes round and helps me clean up if I'm not very tidy. I asked her to come [to Review at the Centre], just be there and tell a bit about me...she said good things about me.

In fact, with Beryl's help a home carer and more hours at the playgroup were agreed at Jane's review. Beryl adopted an authoritative style when addressing Jane:

> Beryl: Didn't settle nowhere did you? …When she was young she didn't settle at nothing…she can read, she can write so I think she could done a job if she played her cards right. I speak up better for her than she speak up for herself.

Beryl told me that Jane had wanted to cut down her days at the Centre but staff at the Centre wouldn't let her because it would be too great a burden on Beryl: 'They think it's too much for me,' reported Beryl.

Beryl's account of her life suggests that caring is an important part of her identity. The caring she offered to others, her mother and her friends, Jane and Eileen, was however in a very private sphere. The sole indication that it was in any way publicly recognized was that the Centre staff prevented Jane from cutting back on her time there because it would be 'too much' for Beryl. So, although caring was important to Beryl, indeed seemed to give purpose to her existence, it was not in any way a route to a place in the wider world, outside the narrow sphere of family and friendship. Like Alice, she claimed not to be bothered about the absence of marriage or sexual relationships. It is a moot point whether she had internalized the prohibitions on people like her mixing with men that were the explicit policy of care services in her youth. Or was this a statement for public consumption?

What of being a person who needs caring for? As far as public care services were concerned, Beryl apparently remained out of sight until her mother died. She did not go to school and says she was visited by a home tutor. Her description of teaching herself to walk when she was seven suggests the absence of medical interventions. She led an uneventful life at home until her thirties. Probably this would be seen publicly as care within the family, but Beryl did not describe it as such. It was just her life. The provision of a flat only after her brother's death ('see before my brother died they wouldn't even think about me getting a flat') shows the local authority acting only when the family could no longer provide even minimal support. Beryl's concession to being a dependent person in social terms was limited to acknowledging that her brother and staff at the Centre 'keep an eye' on her. The main area where she needed practical support was in writing cheques; she cannot read or write. Once she retired, attending the Centre only two days a week, she began to live a lifestyle less untypical of other women of her generation than she had since early childhood. In this respect she was like the older people with intellectual disabilities interviewed by Robert Edgerton (1989).

There is no doubt in my mind that Beryl knew she had been labelled and dealt with accordingly, but this did not diminish her. Her narrative is one in which she appears as an actor, someone who makes decisions, and who makes the best of things. She was happy to be at home with her parents, pleased to look after her mother, looking forward to retirement ('I'll go out and about. I won't sit in. I ain't one of those what sits in'), and only a little resentful of the family which had turned its back on her. She did admit to being someone who appreciated having an eye kept on her, but she certainly conveyed the idea that she was more a carer than cared for.

Alanna

Alanna's is the third life story. She is the youngest of the three women. Alanna's story has been included because she has a son and her main caring activity was in relation to him.

Like Beryl's, the story was told to me in a series of interviews. The account of her life is, again, told as far as possible in her own words. She was not prepared to tell me her age, beyond the information that she was in her thirties, meaning she was born during the 1960s.

> I was born in Ireland only I been in Luton a long time so I probably lost my Irish accent…in those days Ireland was a lovely place, it was all nice…the people are very friendly, not like here, well most of them are but it's sometimes because the men are drunk.

The family came to England when she was 3 years old. She initially went to local schools, but was later sent away to a school for all kinds of girls with 'an illness that didn't show' on the south coast. She explained this by reference to her father's violent behaviour:

> Me mum only did it for me own good because of me dad being drunk all the time and swearing and cursing and that she didn't want me growing up that way she did it for me own good. Once he hit me and he said he'd never do it again. It was only 'cos I couldn't get me own way. He hit me 'cos most probably I was playing up.

In these statements Alanna hints at being abused, but she was at no point any more explicit. She enjoyed the girls school on the south coast. She liked the all-female environment. Later, she was sent to a mixed boarding school, which she enjoyed much less:

> I was always afraid of that school, that was a problem with me learning
> ...I hated it I really did, one teacher there that was strict and made me
> more nervous than I really am and when people make me nervous I'm
> just not able to do anything you know, like reading and writing... I
> mean when we came home for a holiday 'cos I didn't want to go back I
> hid meself in the wardrobe at home and mum of course was worried
> she couldn't find me anywhere.

She left school at 16 and went to work:

> See me mum got all the jobs for me because you still had to write forms
> and be able to talk to people and explain see I could only do certain
> things like washing up, cleaning all those kind of things.

She had two jobs she could remember, one in a hotel and one as a hospital domestic. Unlike Alice and Beryl, Alanna discussed her relationships with men. After she left school and while living at home with her mother she began to go out at night alone:

> I always wanted to go out, didn't have many friends to go out with, so
> mum only kind of took me to the pictures kind of thing, you can't do
> much with your mum there with you kind of thing...that's when I
> used to go out on me own when I was at home you know and got
> meself in um [pause] trouble...you see, this is where I wandered away
> from home, like, to these kind of places on me own, and that's how I
> got in trouble a lot. I regret being with the coloured person now 'cos I
> know it was wrong to be going out with a coloured man and I fell
> pregnant with him and I had to have the child killed which I don't
> think I liked, I mean to kill a human being.

She found another boyfriend who was the father of her child:

> We used to do it in different places and not always the right places and
> he was in a hurry the last time we did it like he wanted me to have John
> and just go like, not be bothered any more. I went out with a coloured
> bloke once...he just wanted me to be for him like, wasn't rape or
> anything like that. He just didn't want me any more which I was kind
> of sad and crying me eyes out.

While she was pregnant:

> She [mum] came and got me which I regret, see I was at a friend's house
> and they were letting me stay for a while you know, but I think I
> would've been able to sort it out but me mum and dad come to the
> house and brought me home, they didn't say anything, they were very
> quiet, but I regretted it because I didn't want to go back home... At the
> hospital I had John, then I went to a place where I met more nuns, a
> place to know the baby a bit more and how to handle them and wash
> clothes... Then I was brought home to me mum and things didn't go
> too well there 'cos of me dad being the way he was with John crying,
> mum and me had to keep him quiet, if he woke up he'd be shouting...
> I stayed with me mum a couple of years then mum wrote away for me
> 'cos I still couldn't fill in forms...then I er went into a flat...then after
> that mum found a house for me, it was only just across the road.

Throughout her life Alanna's most significant relationships were within
the family. The two major relationships in Alanna's life at the time were
with her mother and her son. They are intimately intertwined. Alanna
regarded John as having been her route to independence from her mother:

> I think I'd be worse now if I didn't go out, then I'd be very quiet and by
> meself always washing up at home, always doing things for me mum
> ... She's not strict or anything but I think she'd like to keep me in my
> place.

Her bid for independence was only partially successful. Her parents
reclaimed her when she was pregnant, against her will. She said it was a
struggle to bring John up:

> He's just got a learning difficulty, he's not able to read or write, you see
> it's like meself when I used to go to school, I couldn't learn.

> He's very strong, he's a big lad, he's hard to manage, he get annoyed at
> you when you tell him what to do. He's lovely really, it's just that he's
> very hard to cope with.

Alanna seemed to lack confidence in her mothering. There was a constant
questioning about getting it right. She made uneasy comparisons with
other children:

> I don't know if an ordinary boy would get up, wash himself, see I don't
> know if boys of 15 gets their own breakfast or does their mum get

their own breakfasts…well specially her, the one across the way, she's young and she got four kids…one's a baby, she can cope with that too. You see as well as me being nervous I'm very shy and usually very nervous if you see what I mean and I suppose that doesn't really help John. When he comes home in the evenings we don't really have a chat, a nice chat, he won't really sit still for me to talk to, that's where he misses out.

While her mother had been on hand throughout, Alanna was less than enthusiastic about the help she offered:

He will do what he's told for her, for me mum like, it's just that she don't like to look after him.

It wasn't until the end of the second interview that Alanna revealed the extent of her mother's influence:

Yeah, well she thinks that I can't cope… I've always got the feeling that me mum is putting John down a lot, I mean she'd like him to go to this other place where they look after him and that…like have parents to look after him like a mother and father.

Alanna's mother's efforts to help undermined her confidence. Alanna summed up the situation like this:

I think other mothers let their daughters do what they want to do and I think I'm a bit left behind if you know what I mean, I'm doing what me mum wants me to do, maybe she thinks I want to do the things I did years ago, but it's not the case, not now… Mum says I'm moody a lot of the time, I don't think I'm that bad, I think it's because I can't tell her what I think.

Alanna was aware of the limitations of relying on her family. She felt she'd missed out: 'I used to like dancing but got no one to take me dancing.' It was lack of friends which drove her to go out alone in her teens. Her mother was her companion on shopping trips and the like, 'apart from that I'm on me own kind of thing'. She attributed this lack of friends to shyness:

I never was any good at joining in even when I was at school… I always have to have a whiskey before I go out anywhere.

This was one of many references to what she regarded as a crippling shyness.

Although Alanna was a long-term resident of Luton she had none of the close relationships with other women with intellectual disabilities which gave meaning and structure to Beryl's life. This threw her into dependence on her family for companionship. She attributed this social isolation to her shyness, though in fact she had few opportunities to meet other people because she had no job and did not go to a centre.

What insights can be gained from Alanna's story about women with intellectual disabilities and caring? Of the three women in this chapter Alanna's life appears least affected by learning disability services. Other than through schools she had had no contact with the sorts of services – hospital, hostel and centres – which were significant for Alice and Beryl.

Certainly in terms of controlling her sexuality, the services had been less successful than with Alice and Beryl, but she was born at a time when control of sexuality was less paramount in the minds of the authorities.

Caring in the form of parenting was absolutely central to Alanna. Unlike many women with intellectual disabilities who have children, Alanna had managed to hold on to her son. She aspired to be a good mother. Being a good daughter was also something she struggled with. As a mother she was a willing carer. As a daughter she was an unwilling dependant, despite being a householder who controlled her own income. Being cared for was oppressive to Alanna. It was not only her mother's over-protectiveness that was at issue. The possibility that she had been abused, by her father and/or by the various boyfriends she described, is clearly indicated by some of the interview data.

From the way Alanna described her pregnancy and the significance of having a son it is possible to see her regarding motherhood as a way out of her role in the family. She said that if she had not had John she thought she'd still be closely confined within her family. This bid for independence was only partially successful. Her parents reclaimed her and might well have said it was for her own good. Alanna did not see it like that.

Conclusion

Women with intellectual disabilities and caring

Three life stories have been told to illustrate the complicated way in which the lives of women with intellectual disabilities relate to caring. They do not claim to be typical, but they do represent the experiences of women of three different generations. They allow an appreciation that the rather polarized academic debates on caring described earlier in the chapter are insufficient to incorporate the experiences of women with intellectual disabilities. On the evidence presented here, the relationship between women with intellectual disabilities and caring is complex and subtle.

It is now time to attempt to answer the three questions posed earlier in the chapter, arising out of the review of the literature on women and caring.

1. Do women with intellectual disabilities find a place in the world through caring?

A cautious affirmative answer can be given to this question. All three women whose lives were described present caring as a central activity in their lives: in Alice's case, as a worker; in Beryl's as a daughter and later as a friend; and in Alanna's as a mother. However, their caring gave them very limited access to life in the public arena, the world outside close relationships with friends and family. Alice is the only one of the three whose caring was outside the private sphere. Even in her case, caring was a route to a family life which the circumstances of her life had denied her.

I deliberately chose examples in which caring played a significant role, and I also chose to feature the lives of women for whom caring was apparently welcome. However, it would be a mistake to see this as always the case. In the course of the interviews I did for my PhD there were several women for whom caring, especially for elderly parents, was described as burdensome (see Walmsley 1993, 1995). This does not invalidate the idea that it gave them a place in the world, but does suggest that it may not have been the place of first choice.

2. If the world is divided into those who give care and those who receive it, where do women with intellectual disabilities fit?

The three life stories suggest that there is no straightforward answer to this question. Alice was formally cared for most of her life as a 'mental defective', subject to the legislation which saw them as people who needed care. Yet in terms of care, she apparently gave at least as much as she got, and clearly she had what might be now termed a paid carer role with Mrs P's family.

Beryl was cared for within her own family until her parents died, though she never described it as such. Within the family she became a carer as her mother became incapacitated by rheumatoid arthritis. On the death of her mother she formally entered the sphere of the care services. She became someone who went to what was called 'day care' at the Centre. She acknowledged that she needed someone to 'keep an eye on her'. But she simultaneously carved out a role for herself in caring for her friends, particularly Jane.

Alanna appears never to have been labelled as someone who needed 'care' as such, yet her mother's continued role in her life appears to suggest that she at least saw Alanna as needing care beyond the age most daughters require it. Through her mothering, Alanna continued to claim the status of a carer.

3. How do women with intellectual disabilities view themselves in relation to caring? Do they regard themselves as needing care from others or do they view themselves as carers?

Again, the life stories suggest a great deal of complexity. In fact, care was not a word used in any of these accounts. Helping out, looking after, being a mum, a daughter, a friend, but not caring, carer or cared for. The care tasks they took on, or others took in relation to them, were seen as natural extensions of these more everyday ideas about relationships. These women did not have access to the language of care familiar from the academic debate, and therefore positioning them in relation to it is a top-down exercise. To relate their lives to care demands a particular frame of reference, one to which they were not privy, and that framework has been imposed by the author. To claim the role of carer was beyond their linguistic competence, if not beyond their aspirations. Giving women with intellectual disabilities access to these kinds of discussions is one way of paving their way to a place in the world.

I claimed at the beginning of the chapter that it is important to consider the relationship between women with intellectual disabilities and caring if, as Graham (1983) claimed, care is so important to women. In most of what is written about women with intellectual disabilities, they are viewed as unquestionably dependants, the objects of the care of others. To be an unpaid carer may, as some feminists argue, burden women and exclude them from the benefits of full citizenship (Lister 1990). But to be labelled as dependent gives even less access to a place in the world. As Malcolm Johnson (1993) put it:

To carry the label dependent is to carry the burden of being deviant – someone who no longer enjoys a place in the mainstream of society, and whose behaviour is abnormal. (Johnson 1993, p.264)

In private accounts of their lives many women with intellectual disabilities supply a corrective to the view of them as dependants; but in the public world they remain part of the mass of the cared for, the other, the disregarded and excluded. Privileging the private accounts that women give of their own lives has an important role in affirming their place in the world.

PART IV

Finding a Place in Communities

WOMEN WITH INTELLECTUAL DISABILITIES

Introduction

There are many stories and visions of how women are involved or included in their communities. One dominant story in our childhood was women as the voluntary, tireless workers behind the scenes, working and preparing fund-raising efforts for worthy causes. Recent research involving the mothers of children with intellectual disabilities suggests that this story remains a valid one for many women (Traustadóttir 1992). The contributions of women volunteers have kept some communities and causes alive and sustained over long periods of time. But there are many other stories about women and community involvement. They have often been untold and unacknowledged (Daniels 1988). In one country alone, Australia, Kirner and Rayner (1999) have documented across hundreds of years the diverse ways in which women have participated and led movements in their communities. Women warriors defended their people against the invasion of white settlers and have been heavily involved in the recent struggles for Aboriginal land rights. Women have joined and led unions fighting for equal pay and better working conditions. They have established and led social movements and have fought to ensure that women have rights to education and citizenship. They have been leaders and 'movers and shakers' in professional associations, in the arts and in business. We are only now beginning to acknowledge and to promote publicly their achievements.

The inclusion of women with intellectual disabilities in their communities is similarly diverse and even more unacknowledged. Further, and perhaps more than for most other groups of women, their community involvement has been greeted with resistance by other members of the communities in which they live. Only in the last few years have researchers begun to study and document the ways in which women with intellectual disabilities have found a place within their communities. For example, Bogdan (1995) documents the involvement of women in a community choir and Shoultz (1995) describes a woman who is included in a lesbian community. There are also accounts of women who have played important roles in the development of women's refuges (Powerhouse 1996a) and in self-advocacy (Souza 1997; Walmsey and Downer 1997). We have, however, a long way to go before we begin to recognize the contributions that women with intellectual disabilities make to their communities and the diverse means by which they do it.

This final part of the book reflects both the diverse communities in which women with intellectual disabilities become involved and also the creative and very different forms which this involvement takes. In Chapter 15 Pat Felt and Pam Walker describe Pat's life in an alternative community. For Pat such a community provided a way out of the institutional life which she hated. There seemed to be few other choices. Her description of life in L'Arche is both affectionate and critical: it is an appraisal of her family. Her story shows the many roles which she has adopted as a founding member of a particular community. She is a holder of memories and history; she is an advocate and an active participant in its life. The chapter also reveals the reciprocal nature of community inclusion. Pat has given much to her community and has also gained from it. For example she lists, skills, insight and a commitment to particular sets of values and beliefs. But her membership does not stop her yearning for other possible communities and other ways of being.

Pat's community is consciously set up as an alternative to other possibilities. The women in Chapter 16 (by Susan O'Connor, Ellen Fisher and Debra Robinson) have no choice about the intersecting cultures in which they find themselves. The two stories in this chapter reveal the difficulties which women may experience when they are of colour or of a different culture to the dominant one in which they live. The chapter indicates how different cultural views of intellectual disabilities may conflict, creating difficulties for Teresa, a Latina woman, and her family in their interaction with services and community members in the USA. It also shows how discrimination on the basis of colour may be compounded for women who also have intellectual disabilities. Debra Robinson, an African American woman, tells a story of struggle and of discrimination. But both she and Teresa reveal their resilience, in spite of living in intersecting cultures.

Chapter 17 by Amanda Millear and Kelley Johnson demonstrates that for some women with intellectual disabilities 'the personal is political' has particular strength and truth. Amanda Millear is a strong self-advocate who sees her role not only as asserting and protecting her own rights, but doing so in order to secure a better future for other women with intellectual disabilities. She describes how her life has been a constant series of fights with other people's attitudes and social structures in order to be recognized as a woman with skills and knowledge. Her account is given particular strength by the description of a courageous legal battle against her perceived discrimination by a community organization. Her chapter does not really have a happy ending and points to the limits of the law in assisting people with intellectual disabilities to assert their rights and communities to become more inclusive.

Finally, Chapter 18 by Hanna Björg Sigurjónsdóttir and Rannveig Traustadóttir concludes this part with a hopeful account of the changes experienced by three generations of women with intellectual disabilities in Iceland who have become mothers. The chapter illustrates graphically the difficulties which mothers with intellectual disabilities have in being accepted by their communities and in keeping their children. However, it also shows that over time community attitudes, policies and practices change and provide new possibilities for women to take their places as mothers and as contributing members to their families and communities.

CHAPTER FIFTEEN

My Life in L'Arche[1]

Pat Felt with Pam Walker, USA

I first went to an institution after my mother died. I spent 30 years living in institutions. I was really anxious to get out. Finally, in 1975 I moved into the L'Arche home. L'Arche is the name of a worldwide organization. It has many houses which are shared by people with and without disabilities. Right now, I share my home with six other people – some have handicaps, and some are assistants. I wanted to write about both the hard and the good parts of living in L'Arche.

There are some hard parts to living here. For one, it's hard to get a lot of privacy. Some people give me my privacy; others don't. I've also learned to stay out

1   The preparation of this chapter was supported, in part, by the National Resource Center on Supported Living and Choice and the National Resource Center on Community Integration, Center on Human Policy, School of Education, Syracuse University, through the US Department of Education, Office of Special Education and Rehabilitative Services, National Institute on Disability and Rehabilitation Research (NIDRR), through Contract nos. H133D50037 and H133A99001. The opinions expressed herein do not necessarily represent the official position of NIDRR; therefore no official endorsement should be inferred.

of other people's business. Also, sometimes it's hard to get help with things when you need it. Sometimes there aren't enough assistants, or they are too busy. When people do help me, I like it when they ask me how I want things done.

Decisions and rules are sometimes hard for me. I don't like people making decisions or rules for me; I would rather do it on my own, or do it together.

There are some big differences between L'Arche and a regular group home. We do a lot of praying here together. We also have a lot of parties and celebrations. And we do a lot of traveling.

I also like to keep busy doing things besides here in L'Arche. I go to church, and do volunteer work. I sing with the Community Choir. And I'm a part of a self-advocacy group and I've been on state committees for self-advocacy. I especially like to help other women, since some of them seem to have a hard time speaking out for themselves at first.

I've met a lot of friends through L'Arche, and some friends through other things. Sometimes I feel that I would like more friends outside of L'Arche.

Overall, L'Arche is like family to me. I have found people here that I can trust. In the past, there haven't been very many people that I trusted.

L'Arche has helped me change a lot. I've learned ways of speaking up for myself. And I've learned that L'Arche won't send me back to the institution if I do get angry.

It's not easy for me living with a large number of
people. Some day, I might like to live in a smaller
house. But I would want it to be part of L'Arche.

L'Arche is an international federation of intentional faith-based communities founded in France in 1964 by Jean Vanier. The mission of
L'Arche is to create homes where people with and without disabilities live
together. A lifelong commitment is made by L'Arche communities to their
members who have disabilities. There are now over one hundred L'Arche
communities in 30 countries around the world. Although L'Arche is
rooted in the Catholic Church, members of L'Arche have many different
religious affiliations.

The L'Arche community in Syracuse, New York, was founded in 1974.
Within the next year the first houses opened. The director and his wife
moved in with their infant son and soon welcomed three people from the
local institution to share this home – one of these was Pat. At any given
time there was usually at least one more non-disabled assistant living in the
house as well.

Pam came to the Syracuse L'Arche community in 1976 to spend the
summer. It was during this time that she first met Pat and began to get to
know her. That fall, Pam returned to college. The following year she
rejoined the community as a live-in assistant from September 1977 to
September 1978. During this time, L'Arche opened its second house in
Syracuse, which Pat moved into. Since that time, a third house has opened,
and a fourth one is currently being planned.

Since Pam moved out of L'Arche she has lived close by and has
maintained a relationship with Pat and with the community as a whole,
sometimes joining for dinners, celebrations and other community events.

Pat started writing about her life, and the story of the L'Arche
community in Syracuse in 1975, with the help of one of the L'Arche
assistants. Over the years, she has added to this story. Some of the material
that is included in this chapter is taken from the writings Pat has done with
various assistants over the years. However, we have added further

reflections more specifically about her experiences of living in L'Arche. In order to do this, Pat and Pam had free-flowing conversations, which were tape recorded. Pam wrote up the transcript from the tape and then organized Pat's reflections, in her words, into themes or topics. Pam then read these back to Pat, and she would make some changes and additions, which Pam incorporated into a final version. Again, Pam read this version back to Pat to make sure that it accurately reflected her perspectives and experiences.

My background

I was born in 1936. What I was born with, at that time, they called it spastic paralysis; now they call it cerebral palsy. There were six children altogether; I was the youngest. I spent 30 years living in institutions. I first went there after my mother died. I was at the first one 11 years. Then, I went back to live with my father, who had gotten married again. I was with him for five years, until he died. Then, I went to my second institution, where I lived for 18 years. After that I was moved back to Syracuse, and lived in the institution there for a year and a half.

Moving into L'Arche

Before I moved into L'Arche I went into family care, but I was only there six days because the house wasn't accessible. I didn't really want to live in the institution, but I didn't want to be dumped some place and not like it there either.

I first met Doug and Perry [Doug was the director of L'Arche then, and Perry is his wife] when they came up to the institution in Syracuse. They told me about L'Arche, and said they were trying to find people who were interested in moving in with them. They wanted me to come visit and try it out. They would invite me to come visit for meals or for a weekend. When I would come, I didn't want to go back to the institution. I was so anxious to get out. I kept repeating these words, 'When can I get out? When am I getting out?' 'I don't want to stay here.' After I met Doug and Perry, I started to feel, 'I'm finally going to be free.'

Then, I remember my team leader called me to his office to let me know that Doug and Perry asked if I wanted to come live with them. I was feeling joy; I was feeling so happy. I could have said 'no' for several reasons. The house was not very accessible; some of the bedrooms were upstairs, the kitchen was upstairs, the dining room; I had to put up with 15 steps every single day in order to have breakfast. But I knew that, and I still wanted to try it and get away from the institution.

I lived in that house for three years, and then when L'Arche opened up a second house that was more accessible, I moved in there. The house I am in now has five core members [L'Arche members who have disabilities] and two assistants who live here, plus some others who work here. The number changes a lot.

I'm what's known as one of the founders of L'Arche. I think about one of the songs they wrote here for one of my birthdays, 'She founded L'Arche, with love in her heart.' Besides Doug and Perry, I was the first to move in. When I came into L'Arche, to be honest, it was like heaven. Since living here, though, I've learned that life in L'Arche isn't all heaven. There's hard parts, too, especially living with so many people, which isn't easy for me. It's taken me a long time to get used to it. In this chapter, I wanted to write about both the hard and the good parts of living in L'Arche.

Privacy

It's hard to live in a house like this, with lots of people. Some people are good at respecting my privacy. But, there's others that don't. I'm still trying to teach people, assistants and core members, don't come into my bedroom unless you knock. A lot of them just open the door, and I could be stark naked in here. This can make it very hard to live in community.

I've also learned for myself to stay out of other people's business. If there is problems in the home, I've learned, as long as it's not with me, to stay out of it. That's been hard for me.

Getting help with things

Sometimes it's hard to get things done when you need them. Like last week, I asked them to get my suitcase out, and no one did it until two days later. Also, I find it hard to find somebody to come here and help me straighten up my shelves. Sometimes it's because there aren't enough assistants; other times, it's because they're just busy.

When people do help me, I like it when they ask me how I want things done, instead of just going and doing them. Some of the people here do ask me, but others don't so much. I got my own mouth. I can tell people what I want and what I don't.

Decision making and rules

Living in community, there are some things I get to decide for myself, like my own schedule for bed and other things, and there are some things everyone decides together, at house meetings. The assistants also have their own meetings. This used to make me angry, but I realize there's nothing I can do about it. But, if there's something about me, I would like them to let me know. Sometimes they do, but I'm not sure if they always do.

For my personal things, some of the assistants give me more say in decisions than other ones. It's frustrating with the ones who don't. Like, one time, someone cancelled a meeting for me, because there wasn't any way for me to get there. What I said is, come talk to me, and let me decide what to do, and maybe cancel it myself if I have to.

Also, rules make me angry, like when people would try to tell me when to go to bed or get up. But, I realize that most people here don't treat me that way. I have a lot more choices here, and can make a lot more decisions about what I do. It's just hard for me to remember that sometimes, when I'm frustrated or angry. What I like is to make decisions and figure out house rules either on my own or together with people, but not with them doing it for me.

Roles and relationships in the community

It's been important to me to keep track of all the people that lived here. It also has helped make me feel more at home when people would say, 'Anything you need to know, ask Pat, 'cause she knows it.' I do have pictures of just about everyone that was here. One time, one of the former assistants came by the house to visit. One of the assistants who was working in the house at the time said, 'There's a stranger here.' I said, 'He's no stranger to those of us who've been here a long time.'

There is lots of change in this house – people always coming and going. It's hard for me when someone's getting ready to leave. Lots of people have left lately. I get to know a lot of people, but with some of them it seems like it's just 'hi' and then 'bye'. It's hard to have new people, sometimes, 'cause you're used to the older ones. Also, sometimes this makes me think, gee when can I leave. Sometimes it feels like there's only a few old timers left. It helps me feel better that there are a few others, core members and assistants, who have been around a long time, that I'm not the only one.

One thing that's hard is having assistants who act like friends sometimes and staff other times. I don't want staff people anymore. I put up with it for 30 years; who wants it now? It's confusing. In my mind, I'm thinking they are my friends, then all of a sudden they go and do something where I'm not sure. All in all, I do know that there are some assistants who are my friends. They may say or do things I don't like sometimes, but I do know they're my friends. They've stuck by me for a long time. I do feel like living in L'Arche has given me the opportunity to have lots of friends, both people in the community and other people who I know through L'Arche, but who don't live with us.

I also do get jealous sometimes. When other people get to do something and I don't, that can make me jealous. I can't help myself, it just does. That's another thing that's hard about living with so many people.

In my past, there haven't been very many people that I trusted. A few, but not very many. In my family, I trusted a few people. But the way I was raised made it hard for me to trust. I didn't feel some of them trusted me. The family talked for you; it wasn't you talking for yourself. They made lots of decisions for me without asking. The biggest one was sending me to the institution. Also, in the institutions I was in, I only trusted a very few people. It's hard to trust people who act like they don't trust you. There were a few who I could trust, but not very many.

It's also hard to trust people who keep on bringing up my past. In my past, I've said and done things I wished I hadn't. Nobody's an angel. I have had problems with my temper at times. But, I don't appreciate people who keep bringing up the problems in my past over and over. Some people in my family and in the institution did this to me; some people in L'Arche have, too.

But overall, mostly, L'Arche has been accepting of me. I don't feel I might wake up tomorrow and get told, 'Pat, we're going to have to move you away.' I have found ones that I can trust here. The ones I trust are the ones who have stuck by me.

Difference between L'Arche and group homes

If this had been like a regular group home, I wouldn't have stayed around that long, as long as I have here. I haven't lived in a group home, but I know a lot of people that do live in group homes. That's how I know this is not like group homes. For one thing, we pray a lot here. For another, we do a lot of traveling. And a lot of partying, and celebration. Overall, I feel we have more freedom than people do in group homes.

Prayer

It took me a long time to get used to the way they pray here. My way of praying was nothing like the L'Arche way of praying, in the open. Growing up, my way of praying would be like in a room with the door closed, or else inviting one person in and I would say the Hail Mary. But here we pray a lot together, in the open. It was hard to get used to. L'Arche also helped me find a church that I really like. They didn't mind if I tried out a lot of different churches, of different kinds. In fact, they helped me do that. Finally, I said to myself, why do you keep going to churches that you're not happy with, and that aren't accessible. Find a church that you're happy with. Now, I go to a church that I love, with some others from this house. I don't go there just because they go there. I go there partly because I like the singing in the church, and I like the people there a lot.

Also, we have special retreats, sometimes with friends of the community here in Syracuse, and sometimes with people from L'Arche communities in other places. Once in a while, but not very often, Jean Vanier comes to a retreat.

Celebrations

We do a lot of partying here, too. We celebrate birthdays, and anniversaries of when people moved in. I'm in charge of keeping track of birthdays and anniversaries, because I'm good at remembering that kind of thing. At holidays, we have special meals, or go out on picnics and things like that. Sometimes, we just have parties for no special reason at all. Lot of times, when we celebrate, people from all the houses here in Syracuse will get together, as well as lots of our other friends in Syracuse.

Traveling

We also do a lot of traveling. One time, back in 1975, I got to go to Winnipeg, in Canada, to hear Jean Vanier speak. I also got to go to Ottawa once to talk about L'Arche. We take trips to visit people in other L'Arche communities. Sometimes it's for meetings, and other times just for vacation. I've been to Ottawa a lot of times, and I've known some people there for a long time. I've also been to visit L'Arche communities in Erie, Pennsylvania, Washington DC, Boston, and other places here and in Canada.

Outside involvements

I've always liked keeping busy doing things besides here at L'Arche. I like having outside friends, as well as friends I already know through L'Arche. I always figure, it's nice to know people who you live with, but it's also nice to know other people out there, too.

Besides church, I've been involved in a lot of other things. Like, I worked with Citizen Advocacy, a group that finds people to be advocates and friends for people who want one; I was on their Board at one time. I get together for dinner with people from Amicus Club nearly every month. It's a club that was first started by some people who are blind, but then they started inviting some of their friends who aren't blind, so that's how I got there. I used to volunteer for help with mailing at the Rescue Mission, a place that helps homeless people. And sometimes I go speak about L'Arche at different places, like classes, or workshops, or schools.

I am also involved with Self-Advocates of Central New York. We meet once a month, and have conferences every year. I'm also on the state steering committee for self-advocacy. I travel to Albany for that, a couple of times a year. Self-advocacy is about trying to make ourselves understood. It's taught me how to do for myself, and to control my own way of living. And then I can teach others what I've been taught. With self-advocacy, I've also gotten to travel to different places besides Albany. I went to Toronto for a conference, and I went to Oklahoma for another conference.

Because of what I've learned in self-advocacy, in my mind, I want to be an advocate to other people. I can still do that, unless they don't want my help. I've also learned, when people see you doing for yourself, then they might follow you.

I like helping people out. I've been helped out a lot, so now I want to help others out. Self-advocacy is one way I can do that. I especially like to help other women, since some of them seem to have a harder time speaking out for themselves. Like, I kept pushing them for Genevieve to move out of the institution and into L'Arche, which finally happened.

I also sing with the Syracuse Community Choir. I've always liked singing. Back in the institution, I sang in the choir. Now, I've found another choir that I can sing with. One of my friends who used to live in the institution with me and lives in a group home now told me about the choir. To me, it's a special kind of choir because it's very accessible. People will help me and others get rides. We print our music in Braille so people who are blind can sing with us.

I have made some friends, through choir and self-advocacy and other things. I would like more friends, though. Going to visit other people is a problem, like getting into their houses. I have told people, on a nice evening, your back yard would be just as good as your home. It's harder to get around and meet people now that I can't walk. But, since I've gotten Quickie (my electric wheelchair), I get around much better than I did with my other wheelchair.

L'Arche is like family

Most of my family doesn't stay in touch; but there are some of them that do. Mostly, one of my brothers did when he was alive. Now, my other brother tries to do what the other one did when he was alive. My brother sometimes comes to my annual review at L'Arche. And he does things to help me out, once in a while. Like, he made me a loom. But, it's mostly me who calls, rather than him. Sometimes I go there for holidays, but not all the time. I am also in touch, once in a while, with a few other relatives, like my nieces and nephew, and my cousin.

My family didn't want me to go to their funerals. I missed my father's. When my brother died, the family said no about that one too, but L'Arche and I said yes. So, in other words, I had somebody behind me, with me, that said, tough, she's his sister, and she's going. I wish I could have gone to my father's funeral.

So, there are some family members who have supported me and some who have not. I think it would be hard for me to live with my family. I want to still have contact with them, but not live with them. In L'Arche, even though I do have my hard times, some of the people here have been more accepting of me than some of my family were. So, it does feel like family here.

Personal transformation

L'Arche has helped me change a lot. I did start changing, though, when I was in the institution and started speaking up for myself and others. But, because of that, I became what's known as a troublemaker. Since I moved into L'Arche, I've learned that it is OK to speak up for myself. But I've learned ways of speaking up that don't get me into so much trouble. I've learned ways of dealing with my anger. I didn't learn that from my family or in the institution. I used to be afraid of being told if I got too mad at people, I'd be told I had to leave. But that was all in my mind, 'cause I've already been informed by people at L'Arche 150 times it would never happen, unless I started beating people.

I started going to people, whether they were busy or not, and saying, I need to talk to someone. So, I now go to people when I'm angry. I've been doing that for just about seven years now. I also learned other things, like to stay out of other people's business. And to keep busy; that helps me from getting so jealous as I used to. And I shocked just about everybody in L'Arche. People say, she has changed a lot. My spirituality has also helped me deal with my anger. Sometimes it helps stop me from saying things I don't want to say. Or, it helps remind me of the good things in my life.

Future

My dream for a long time has been to have my own home. If I did that, I would still want to be part of the L'Arche community. I would still want to come here to visit, come for prayer, things like that. I don't think I'd want to live all by myself. Maybe with a few others. If I had my own home, I'd like to open it up and share it with others who need a place to live, like Jean Vanier did. The community has said to me, 'If you decided to live on your own, we won't hold you back.' I know they would help me out. They have said, too, they would hold my bedroom until I told them I'm all set and I'm sure I don't need it.

I've decided, though, to stay here, at least for now. Even though there's hard parts. Sometimes I say I don't like it. But, in my experience, how can a person say they don't like L'Arche when they know deep down in their hearts they're lying? Because my experience of L'Arche altogether is of L'Arche as a home and a family, with many good things. I have said, though, living with a large number of people is not easy for me. If they do open a smaller house that's accessible, I would like to move to one.

A few years ago, I was in the hospital; people were there with me all the time. It's confusing to explain to outsiders, but, to me, L'Arche is the only home I know of that sticks by you no matter what. If I left, who knows, I could be in a nursing home by now. It isn't so easy to get help for people who want to live on their own. I wouldn't feel comfortable landing in a nursing home. But I'm afraid I might because of my medical problems. But, living here, I feel L'Arche would do all they could to keep me from having to go to one. I've lived in L'Arche so long, now, it would be very hard to leave, 'cause I'm used to it. If I left, I would miss having L'Arche to come home to.

CHAPTER SIXTEEN

Intersecting Cultures
Women of Color With Intellectual Disabilities

Susan O'Connor, Ellen Fisher
and Debra Robinson, USA

Women of color with intellectual disabilities are
often looked at by other people in ways that have
nothing to do with who they really are. People may
look down on them because they are women, because they are people of color, or because they have
a disability. These different types of negative attitudes can make things difficult.

This chapter is about the lives of two women of
color with intellectual disabilities: one who is Latina
and one who is African American. They both live in
the USA. The two women are very different from
each other, but they have both had to deal with some
of the same types of negative attitudes from other
people.

The first woman in the chapter, Teresa, is a Latina
woman in her mid-twenties. She is the mother of
two children. She is very important to her family, and

they are important to her. She is visited by different professionals who see her as a 'client' needing help in doing things. This is not how she sees herself or how her family sees her. To herself and to her family, she is first of all a wife and mom. Teresa needs support but she does not always like how the support is given.

The second woman in the chapter, Debbie Robinson, is African American. Here is her story. I was born in 1960. My five brothers loved me to death. I was also very much loved by my mom and dad. But it was rough growing up. There were six of us kids and I had a lot of needs. In 1986, I became a member of Speaking for Ourselves (the self-advocacy organization) and that's what turned my life around: advocacy! I was the first African American woman to be a board president of Speaking for Ourselves. While I was in office, the board gave me a really hard time because I was a woman. The last few years of my life have been very busy and very good.

It is important to find out about the lives of women of color with intellectual disabilities, and to hear what they have to tell us, so that we can work together to change things. We hope that this chapter will help people to begin thinking about this.

As diversity increases in the USA, there has been a growing focus on multi-cultural issues which encourages us to look at the multi-dimensional aspects of a person's life; especially as they relate to key areas such as race, gender, social class and disability. Areas that greatly impact a person's life and affect how they interpret or are interpreted in the broader culture. Central to such understanding is the degree of societal discrimination that exists in each category and then how that discrimination becomes compounded for those who are members of groups that face multiple forms of discrimination.

For example, being a woman of color with an intellectual disability lends itself to discrimination on a number of levels. While certainly all women of color do not have the same experiences, there may be common issues they face based on societal attitudes toward gender, race and ethnicity. To add yet another dimension, women with disabilities, and specifically women with intellectual disabilities, are viewed in a particular way within this society. It is important then to see the multifaceted experiences in which women come to maneuver and understand their world.

In this chapter, we briefly discuss how multiple roles impact on women labelled with intellectual disabilities. We will highlight the experiences of two women, one who is Latina and one who is African American. The stories are quite different but are also interrelated. While they are not meant to represent the experiences of all women of color with intellectual disabilities, they serve to highlight some of the issues that women of color with these labels may encounter. They also begin to provide a forum in which these women's unique voices can be heard.

In the next section, we will highlight some issues that have arisen in the life of a Latina woman, Teresa. One of the authors got to know Teresa over the course of a year. The following story is based on discussions and time spent with Teresa in her home and community.

Teresa

Teresa appears to be a woman of few words. Upon first meeting her, you see a quiet, very shy woman in her mid-twenties. This image changes as you get to know her and she becomes more comfortable with you. Teresa is also more talkative when her common law husband is not present. To some she presents a rather dishevelled appearance, especially to those 'professional' people (social workers and case managers) who enter her life on an ongoing basis. Teresa's hair is frequently tied back tightly in a ponytail, stretching what looks to be natural curl. She often wears a lightweight white cotton skirt and walks about her house barefooted. Teresa remains at home except for her near bi-weekly attendance at church. Her daily routine is fairly predictable as she describes getting up at 6: 00 am to get her children ready for school, and doing the ritual cleaning and cooking. When alone she often watches television. Teresa speaks only Spanish but has been attempting, over the years, to learn some English. She was born in Puerto Rico but moved to the USA some 15 years ago. She lives with her common-law husband and her two children. Since coming to the USA she has been labeled mildly 'mentally retarded'.

Teresa's role in the family is a traditional one. She is at home when her two school-age children return from school and she is left responsible for the upkeep of the family's apartment. In traditional Puerto Rican culture, prestige comes to a woman through taking care of the family. Though this is her primary role, she is visited by three professionals who are working with her on a multitude of issues that range from caring for the home, taking care of her children and her relationship with her husband.

As a woman of color and a woman who has been labeled, Teresa and her family are of lower socio-economic status. Teresa faces a number of issues, the first of which is the label itself. It wasn't until Teresa came to the USA that she was given her label. For Teresa, and within the context of her family, the label is confusing. As Harry found in her study of Puerto Rican families: 'If daily affairs can be managed by a healthy body, common sense, and elementary academic skills, labels of retarded or handicapped became unclear' (1992, p.147). This is particularly complicated for people whose second language is English. Harry points out that the term *retardo* (retarded), is used in Puerto Rico to refer to someone with mental illness and is a highly stigmatized label.

Teresa sees herself within her family, not as a woman with a label, but in the traditionally valued role of mother and caregiver. In fact, according to her husband who asks 'what is this mentally retarded anyway?' the label has little meaning to their functioning.

Many of Teresa's parenting styles match those of others in her neighborhood. For example, she is not overprotective of her children who have also been labeled. Rather as a parent she expects her children to function in their neighborhood environment and her children run freely with other neighborhood children, yet she was aware of limits regarding safety after dark. She is sometimes successful with disciplining her children and sometimes she is not. Teresa does struggle with this aspect of childrearing.

In many ways she carries a dual identity. Within the context of the system she is seen as 'retarded'; yet within the context of her family, she has a valued caregiving role.

Often people with disabilities are seen only through a disability lens by others, although they and their families see them differently. Within the family they have roles that relate more to needs in their family or expected cultural roles. In spite of her label, Teresa has a valued role not only within her family, but within her church. Involvement in her local Catholic church on a bi-weekly basis gives Teresa a sense of community, as well as the ability to express a very important part of herself through her religion. Here she gains a comfort level and sense of herself. Despite her label, membership within two socially valued institutions adds meaning and routine to Teresa's life. It is how she defines herself, even though outsiders may define her by her needs: i.e. needing work on her skills in parenting, housekeeping, childrearing and relationships.

This does not mean that Teresa's life is without difficulties and that some of those needs are not real. She frequently fights with her husband and has left him on several occasions. She was very alone at these times, as her extended family lives some four hours from her. She frequently gets tired of taking care of her children and suggests that she has a hard time disciplining them. Her life, as is true of the lives of many women, is multifaceted.

One issue that can be critical for some women of color who have intellectual disabilities, especially if they are parents, is the number of services that are in their lives. This is true for Teresa as well. Often those providing the service are from white middle-class backgrounds and they have their own standards as they relate to childrearing, housekeeping and what it means to live a quality life. When these cultures interface, it is often the more vulnerable party that is called upon to change.

Teresa, who has workers from three different agencies working with her at one time, is not quite certain who does what. They have identified areas of need such as learning how to care for her children better, housekeeping skills and relationship skills and work with her on them. But when asked what they did, Teresa commented, 'Just talking!' In her eyes, she got up at 6: 00 am and did the cleaning for the day, cooked and was there when her children got home. Her ideas and theirs were different in many areas. Though this does not mean that Teresa doesn't need or want support, it is how that support is provided and how Teresa is involved that is critical.

The challenges of how to support and respect women and more specifically mothers with intellectual disabilities – particularly those from diverse cultures – are issues faced daily at many agencies. The director of one agency supporting mothers with intellectual disabilities, Audrey Kvist, discussed the major issues that she sees the women in her agency face. One major issue with some women who come to receive support is that of poverty. Because so many of the women live in poverty they are faced with a multitude of issues. Self-esteem is one. Many have had poor role models growing up and have not learned the skills necessary to best raise their children (Kvist 1998). They have difficulty finding long-term affordable housing, have had poor or limited educational experiences and often feel they have little control over their lives (Kvist 1999). In Teresa's situation, her lack of knowing English is a huge issue that may also contribute to her shyness. She also had limited schooling and was faced with her children knowing English and choosing it over Spanish, which added to her feeling a lack of control over them. While she struggled to learn English, it was difficult for her when she did not know how to read in her native language. As a mother with children within the school system, this left her open to judgement by the teachers of her children. She said nothing when involved in planning meetings for her children.

Responsive agencies recognize the potential of the woman and the constrictions often placed on her by the lack of valued educational, family and economic opportunities. Walking the fine line of respecting the diversity and skill that these women already possess and building on those skills is a challenge.

Some women experience much of the discrimination described above and emerge as leaders within a movement working to change the systems they felt worked against them. The following is the story of one such woman, Debbie Robinson. Debbie's story is best told by her, so that is how it has been recounted.

Debbie

Debbie Robinson is a 39-year-old African American woman, who lives in Philadelphia, Pennsylvania, in the USA. She is a leader in the self-advocacy movement at the local, state and national levels. She spends much of her time working on inclusion issues and trying to improve the lives of others. But until now she has not had the opportunity to tell her own story.

While Debbie and Teresa are both women of color with labels of intellectual disability and have therefore encountered and dealt with some of the same obstacles, their life paths and self-definitions are as diverse as those of any two people might be. Yet, there are elements in common that grow out of the discrimination that they have experienced during the course of their lives. Here is Debbie's story in her own words.

I was born in 1960 in Philadelphia, where I live now, but I was raised in Queens, New York. I have five brothers. Three of my brothers were older and two were younger. When I was about six months old, they found out that I had cerebral palsy. I had a lot of operations as a kid. We lived in the projects for a couple of years. ['The projects' are groups of homes made available by the government for low-income families.] Living there was rough. But, for me, the hardest part of my childhood was having all of those operations. That's what I remember most about growing up. I spent most of my life in hospitals. I went to public school in a special education class; I had a tutor when I missed school.

My brothers loved me to death. I was also very much loved by my mom and dad. But it was rough growing up. There were six of us kids and I had a lot of needs. My parents didn't put me in an institution. They wouldn't do that. But they received no help at home either. I grew up in the 1960s, which was when all of the radical groups started. But we had nothing in place for people with disabilities!

At the time, I didn't understand why I was the only one with a disability and my brothers came out 'normal'. In the disability rights movement, things are different now. But, growing up, I felt like I was the only one. And I kept all that stuff inside of me. I didn't understand yet what my purpose in life was.

When I left junior high school, I went into a workshop/training program. I was in that program until I was 21 years old. After the training program, I went to the United Cerebral Palsy workshop. [UCP is a large agency that serves people with cerebral palsy and other developmental disabilities.]

In 1986, when I was 26, I moved back to Philadelphia. I was on a waiting list for services when I first came, because I was still living at home. (I lived at home until 1991 or 1992.) I went to the UCP here then. That's where I began to meet a lot of people. When I went to a Speaking for Ourselves [the self-advocacy organization] Job Fair and then to the chapter meeting in Philadelphia, that's what turned my life around: advocacy!

Six months after I joined the Philadelphia Speaking for Ourselves chapter, I became president. I was the first African American, and also the first woman, to be a board president of SFO. It had been all male run up to that point, and there weren't even very many women *members*. I was still at UCP and knew lots of African American women there, so I recruited them. I recruited Octavia and Carolyn, who both became presidents after me. While I was in office, the board gave me a hard time. Because I was African American, and because I was a woman, people really tested my leadership. I'll never forget how hard it was.

At Speaking for Ourselves, I met Roland Johnson, a great leader who became my mentor. I first learned about institutions at this time in my life by visiting a dear friend who lived in one and by visiting Pennhurst [a large institution for people with intellectual disabilities] when they were closing it, with Roland and Mark Friedman. We were called the three musketeers at that time: we went everywhere together! It was Roland who helped me find my strength and saw something in me that I had found unimaginable until then. He would say to me, 'I might not be there with you when you get there, but you'll be up in Washington and have all these great things happen.' I would say, 'I don't believe it.' But he was like Martin Luther King. He visualized things that later came to be.

During the same time period, I worked at UCP for five years. From there, I got a job at Philadelphia Coordinated Health Care. I was there for five years too. Then, several years ago, Vision for Equality was developed here in Philly and I was the first person with a disability to work there.

The last few years of my life have been very busy and very good. I began to receive awards for my work. And in 1997 I got approved to be on the National Council on Disabilities. My friend Justin Dart recommended me. I'm in my last term now on the National Council on Disabilities, and

I'm Financial Director/Treasurer at Self Advocates Becoming Empowered [SABE, the national self-advocacy organization in the USA].

When I think about my life, and about being an African American woman, and also a woman with disabilities, I think that being a minority has affected what I have done and how I have felt a lot. Being African American, I have really felt out of place at times. There are not too many minorities on government boards, for example. So, for me, being the first self-advocate in some places, as well as being a minority, has made a combination effect. African Americans, Puerto Ricans and other minorities are not represented enough in the places where decisions are made. And I have seen that across the country. Now people are finally getting the idea to put people with disabilities into places of power. But if you look at how many of these people are from different races, there aren't many! As minorities, and also as people with disabilities, we always have to prove that we are capable of doing things!

Another issue has been that the information that comes out of these places of power is not circulated in a way that people with disabilities of all colors can understand. People are often talking in another language, one that people of color may not understand. They talk at you; they talk around you. But they don't talk *to* you. I would like to see us doing outreach into *all* of the neighborhoods. People don't necessarily have computers. One woman I know doesn't even have a phone. How will we reach out to *her*? The country I live in tells me that they are reaching out to people with disabilities. But which ones? There has been no outreach yet to minorities. We are just beginning to work on that at the national level now. We are working on putting a plan into action that will reach *all* people with disabilities.

So, some issues have been the same for me as a person with a disability, whether I am a person of color or not. And other issues have been different. Looking at my life, I know that, if it hadn't been for my family and then Speaking for Ourselves and people like Justin Dart, Roland Johnson and Mark Freidman, I would be one of those people today that has nothing. My family loved me and gave me the background and support and values. And Speaking for Ourselves showed me that I have something to contribute and helped me find my purpose in life. I'm who I am today because of all of them. I have been luckier than most people in my career. I didn't expect all of this. When I got into advocacy, I didn't have a degree. Instead, what I brought with me was being an African American woman self-advocate, and bringing all of those ways of seeing things with me. So, I came to the table that way. And that's what I do in my life.

Conclusion

It is clear that multiculturalism as we have described it here is providing us with ways to better hear the voices and understand the experiences of women of color who are also labeled with intellectual disabilities. Their experiences, like the experiences of all women, are very diverse. Many of the issues that need to be addressed (e.g. poverty, housing, the exclusionary nature of the workforce) have at their core the pervasive discrimination that impacts the lives of people facing multiple oppressions. It is only when we focus on the complexity of issues surrounding women of color with intellectual disabilities and begin to hear their stories that we can successfully work beside them to create change.

CHAPTER SEVENTEEN

Thirty-Nine Months under the Disability Discrimination Act[1]

Amanda Millear with Kelley Johnson, Australia

Life always seems to be fights, settle fights and on and on and on. It hasn't stopped since the day I was born. In my chapter I write about some of the fights I have had in my life. It has not been easy. I have had to fight my disability and to have a go at things in spite of having an intellectual disability, hearing and sight problems. When I was a child I had to leave my family

[1] The Disability Discrimination Act 1992 is Australian national legislation, the objects of which are:
(a) to eliminate as far as possible, discrimination against persons on the grounds of disability in the areas of:
(i) work, accommodation, education, access to premises, clubs and sport; and
(ii) the provision of goods, facilities, services and land; and
(iii) the administration of Commonwealth laws and programs; and
(b) to ensure, as far as practicable, that persons with disabilities have the same rights to equality before the law as the rest of the community; and
(c) to promote recognition and acceptance within the community of the principle that persons with disabilities have the same fundamental rights as the rest of the community. Complaints of discrimination are taken to the Human Rights and Equal Opportunity Commission where there are opportunities for conciliation, mediation and a full hearing and judgement on the issue.

to go to a special school in the city. I was very lonely a lot of the time. That was a fight. And I have had to fight other people's attitudes. That is really hard. When I grew up I had to fight to try and get good conditions for work, to set myself up independently and to make decisions like having children.

In 1993 I wanted to become a trained leader in the Scouts. But the Scouts said I couldn't do this because of my disabilities. I thought this was discrimination. In Australia we have a Disability Discrimination Act that says that you cannot be discriminated against because of your disability. Over 39 months the Scouts and I met with the Human Rights and Equal Opportunity Commission which hears complaints to try and reach an agreement. We finally did it. I did not get everything I wanted and sometimes I think that I only won 75 per cent of the battle. But it is important to fight for your rights.

The things that have helped me to fight have been my belief in God, my friends and family and being involved in self-advocacy groups. I think it is important to struggle and fight for your rights because then you help other people in the future as well as yourself.

Life seems to be fights

Life always seems to be fights, settle fights, settle fights and on and on and on and on.

It hasn't stopped since the day I was born, I don't think. It's just being aware of what rights you have and what you haven't. It's a matter of just standing up and just leaping in for it I guess and not being scared to take a stand. I've been fighting ever since the day I was born and I'm still doing it.

Fighting my disability

I was born with my disability. I was one and a half pounds small [when I was born]. I must have fought even to stay alive for the first three months of my life. I must have been fighting against a real big subject called death. And that was the first biggest fight in my life I've ever had.

Well I didn't know I had an intellectual disability or ear problem or sight problem until I started to get older and realized I was different and I couldn't do certain things. I must have started realising it in a hard way. I was a different person to my brother and sisters. I don't know where I found that out but boy it was a shock and there was two or three times where I would cry at the beach with mum. And I told her, 'I feel different and I'm jealous of my brother and sisters.' I think she said she knew how I was feeling. I think she could understand where I was coming from. I was literally just opening up a book. This is me. This is how I'm feeling. And there were other times I felt that I was a second-class citizen and it was having to realize that I can't do the things that my brother and sisters can do. Why? I begin to realize that all these friends of my brothers and sisters do they know I'm a different person or haven't [they] woken up? And it was always continually haunting me.

I tried to do some of the things. I would have a go. Mum gave me a driving lesson in an automatic utility and I discovered that my eyes were off in different directions. I've always had that problem anyway and I knew my limitations but I wanted to have a go at it. But the real jealousy comes from deep down; it's been building up like a brick wall. And all of the jealousy is in all of those bricks and gradually seeps out and I had to tell mum this. It's most annoying being different and therefore how can I blend in with today's society and the stupid attitudes against people with disabilities? Because their mind and attitude and all that doesn't let us blend in. And a lot of people with disabilities don't have the same opportunities, the same support, whether it's moving out of home or being saved from an institution. Mum and dad must have thought about me twice and not once. And lots of my friends have been in institutions. It's enough to make you walk on your hair. I'm so lucky mum and dad saved me from that crap.

Fighting people's attitudes

I was born with this and there is nothing I could do about it. You are literally having to grapple with people's thoughts and their attitudes about you in the main instance. It's all right if people see me actually, but it's people who won't give you a go and won't let you have your chance to see what you can or can't do and that's been very painful. They just probably don't see you as a real person. I wouldn't mind if I was able to explain to them. I can't pass them my disabilities because it just doesn't work that way. I'm not going to hurt anybody. Just to reassure them that I'm a person, that I can do this or that. I've done all these different things and that and I still come against people who don't have a knowledge or understanding of any kind of disability. I'm always coming up against that and that is most annoying. They may or may not know; they may or may not be discriminating or might be putting me through pain or agony, but they don't know me. If they do wrong I get up and fight and get my fangs and claws out and try and do something about it. They can accept the way that you are. If they don't, it's in their mind and attitude and you are forced to throw your hat in the ring if you know what I mean and stand up and fight.

Fighting loneliness

I moved down to Melbourne at 6 years of age [from a remote farm]. To go to special school. And I still remember even now going into the mistress's house. I remember sitting at this big table and I was only a small tacker[2] then and sitting at this big table and I was one of the first students that started off at a special school which was called originally Selbourne House. I guess I must have been very alone because I'd never been down the big smoke before and at 6 years of age it must have been very scary stuff. Like walking into a big room as if I was a little mouse. I lived at a

2   Tacker is a colloquial expression for small child.

special day centre for people who can leave their kids in care. I used to go to the special school by taxi. Mum and dad used to take me back and forth between Melbourne and Deniliquin and every time they dropped me off [in Melbourne] I would howl like a wolf because I'd say, 'Mummy I don't want to go, mummy this, mummy that.' That went on for years and years I presume. Then I must have grown out of it and all this other stuff and I was getting more independent and I was able to do a little bit more. Well and through leaving home at 6 years, well I reckon that's done me a lot of good and it's had its good and bad times full stop.

Fighting for work

I had to leave school at the end of 1972. I felt really sad because my school life had been over. It took me some months or about a year to try and forget about school because my mind and heart were back at school but my flesh and blood was somewhere else, if you know what I mean. I stayed at home [on the farm] after that and in the meantime I was waiting to get into this rehabilitation place that allowed people like me to go there. And I come down to Melbourne and I lived in this place and I had to do a particular program. It was fine. I didn't mind the majority of the stuff but there were things I *hated*. Really hated indeed. And I had to go in this big room and count up a pile of bottle tops or whatever. I plodded on as long as I could and they kept a record of how fast I went and how fast I could do the work and there was a certain line that each person had to get up to. I was below it. I hated it. I think they were finding out at the process room what speed I could have and how much work I could put in a bucket. I found out that factory work is out of the question. Oh boring! My mind was asleep. Nothing to keep it from going to sleep. My hands were busy but me mind was off the planet. It was dead. And so my term was up there. And I started going to St Nich's workshop[3] and all this other stuff. I was doing things that I hated. Pegs! Curtain rods. Counting nails, screws. And when I first started at St Nich's guess what how much we got paid? $2.50 per week. Looking back now I see this as slave labour. And I was in that workshop from 1974 or starting from 1975 up until 1980. I left because they were not allowed to have married people in the workshop because

---

3   A sheltered workshop attached to a large institution which is now closed.

they couldn't pay them. That was their rules and regulations at St Nich's at that time.

I think I managed to go out away from St Nich's and do some voluntary work. I think it was for the Red Cross in the city and I thought this is grand I've never done voluntary work before and I liked it and I was glad to get away from St Nich's because there were things that I hated and two of the things that I hated is when visitors come they would watch you do your work. I thought they were watching me work and I felt like I was in a cage. And I had to ask to go down the street. And the babyish things. You had to ask to go to the toilet. Oh my stars. I felt like a kid of 6 years of age.

And the people got into the work and they had no workers' compensation back then. They were not even covered by work care and all this other stuff. And then there were always work accidents happening in the workshop and they were not covered and there was no sick leave, no this, no that. There was hardly nothing.

I took St Nich's to the Equal Opportunity Board because they were not going to allow married people into the workshop because there was something to do with the money. I thought that was discriminatory. I s'pose I did [win] because somebody said to me they had married people in. And that place doesn't exist [now] thank goodness.

Fighting for independence

I went into this house that was a flat on the grounds of St Nich's because this is where I begin to get my budgeting skills, cooking skills and all the rest of it. And there were certain women picked to have this trial run in this flat at St Nich's and there was a house out in Ascot Vale so I went in that house. I didn't feel happy. I wanted to get out. I was glad that I was getting out because I was getting married and I wouldn't be back in the dump.

Fighting to decide about children

It took two and a half years to decide not to have kids because [of] the whole heap of things that I had to take into kind of consideration. The money, child, big responsibility and all the rest of it too. The doctors didn't gang [up] on me because I knew the law gave me that choice and I used the law as my guiding stick at the time. I was given all the good and bad sides. And the decision was left in our back pocket. Not mum and dad's, not the doctor's, not Peter's [husband] mum and dad. It was made a joint decision and that decision was made by me and my husband. I had the tubal ligation in January 1983 and soon after I had that I felt this tremendous... I still can't even describe it even today. I had a great big burden off my shoulders. And I still think looking back from today I still made the right decision. That's allowed me to do the things I've been doing since then. It's freed me up and I haven't been tied down or anything like that. And a lot of people don't get that choice either.

Fighting discrimination

Under the old Equal Opportunity Act I fought a number of areas of discrimination and one of those was on sexual harassment and the other one was against a record shop and a third one was against a stupid workshop that didn't believe having married people in it. In the record shop they asked me for my driver's licence (as guarantee for a cheque). I said excuse me visually impaired people don't have a driver's licence and I thought that was discriminatory and I went through an outside conciliatory meeting with the person and they hopefully improved their things with people like me. Later they developed a simple system that I could use. And this sexual harassment thing, I had a guy calling me lady in a group I was involved in at the time and I didn't like it and I told him to stop time and time again but it wouldn't sink in. So I took him into the equal opportunity thing and complained about him calling me lady and that got sorted up and now me and that guy are friends because it pays to stand up for one's rights because you either get what you want or pretty close to it.

Finding strength in God

And there's just something else that dawned on me. Even God has accepted me the way I am. He's not discriminating against me. I'm a person with disabilities and He's accepting me as I am. That just dawned on me out of thin air. I'd just like to put that in the book too. And the two or three people have said to me you can pray to God in the bush or upstairs or anywhere you want because He can hear you. I've often prayed sitting on the throne.[4] Sometimes I think God upstairs has been with me from the

4   Colloquial expression for toilet.

beginning to now with my big fight. And if I didn't believe in God or prayer I don't know where I would be. And because it must have been Him helping me to fight for the first three months of my life and I'm still fighting even now. Do you get my drift?

Finding strength in friends and family

I've had friends and support and special friends but nobody could ever take the place of mum and dad so to speak. And most of my friends accept me for what I am and they know that when I get angry and say something I do say my piece. This is a good and bad time but when I got something on my mind and I want to share it with somebody I go ahead and share it.

Finding strength in self-advocacy

People with an intellectual disability had no group that they could belong to and no standing up and no support and nothing. And that's what Reinforce[5] – we originally called it Force 10 – was started up [for]. There was a church group in Sydney had Force 10 and then we renamed ourselves as Reinforce. I was also helping to set up the early years of AMIDA.[6] And you could say that I am one of the foundation members of AMIDA and one of the early foundation members of getting Reinforce off the floor too. And that's how I got involved in the rights issues and all this other stuff and been there ever since. I did lots and lots of things to help myself get more skills and into groups and committees and that's how I know how a committee runs and I've had various jobs on committees. I just wanted to do more and more.

The big fight: 39 months under the Disability Discrimination Act

Between 1993 and 1996 Amanda took a complaint of discrimination against the Scouts Association of Australia (Victorian Branch) and later the Scout Association of Australia (Victorian Branch Council) to the Human Rights and Equal Opportunity Commission under the Australian Disability Discrimination Act 1992. This part of the chapter describes how the

5   Reinforce is a statewide self-advocacy group in Victoria, Australia.
6   AMIDA (Action for More Independence and Dignity in Accommodation) provides individual and systemic advocacy to help people acquire the accommodation that they want.

complaint arose and what happened during and after the complaint was heard. It uses transcripts from the hearings, Amanda's written account of her experience and transcripts of discussions over an extended period of time.

The complaint

In early August of 1993 I was working in a voluntary capacity for the Scouts. I had worked for them since November 1989. I was getting a bit restless. I wanted a little bit more. I wanted to spread my wings out a little bit more. And I wrote a letter to the Assistant District Commissioner asking if I could get back with the Cub Scouts [as a warranted leader]. I've done my leader training and all the rest of it and I'd done a first aid training. Then on 4 August 1993 I hopped into my District Commissioner's car after a district meeting and I saw this letter kind of sticking up out of a book and I thought I wonder what that is.

Dear Amanda,

Re your inquiry to have a warranted position in the District.

Your job description clearly indicates that you are not to be 'in charge' of any youth member or members of the Association. As you have indicated to me you understand this is because of the necessity for all leaders in charge of youth members to take 'all due care'.

As you have been legally classified as blind and the slowness, at times, of your thought processes would not make you able to act quickly if a dangerous situation arose. I am sure that you can understand that the Cub Scouts are very boisterous and unpredictable in their actions and that any Cub Scout Leader must ensure that they are watching and assessing any situation in the hall.

My concerns are for yourself and ultimately me if any litigation was taken against you as a warranted leader in the case of an accident. Therefore I cannot offer you a warranted position in this District and I am sure that this situation would be similar in any District.

However I recently received a piece of memorabilia from...and I thought it would be good to try to put together a history of scouting in... To this end I thought with your good clerical skills that you may be interested in the job of archivist for...

That was fine. Until it mentioned about me being legally blind and slow in my thoughts and actions to do with dangerous situations. And boy my insides what the ... you're talking about my disability. And she reads on and she said I can't offer you a warrant and I said [to myself] wait a minute this sounds like discrimination. I said I'm not going to sit down and take this shit. I'm going to fight. I was actually calm and collected outside but inside I was really tearing apart.

And so we went through the rest of the letter. And after I got out of her car I howled and I yelled and I screamed and I was in shock and I said, 'Not again. This is my disability, why, why, why? I ask a simple question and this is what I get back and all this is at home in my house.' And what did you think I do on 9 August 1993? Go and put a complaint in [to the Human Rights and Equal Opportunity Commission] and that's how this long matter started up.

> The complainant alleges that she has been discriminated against on the grounds of her disability, namely an intellectual disability and a vision impairment. The complainant alleges that she has been denied appointment to a warranted position and has not been considered for appointment to any position as Assistant Club Scout Leader within the scouting movement and that these actions are in breach of s27 of the Act.

Attempted conciliations

The process was very slow. Amanda wrote in 1995:

> It's still up in the air as to when a conciliation or hearing will take place even though it is almost twenty-eight months since I lodged [the complaint]. So far the process has been a hard road because I was not prepared for it to drag on for so long. I have been learning new skills and new knowledge and new experience with each step of the process. I have stuck it out and not thrown in the towel as they say. It's not only for me but also for other people and the future too. I am fighting for a principle too.

Two attempts at conciliation were made. Both failed. Amanda writes of the second meeting:

> After we [both parties involved in the complaint] had talked about things and the [second] conciliation meeting ended we went our separate ways. I had to do some *real thinking* afterwards. I felt I was in two minds about things. I told my legal advocate what I was feeling and then I decided of my own free will. I said this [proposed agreement] is against my principles and threw everything out of the window. I said I will go to my hearing. I have felt a lot better since I made my decision. Now my legal advocate has some work to do! It is the calm before the storm.

The hearings

At the hearing the respondent(s) sought to have the case dismissed on a number of legal grounds. Arguments were made by both sides leading to an adjournment. The second hearing again involved detailed argument between two barristers:

> I went to the hearing with my legal advocate, my support person and my barrister. Each side had their own table and the Commissioner had his own long table. My barrister spoke first and then the other side spoke next. I sat like a mouse in the hearing and watched my barrister in action. The other side had a big wad of papers and threw them at us and the Commissioner *unexpectedly* ... The Commissioner adjourned the hearing until 19 March.

> On the 19th I was there nice and early. I was still numb and shocked inside from Monday's activities. I and my barrister went in and sat at our table. They had four people at their table. The hearing started again, then my barrister said his words of wisdom. He was referring to lots of documents. It looked to me like my barrister had found lots of good points. I sat like a mouse and watched him in action again. I tried to follow him but I got lost. I felt that my barrister was a lion with claws. The Commissioner started talking...and adjourned the hearing again.

These hearings were not in fact to decide about Amanda's complaint. They were to assess whether the Human Rights and Equal Opportunity

Commission had the jurisdiction to hear the case. In July 1996 the Commissioner found that it did.

> I find that the Human Rights and Equal Opportunity Commission has jurisdiction to conduct this inquiry against the first respondent.

By having this document I can say I've been there and done that and that I'm not scared to fight. [It] meant that we were going to go back to a partly heard hearing. They were saying that 'oh we're not under the Act here.' The Act has got nothing to do with this. Sorry you guys you are under the Act. And I had my photo etc in the newspaper in April 1996.

Conciliation meetings

Amanda's hearing was scheduled for November but prior to it, there was a private conciliation meeting to try and come yet again to an agreement:

> Monday came which was the first day of conciliation. I felt really scared and nervous as I did not know what was going to happen. Inside I was scared, petrified, wondering what was going to happen. Then the independent person came in and told us the other side had arrived. And the private meeting began. I waited with my support person in the room. My legal people went in and out three times. Each time my legal people brought back an offer from the other side. I knocked back two offers. The third offer was a better offer than the others. After a long while the four of us went back into the big room and we talked about the offer from them and other issues relating to it. I said I was going to think about the offer. And the independent person suggested another meeting. My legal people said 'Congratulations on what you have done so far' and they were smiling too at the same time. On the way home in the taxi I felt 10 feet tall and 10 feet wide and felt different too! And very, very tired and exhausted.

> At the second meeting my lawyers explained things to me and the independent person came in and out with pieces of paper from the other side. At one point I got really emotional and started to cry and told them how I felt. The inside of me was fighting against feeling and it was like World War III. Shall I accept this offer or go to my hearing?

Plain English version of the legal agreement provided for Amanda by her lawyer

Mrs Tuttleby[7] says that the Scouts have discriminated against her and has taken her case to the HREOC.

The Scouts deny having done anything wrong.

To save unpleasantness and money Mrs Tuttleby and the Scouts have come to an agreement.

The Scouts promise to pay all of Mrs Tuttleby's legal costs and to pay their legal costs.

The Scouts promise to give Mrs Tuttleby a new Cub Scout uniform.

The Scouts promise to give Mrs Tuttleby a personal leader adviser who is experienced in the Scouts and familiar with disability issues.

The Scouts promise to make a real effort to help Mrs Tuttleby find a Scout group which will appoint her as a leader with a restricted warrant. This will include giving her a letter of introduction to Scouts groups.

As long as Mrs Tuttleby finds a Scout group that wants her as a leader, the Scouts promise to offer Mrs Tuttleby prewarrant training. [It is Mrs Tuttleby's responsibility to find this group.]

The training will be modified to take into account Mrs Tuttleby's disability. And she will be able to take extra time in finishing the training if that is necessary.

When she has finished her training successfully the Scouts promise that Mrs Tuttleby will receive a restricted warrant. The restrictions on the warrant mean that Mrs Tuttleby will always be with two other warranted leaders and will have to obey the reasonable instructions of the section leader.

The Scouts promise to present Mrs Tuttleby in the usual way everything in the way of badges, certificates, awards that she is entitled to.

Mrs Tuttleby will not take any further legal action on the matters involved.

The Scouts promise to allow Mrs Tuttleby to work at the Disability Resource Centre as they both agree.

Mrs Tuttleby promises not to bring legal action against the Scouts in relation to anything that has happened before now.

Mrs Tuttleby promises not to go to the media in relation to the decision.

Neither the Scouts or Mrs Tuttleby will make negative remarks about each other.

---

7   Amanda has since changed her surname from Tuttleby to Millear.

And I sat and looked at my legal people and my support person. I felt that I was torn between two things and would either sink or swim. After that I had to follow my instincts and then I looked into their eyes first and then I said I will accept this offer and I dropped my complaint. And I just sat there at the table with them, feeling stunned with the mammoth decision I had just made. The three of them were delighted and smiling like Cheshire cats.

The agreement

I felt very proud of what I had just achieved. I still had other people in the future in my heart. I wonder if I have made a crack in the door for other people who have disabilities. That document I had just signed is a legal document binding on both parties and each party had to do certain things in the document. Both parties have taken a big step in mutual agreement. On the way home I was thinking of telling and urging people to stand up and use the Disability Discrimination Act and to fight for their rights. It is not an easy road to go along and I spent 39 months on it. Stand up and use it and fight!

After the decision

Four months later Amanda had celebrated the decision with advocacy groups, had received a new uniform and a letter of introduction to Scout groups. She did not yet have a personal adviser, nor had she been accepted into a Scout group and so was not eligible for training.

You can say I was under legal stress for nearly 12 months straight. I'm still unwinding from the 39 months that was one thing and at the meantime I'm still comparing [things] to this time last year. Do you know what I'm trying to say? And now I'm fighting on all fours…and it's not a very easy job selling yourself to a Scout group. I'm only trying to keep my side of the legal agreement. [I've tried] three [Scout groups] so far and I'm about to look at another two. Because these people either don't want me but they're not letting me know and it's that hard to sell myself.

I've won three-quarters but I've still got that one-quarter to go and it's that quarter that's going to be hard to get if you know what I mean. Now I've been thinking I've been trying to toss and focus in my head in and out. Have I won the War? Have I won the fight? I don't know.

CHAPTER EIGHTEEN

Motherhood, Family and Community Life

Hanna Björg Sigurjónsdóttir
and Rannveig Traustadóttir, Iceland

More women with intellectual disabilities are having children than before. This means that there is also more need for support for these families than before. We need to listen to the mothers to understand what kinds of services are best for them. And there is a need for more training in disability for support workers.

Over the past three years Hanna Björg and Rannveig have spent time with ten Icelandic mothers who have intellectual disabilities and have talked to them about having children, families and living in the community. There were three groups of mothers:

1. Three elderly mothers in their seventies and eighties who had their children a long time ago. Their children are now middle-aged people. When these women had their children in the

1950s it was very difficult for them to be mothers because no one believed they could take care of their children. Two of these women were not allowed to raise their children and were placed in an institution. One of the mothers lived with her children in her mother's house.

2. Two middle-aged mothers who are in their forties. Their children were born in the 1970s and are teenagers now. Although it was easier for these mothers to keep their children, one of them lost custody of her two boys. The other mother kept her children with the help of her family.

3. Five young mothers in their twenties and thirties who have young children. All of them are raising their children with the help of their families and the service system. Although these women have kept their children, most of them are afraid their children will be taken away from them.

Mothers with intellectual disabilities need help to take care of their children and their families. It is very important to give them good support that meets their needs and their children's needs. What worked best for the mothers in this study was when the mothers got help, both from their extended family and the service system. The mothers said that their families gave them the most important support to keep their children.

This chapter is about women with intellectual disabilities and their experiences of motherhood, family and community life. It is based on an ethnographic study with ten Icelandic mothers from three generations:

1. Three elderly mothers who had their children around the 1950s.

2. Two middle-aged mothers whose children were born in the 1970s.

3. Five young mothers who had their children in the 1990s.

We will trace how ideas and attitudes, policies and services have changed over these 50 years and how they have influenced the women's possibilities of motherhood and family life. However, before we turn to the study, we provide a brief overview of what is known about mothers with intellectual disabilities and their families through research and professional practice.

A growing population and a growing international interest

Mothers with intellectual disabilities are a largely invisible population in most countries. No one knows how many there are. Some researchers believe their number is 'probably unknowable' (Booth and Booth 1998, p.1), while others call for more epidemiological data to determine how many there are (Tymchuk, Llewellyn, and Feldman 1999). Most sources, however, agree that the number of mothers with intellectual disabilities is increasing and predict it will continue to grow (Feldman 1986; Llewellyn, McConnell and Bye 1995; Tymchuk *et al.* 1999; Withman and Accardo 1990). The reasons are new ideas about the rights of people with intellectual disabilities to lead a regular life in the community, including family life, and subsequent closure of many institutions and long-stay hospitals. In addition, most countries have banned mass sterilization of women with intellectual disabilities and attitudes about their sexuality have changed so they have more freedom to live independently and live sexual lives. This trend has been observed in most European countries, including Britain, Germany and the Nordic Countries, in Canada, the USA and Australia (Booth and Booth 1998; Danish Ministry of Social Affairs 1996; Tymchuk *et al.* 1999).

As a result of the increasing number of families headed by parents with intellectual disabilities, local services are experiencing growing demands to support them and the need to know more about them is increasing (Tymchuk *et al.* 1999; Tymchuk and Feldman 1991). In the fall of 1996, the European Union, in co-operation with the Danish Ministry of Social Affairs, called experts from across the world to a meeting in Denmark to discuss the topic of 'Parenting with Intellectual Disability'. The meeting provided an opportunity to share thoughts and research findings from European countries, as well as from countries such as the USA, Canada and Australia (Danish Ministry of Social Affairs 1996; Tymchuk *et al.* 1999). All the nations present were struggling to address the topic, but were doing so in relative isolation from each other. They all expressed a wish and a need to develop more appropriate services for these families that would adequately meet their requirements. It was emphasized that services needed to recognize the principle of full citizenship of parents with intellectual disabilities and respect their participation in decision making. All nations, however, admitted that they were far from providing optimal supports and recognized the need for more information and knowledge about families headed by parents with intellectual disabilities (Danish Ministry of Social Affairs 1996).

Another example of the growing international interest in the lives of mothers with intellectual disabilities and their families is a recent special issue of the *Journal of Intellectual and Developmental Disability* on parents with intellectual disabilities, published 'to facilitate the international sharing of information about this population' (Tymchuk *et al.* 1999, p.6). In their introductory article to the special issue, Tymchuk *et al.* (1999) point out that although parents with intellectual disabilities are a growing population they have not yet reached a 'critical mass'. That is, they have not reached the critical number that is needed before a group and its needs become clearly noticeable to social planners.

Research findings and mothers with intellectual disabilities

The study of parenting and family life of people with intellectual disabilities has a long history. In the Foreword to the special issue of the *Journal of Intellectual and Developmental Disability*, Edgerton (1999, p.1) dates the beginning of these studies back in the early 1970s. He says that in the early years 'it was clear that the weight of professional opinion was opposed to mentally retarded persons becoming parents', although a few studies documented positive findings about their parenting skills and family life. These studies, however, were few and far between. It was not until a little over a decade ago that researchers across the world began intensive study of parents with intellectual disabilities and their children.[1]

This research shows that attitudes still prevail that women with intellectual disabilities are incompetent as mothers and that they are at a high risk of losing custody over their children. Studies have documented that between 40 and 60% of them have had their children removed from their homes (Booth and Booth 1998). Because of widespread concern about the welfare of the children in these families, most studies have addressed issues of parenting adequacy (Feldman 1994; Keltner, Wise and Taylor 1999; Llewellyn 1993; Pixa-Kettner 1999; Tymchuk and Feldman 1991). These studies have shown that IQ is not a good predictor for parental success. Many other factors are equally important such as poverty, unemployment and history of abuse (Hoffman and Mandeville 1998, Tymchuk and Andron 1990). Researchers have found that many mothers with intellectual disabilities have problematic personal histories and have experienced physical, emotional and/or sexual abuse as children. Some had been removed from their parents as children and raised within the service system. As a result, many of them grew up with 'inappropriate or non-existent parenting role models, little or no experience of children's developmental needs, relationship problems, and poor financial, living and employment situations' (Llewellyn 1998, p.17; see also Booth and Booth 1994; Tymchuk 1992).

Thus, although intellectual disability can bring obstacles to successful mothering, for most mothers their disability does not seem to be the primary reason for their parenting problems. Instead, stress factors that are not related to the intellectual disability seemed to create more difficulties, as has been noted by many researchers (Booth and Booth 1998; Pixa-Kettner 1999). One of the most disturbing issues is sexual abuse. Research on sexual abuse of women with intellectual disabilities indicates disturbingly high percentages of abuse (Sobsey 1994, see also McCarthy 1999b and Chapter 9). This is of particular concern because of the effects of

---

1   Most researchers talk about 'parents' with intellectual disabilities or 'families' headed by parents with intellectual disabilities. The research itself, however, is overwhelmingly focused on mothers. This is not surprising as the same is true of most other family studies (Traustadóttir 1992).

sexual abuse on women's self-esteem and their capacity to develop healthy relationships with family members (Mandeville and Snodgrass 1998; see also Chapter 4).

Overall, however, the lives of mothers with intellectual disabilities are influenced by issues of motherhood and family life common to most mothers. Researchers who have examined their lives through personal accounts of their own experiences of childrearing and motherhood claim that 'blank judgements of parental incompetence are not grounded in the lives of parents themselves' (Booth and Booth 1997, p.5). Instead, the high incidences of child removal are as much due to the decisions of professionals as to the performance of the mothers. In fact, when mothers with intellectual disabilities are suspected of parental inadequacy, this is frequently made real through decisions and actions of those who have the power to intervene in their lives (Booth and Booth 1994, 1996).

There is a considerable amount of agreement among those who write about mothers with intellectual disabilities and their families. First, most researchers agree that, like all parents, mothers with intellectual disabilities need appropriate services and supports in order to secure the health, well-being and safety of themselves and their children. Second, substantial research and clinical data have documented that, given appropriate supports that are matched to their needs, parents with intellectual disabilities can successfully raise their children. Third, despite the well-documented need for support and the evidence of success if given supports, suitable services for these families continue to be non-existent, limited, fragmented and/or unreliable (Danish Ministry of Social Affairs 1996; Tymchuk 1999).

The study

Our research with women with intellectual disabilities in Iceland started in 1994 with a small project which focused on a woman with intellectual disability who was a leader in the Icelandic self-advocacy movement. During interviews with her we learned that it was not her leadership career she was most interested in talking about. Instead, her major concerns were with motherhood, the recent abortion her family had forced her to have, her fight against being sterilized and her strong desire to have a child. When we started a larger study of women with intellectual disabilities in 1996, we placed a strong emphasis on motherhood and family life.[2] Over a three-year period we have conducted long-term participant observations and/or interviews with 30 women with intellectual disabilities.[3] Ten of the women are mothers. Many of the 20 women who do not have children have been sterilized. Some have a strong desire to have children and some do not want to become mothers.

In this chapter we focus on the ten mothers. To learn about their lives in context we also interviewed and spent time with their partners, young children and extended family members. On some occasions we talked to support workers and professionals who provide services to the mothers. Additionally, we interviewed three of their adult children. The research was conducted using ethnographic methods (Hammersley and Atkinson 1994; Taylor and Bogdan 1998). We have spent a considerable amount of time with each of the women and taken part in their daily lives. We wanted to gain as good a knowledge of their lives as possible and attempted to understand things from their perspectives. We have kept in touch with most of the mothers over a period of few months and up to three years. We still keep in touch with the woman in our initial study in 1994. We have considered it important to have this long-term involvement with the mothers. This is the first research with mothers with intellectual disabilities in Iceland and we wanted to make sure we 'got it right' and gained in-depth understanding of their lives. In addition, many of the mothers live in fear of losing custody of their children and are afraid of strangers who might report them to Child Protective Services. Due to this it sometimes took us a long time to gain their trust. Some of the women were inarticulate and found it difficult to explain things in interviews. In such cases observations and visits to their homes over an extended period were the best way for us to learn about their lives. Because we have stayed in touch with the women over such a long time we have observed many changes in their lives: children being born, children entering pre-school,

2   This research has been supported by grants from the Research Fund of the University of Iceland and the Icelandic Research Council.

3   We would like to express our gratitude to the women with intellectual disabilities who have gracefully invited us into their lives and shared their experiences with us.

moves to new homes, divorce, changes in support services, service workers coming and going, changes in the support from extended family, and so on.

The mothers

The ten mothers who participated in this study compose a diverse group and their living situations varied. The oldest woman was 83 years old and the youngest was 25 years of age. Based on their ages, the mothers can be divided into three groups:

1. Three *elderly mothers* in their late seventies and early eighties. Their children were middle aged at the time of the study.

2. Two *middle-aged mothers* in their forties who had teenage children.

3. A group of five *young mothers* in their twenties and thirties who had young children of pre-school and early school age.

Between them the women had 19 children, 7 of whom have been labelled as having mild intellectual disabilities. Three of the mothers in the two older groups have lost custody over their children while all five young mothers have kept their children. Despite the fact that all the younger mothers have kept their children, most of them live in constant and in some cases debilitating fear of losing their children.

Possibility of motherhood and family life

The wide age range in the group of mothers in this study helps us see how ideas, attitudes, policies and services have changed over the years and the important influence these have on the possibilities of motherhood and family life for women with intellectual disabilities. In this section we examine the historical development as it is reflected in the lives of these women.

The elderly mothers

When the three elderly mothers had their children in the 1950s, there were no community services as we now know them. The only public services for people with intellectual disabilities were institutions. At the time no one believed mothers with intellectual disabilities had the competence to raise children. As a result, the three mothers in the oldest group did not raise their children themselves. Two of the women became pregnant as a result of sexual abuse. Both of them were sent to an institution: one immediately upon having the child and the other a few years after her son was born. Their children grew up with family members. The third woman lived with her mother who took the primary responsibility for raising her three children. It is interesting to note that all their children, who now are middle-aged people, have good relationships with their mothers. Two of them, siblings in their forties and fifties, live with their 77-year-old mother and take care of her.

When the three elderly mothers were having their children, the prevailing attitudes about women with intellectual disabilities were that they should not be allowed to have children and the 1950s was an era of compulsory surgical sterilisation in many countries (Scheerenberger 1983). The only possibility for these three elderly mothers to be close to their children was if extended family (usually parents) were willing to have them live in their homes and take care of them and their children. Their independent rights to motherhood and family life were usually not considered an option.

The middle-aged mothers

When the two middle-aged mothers had their children in the 1970s, community services were beginning to emerge but were not extended to mothers with intellectual disabilities. In those years, attitudes towards people with intellectual disabilities were becoming more positive as a result of new ideas, usually referred to as normalisation and social integration (Flynn and Nitsch 1980). People were beginning to recognize the rights of those with intellectual disabilities to live in the community and lead regular lives. The possibilities of motherhood and family life were emerging. The two women who had their children in this era struggled to keep their children and raise them with the help of their families. One of them managed to do so, but the other lost custody of her two children when she moved out of her parents' home to live independently. Her two boys were taken away from her and shortly after she was sent to a group home. This was a traumatic experience for her and the children, but she has managed to stay in touch with her boys over the years and has good relationships with them now.

It is interesting to note that the only possibility for these two women to keep their children in the 1970s was through support and protection from extended family. If such support were not available, the mothers were at great risk of having the children removed from their care. Their rights to motherhood and family life, however, were more likely to be recognized, although very tentatively, and the prevailing attitudes still assumed they were incompetent as mothers.

In addition to losing their children, all three women in the two older groups subsequently experienced exclusion from their communities; two were sent to an institution and one to a group home.

The young mothers

The remaining five young mothers who compose the third group have all kept their children with support from their extended families and a varying degree of assistance from local community services. The type of assistance they receive from services ranges from help with filling out forms and claiming benefits to extensive daily in-home support. Although they still battle negative attitudes and scepticism about their abilities as mothers, these five women belong to the first generation of mothers with intellectual disabilities who receive support services for themselves and their families.

The mothers in this group who enjoy the best and most secure forms of support receive services from local community agencies combined with assistance from extended family members. The assistance that the mothers consider most important is to have someone from their extended family (usually their mother) help them deal with the service system. In fact, they view this help as crucial to protect them from the potential power of the service system which they fear will take their children away. This fear comes from knowing that many mothers with intellectual disabilities have lost custody of their children and is heightened by their encounters with some professionals who have threatened to remove the children from their care. Some of the mothers have had support workers who use the fear to control them. This is particularly true of one woman who is constantly reminded by her support persons that they have the power to have her children removed from home if she does not do as they tell her. Her life has become almost unbearable as a result of this, but she feels powerless to do anything about it as the formal power lies with the professionals. She also fears that her complaints might be interpreted in a way that would weaken her position. She could be judged 'unco-operative', which would make her even more vulnerable to child removal.

It is interesting to note that, although their rights to motherhood and family life are beginning to be recognized, the role of the extended family still seems to be crucial in retaining custody of children and successful parenting.

Motherhood, family and community life in different eras

The stories of four of the mothers now follow: one from each of the older groups and two stories of young mothers. The purpose of these stories is to highlight the possibilities of motherhood, family and community life for women with intellectual disabilities over period of close to 50 years, starting in the 1950s. All the names have been changed to protect people's privacy.

Jónína

Jónína is in her early eighties and is one of the elderly mothers. She grew up in a small village with her parents and a large group of siblings. When she was 5 years old the family was split up because the parents could not provide for all the children. Jónína was sent to a farm where she stayed for seven years. She was kept in the barn with a 'mad woman' and treated like an animal. The family was reunited when she was 12 years old. At the time Jónína could neither read nor write and she sometimes found it difficult to control her temper. She was considered 'weird' but no one bothered to understand why or what could be done about it.

At the age of 32 Jónína became pregnant after having been raped. It was never determined who the father was. After the child was born Jónína and her son, Egill, continued to live with her parents and a large extended family. Most of the adults worked outside the home. Jónína stayed at home and did the housework. When her son was 9 years old, Jónína was suddenly removed from the home and sent to an institution in another part of the country. It is unclear who made this decision. Egill, Jónína's son, is still angry at his family for sending his mother away. Egill said, 'No one said anything. She was suddenly gone.' The family did not assist Jónína and her son to stay in touch. They did not see each other until five years later when Egill moved with his grandmother to a town near to the institution where his mother was placed. Since then he has visited her most weekends. Jónína is very proud of her son, his wife and four children. She follows the events in their lives and participates in some of them. Egill is very fond of his mother, although he has on occasions had mixed feelings about her. He feels close to her and says he has never felt ashamed of having her as a mother.

Jónína lived in the institution for 40 years. She was a hard worker and was among a group of inmates who carried out a lot of the work: cleaning, running errands, setting the table, washing dishes and taking care of the more disabled people. For much of her time in the institution, Jónína lived on a ward with women and children. She often helped take care of the children who lived on her ward. She would feed them, dress them, put them to bed, change them and help them go to the bathroom. Jónína never received any payment for her work in the institution. Jónína met her husband in the institution. A few years ago, they moved out of the institution and got married.

Thorbjörg

Thorbjörg is in her forties and has two children. She grew up with her mother and stepfather and a large group of siblings. When she was 10 years old she was diagnosed as being behind her peers in development and sent to a special school. Shortly after she started having epileptic seizures. After graduating from the special school, at the age of 16, she got a job in a factory and has worked there ever since.

Thorbjörg had her first child at the age of 22. At the time she was living with her parents and continued to live there after her son was born. The child's father had no contact with either her or the child. Four years later Thorbjörg fell in love with a man, established a home with him and had another child. Her partner was a heavy drinker and frequently away from home for long periods of time. Their relationship was difficult and Thorbjörg was alone with her two boys much of the time.

When Thorbjörg had seizures she had to rely on her elder son, Johann, to help her because she could get no other assistance. Her mother and her siblings did not help her and community support was not available. When her older boy was 8 years old the staff at his after-school program reported the family to Child Protective Services. This resulted in both her boys being taken away from her and sent to foster homes. She was never told why she was reported or why her sons were removed. Thorbjörg was devastated with grief. She felt she could not continue to live in the same neighbourhood. She broke up with her partner and moved away from the memories and her sons' friends. Shortly after, at her family's initiative, she moved into a group home for people with intellectual disabilities where she lived for a few years.

Thorbjörg's older son, Johann, was very close to his mother and the separation was very difficult for him. To make things even worse, Johann bounced between foster homes in different parts of the country and group homes for children in the city until he finally was placed in a permanent home far away from his mother. All this has had negative effects on Johann and, as a teenager, he has had difficulties with drug abuse and related problems. Thorbjörg believes he would have been better off living with her. Her younger son's placement was more successful. He has been in the same foster home in the town where his mother lives and is a well-adjusted teenager.

Thorbjörg has tried to keep in touch with her sons over the years. It was difficult to stay in touch with Johann as he moved from one place to another and usually lived far away from her. They mostly kept contact through letters which she treasures. She tried to go to visit him and asked the social worker who oversaw his case to take her along when he went to visit Johann. The social worker promised to do so but always broke his promises. It was easier to stay in touch with the younger boy.

For the past year, Thorbjörg has lived independently in a small apartment. She has a good relationship with both her sons and sees them frequently now that they are both old enough to come and visit her on their own.

Halldóra

Halldóra is one of the younger mothers. She and her husband, Kristján, are in their early thirties and their son, Gunnar, is 4 years old. Halldóra is a full-time home maker. Kristján works in a factory. Before they had Gunnar, they lived in a flat owned by the Disability Services which also provided them with in-home support twice a month. When Halldóra became a mother her parents bought a house with two apartments in order to better assist Halldóra and Kristján who live in a small apartment on the first floor with a separate entrance.

Halldóra was born and raised in a small town. At the age of 7, following epileptic fits, she was diagnosed as having brain tumour and had to spend long periods in hospitals away from her family. She remembers little from her childhood. As a child she was lonely, had few friends and little contact with other children. Her mother had to fight hard to get special education supports for her daughter. After leaving school Halldóra got a job in a fish factory which was interrupted on a number of occasions by periods of hospitalization. At the age of 20 she finished vocational training and got a job in a food-processing factory. She worked there until she was seven months pregnant. Since then she has been a housewife.

Halldóra and her husband had often talked about having a child but 'it was not on the agenda to have children so soon,' said Halldóra. They wanted to wait and see how well they could take care of themselves before they had a child. They also thought Halldóra's illness might prevent her from having children. That's why 'we were sometimes saying that we might need to adopt a child,' said Halldóra. She was on the pill when she became pregnant. Her doctor hadn't realized that her other medication affected the pill. Halldóra was three and half months along when she realized she was pregnant. At the outset, Halldóra and Kristján had mixed feelings about the pregnancy. They were looking forward to having a child but worried whether Halldóra could carry the child and how her medication might affect the fetus. Halldóra discussed these worries with her family doctor. He convinced her that everything would be all right.

When Halldóra told her mother about the pregnancy she advised her to have an abortion. Her mother was concerned about possible negative effects of the pregnancy on Halldóra's health and worried that Halldóra and Kristján would not be able to take care of the child. Halldóra and Kristján decided not to have an abortion and prepared themselves for their new role by going to parenting classes. As it turned out, Halldóra's health was good throughout her pregnancy and has remained so since the child was born.

When it became clear that Halldóra was going to have the child, her mother and the rest of the family decided to give Halldóra and Kristján all the assistance they could. Halldóra's mother contacted their support worker from the Disability Services, informed them that Halldóra was expecting a baby and asked for all the assistance that was rightfully theirs.

The worker, who had not supported parents with intellectual disabilities before, contacted the Community Nursing Service and local Social Services. Together those agencies, in co-operation with Halldóra's mother, created a network of support and did everything in their power to enable Halldóra, Kristján and the new baby to succeed as a family.

Halldóra and Kristján have been content with the support they receive. They are aware of their limitations and want to do everything to secure their baby's well-being. Despite the good services and positive attitudes of the professionals they have encountered, Halldóra is afraid of the Social Services. Child Protection is a part of the Social Services and 'I have recently read articles about women who lost custody of their children,' Halldóra says.

Halldóra has liked most of the support workers and some of them became like friends to her. In particular, she liked the fact that her aunt was one of the support workers. It made Halldóra feel more secure to have someone who was close to her, understood her and whom she could trust. The support was most intensive at the beginning. For example, the community nurse came five days a week for the first few weeks. She advised Halldóra on nutrition and how to care for the baby. She also checked whether the boy was meeting the developmental stages. Both the parents and the child were thriving. The support workers, who met regularly, agreed that the support could be gradually reduced.

Halldóra is pleased with her living arrangements. It allows her to live independently and still be close to her parents. The closeness, however, has both positive and negative sides. The positive and most important thing is the security of being close to her mother. Halldóra says her mother 'ensures the child will not be taken away from me'. The negative part, according to Halldóra, is that she feels her mother interferes a bit too much in the upbringing of the child, financial matters, and things like that.

Halldóra wants to have another child. But not yet. She thinks it might be hard for her to care for two small children and that would increase the danger of the children being removed from her care. Although Halldóra has had extensive, well-co-ordinated and very successful supports from many services, she still has a deep-seated fear of professionals. She is afraid they will just look at her disability and take her son away from her.

Birna

Birna is another of the young mothers. She is 30 years old and has three children of pre-school age. She grew up with her parents and three brothers and sisters in Reykjavik. At the age of 7 Birna was diagnosed as having intellectual disability and was moved to a special school where she completed her ten years compulsory schooling. After leaving school Birna had a series of jobs in various factories. In her early twenties she met the father of two of her children and they lived together for five years in a flat they purchased with the assistance of a social housing scheme. Birna stayed at home and enjoyed the daily routine of family life: cooking, shopping and paying the bills. Her major concern was her partner's drinking and the abuse that frequently followed. Eventually, with the assistance of her parents, Birna left him and returned to the family home. She was expecting her first child at the time. Two years later, as the result of a casual relationship, Birna had a second child. Later Birna re-established the relationship with the father of her first child and became pregnant. The relationship did not last, mostly because of Birna's fear of abuse.

Birna continues to live at her parents' home with her children. Her existence revolves around her children and they are the most precious things in her life. Birna has received no support from the children's fathers. Her support comes from her family, especially her mother. Birna and her mother are both full-time homemakers and share housework and child care. They also take turns bringing and fetching the children to the pre-school. Birna's mother also accompanies her to meetings with professionals.

Birna is very close to her mother and is comfortable living in her parents' home. She feels that she and her children are very welcome there. Although she feels content she would like to be able to live more independently, but she doesn't dare. She is frightened that if she moves away from her parents' home she will lose custody of her children. Living with her parents gives her security.

Birna and her mother refuse to accept support from the service system. The reason for this is their negative experiences with professionals in the past. One of these incidents was related to the State Diagnostic Centre which labelled one of her children 'slightly behind in her development'. The Centre assigned a social worker to Birna's case to assist her in filling out some forms. Birna liked the social worker and trusted her completely. It was therefore a big shock to Birna when she received a letter from the Child Protection Services signed by a child protection officer who turned out to be Birna's social worker. Birna and her family felt badly betrayed by the social worker. This incident led to other negative interactions with the service system which, in turn, increased their fear of the system.

Birna also feels that the staff at her older daughter's pre-school had prejudice against her. Birna says she was on good terms with them until she told them she had gone to a special school as a child. After that the staff treated her differently from other parents and both Birna and her mother felt humiliated and talked down to. As a result, they removed the child from the pre-school. The only professionals Birna has a good and trusting relationship with are her middle child's pre-school teachers.

The negative interactions between Birna and her family on the one hand and the service system on the other have led to a deep distrust of professionals. Birna lives in constant fear that she might lose her children. She feels threatened by a system that does not trust her or her mother to raise the children. As a result of her fears Birna doesn't dare live independently; nor does she accept the benefits and services that are rightly hers. She is defensive and feels she has little control of her own life. She seldom leaves the house, scared that 'something might happen at home in the meantime'. Prior to Birna's conflict with the system she occasionally went out on weekends. She no longer goes out as she does not want to give the professionals any reasons to remove her children. The fear of the system has brought Birna and her extended family close together. They rely on each other and are determined not to receive any support or have anything to do with the system.

Conclusion

This chapter has considered the possibilities of motherhood, family and community life for women with intellectual disabilities. Based on the lives of ten Icelandic mothers with intellectual disabilities, we have examined how these possibilities have changed for the better over the past 50 years. It is, however, interesting to note that the young women with intellectual disabilities who are having children today still consider it essential to have the support and protection of their extended families. Most of them believe that if their extended families would not protect and assist them, it would be very difficult, if not impossible, for them to keep their children and lead a family life in the community. Thus, the importance of the extended family in the lives of mothers with intellectual disabilities continues to be crucial.

Research tells us that women with intellectual disabilities can, with appropriate supports, be successful as mothers (Andron and Tymchuk 1987; Booth and Booth 1994; Llewellyn 1994; Traustadóttir and Sigurjónsdóttir 1998; Tymchuk and Feldman 1991). Although such support services are more readily available now and attitudes have changed for the better, there still remains much work in developing both policy and services for families headed by parents with intellectual disabilities.

First, there is a need for a clear policy outlining the types and levels of support that should be available for parents with intellectual disabilities and their children.

Second, it is important to better understand the needs of mothers with intellectual disabilities and their families, and what kinds of programs are most successful in meeting these needs. More studies are needed in this area.

Third, we need better training for professionals and support workers. Today, only a small number of them have expertise or experience in working with families headed by parents with intellectual disabilities. As a result, there is a great variation in the type and quality of support offered. Services are too often fragmented and unreliable, vary highly between agencies and are dependent on the attitudes and/or expertise of individual professionals. This creates a great deal of insecurity in the lives of the mothers and their children.

Finally, it is essential that services approach each family with respect, ensuring fair and just treatment for the family as a whole.

...in the World

Kelley Johnson, Australia
and Rannveig Traustadóttir, Iceland

Many women with intellectual disabilities are now out in the world, finding places in relationships, with their families, at work and doing things in their communities. The stories in this book show that it is not always easy for women to do this. The stories also show that women with intellectual disabilities are doing very interesting and exciting things in the world. This concluding chapter tells about some of the things we have learned from working with women to write this book.

Sometimes having intellectual disabilities makes it harder for women to do what they want in their lives. But the women who have written stories for this book all say that discrimination, lack of support and attitudes of other people are very, very important problems for them.

The stories in this book show that women with intellectual disabilities are doing many things in their lives. They work, care for others, lead organizations and fight for rights. They are mothers, lovers and friends. But we do not read much about their lives. We believe it is time that the work of this group of women was made much more known and that is why this book has been written.

Women with intellectual disabilities from eight different countries have written chapters for this book. Some of their concerns are similar, others are different. Some women are concerned about having any kind of paid work, others are concerned with having well-paid and interesting work. Some of them are mothers, while for some it is just a dream to have a child. In part these things are linked to where women live. But all the women in the book share some common concerns: they want to work, have relationships and be valued in their communities.

Being a woman is important. Sometimes because a woman has a disability her needs and interests as a woman are not seen as important by those around her. The stories in this book show over and over again that it is very important to think about women's needs and rights when services are being planned and when decisions are being made about their lives.

This book has involved 25 women across the world working together to think about it, write chapters and to read it. We hope that the ideas in the book will bring more women together across the world to work for justice and fairness for ourselves now and in the future.

Now, more than ever before, women with intellectual disabilities are 'in the world'. Although some women remain 'locked out' of their communities, living their lives in institutions, many are now taking up the varied community spaces available to other women. This, however, does not happen without a struggle. For many women are still 'locked in' to societal expectations about disabilities, and discriminatory policies and services, which stop them from showing what they can do. And sometimes the social structures and services are simply not present to allow women to live their lives as fully as they would like. Such difficulties exacerbate the problems of women with intellectual disabilities in relation to living with their disability.

When we discussed the writing of this conclusion, it seemed at first superfluous. The women who had contributed chapters had spoken and written articulately and passionately about their positions and about their lives. The structural and social limits placed on them were apparent in their personal stories. What more could we add as editors? In writing a conclusion, were we appropriating the stories which had been written, adding an 'academically legitimate' commentary to them? After much discussion we decided to write a short conclusion that would serve to underline and emphasize some of the learning which we have gained from the work on this book.

Some of this will seem self-evident. But for us, as editors, workers and women, the learning is not an intellectual knowledge about women or disability. It is something that we know through our relationships with the women who have written chapters and it is something which has affected deeply the way we see the world and ourselves. We hope that readers share our experience and that the book, and this conclusion, will mark the beginning of a much more open discussion about women with intellectual disabilities and their place in the world.

Disability and societal discrimination

Many of the women who contributed chapters to this book had been attributed with a label of intellectual disability. For each of them this label meant different things. For Janice and Tamara in part it meant physical difficulties with speech and movement, for Amanda it was linked with poor eyesight and hearing. Most of the women spoke of their attributed disability in functional terms. It was something that prevented them from doing things they wanted to do. None of the women provided textbook style definitions of intellectual disabilities. And it seemed that for some it remained a mystified and undiscussed issue. But if there was diversity in the way they perceived the label and their disability, there was unanimity in the views they expressed about its consequences. All of the women saw the label of intellectual disabilities as leading to a denial of opportunities. Many of these were perceived in terms of social restrictions and discrimination. Some were seen in terms of the inadequacy or absence of services and policies designed to assist women to live in fulfilling ways. Thus, Amanda and Janka were forced to leave their families to go to special schools and many of the women talk of the difficulties in obtaining paid work. Some of the older women in Chapter 5 find themselves living in inappropriate places because of a service failure to consider their needs. And Janice and the Icelandic mothers speak movingly of the issues and difficulties of parenting in a society which devalues women with disabilities and does not acknowledge the possibilities of parenting for them, or does so grudgingly.

We believe that this book carries within each chapter the tension in which individual women are held: between their needs, desires and abilities on the one hand, and the failure of the society to acknowledge these and the difficulties which they experience as a result of a disability on the other. We have come to the end of this book with renewed commitment to the importance of changing social structures and communities so that they are more inclusive of women with intellectual disabilities.

It is true that some women in this book have difficulties living their lives in the ways they would most like. These difficulties are partly due to the nature of their disabilities. However, it is overwhelmingly true that many of the obstacles they confront are not caused directly by their disability but by the social and societal contexts in which they live.

Diversity of places in the world

When we began this book we believed firmly that women with intellectual disabilities held very diverse places in their communities and that this was not often acknowledged. Rather they were seen as in need of care and support and were often perceived by others as a rather homogeneous group. We began with a view that this book should in part celebrate the lives of women who had found places in the world. We have been inspired by the richness and diversity of the ways in which women contributors have seen their lives and have written about them. In this book are women who have led national and statewide self-advocacy groups; who have struggled within the legal and service systems to assert their rights; who have undertaken full-time paid work in a variety of areas from education to process work to the arts. In this book are carers of other people, mothers, lovers, wives and friends. All of the women in this book hold many of these positions simultaneously. They are diverse and strongly individualistic. They speak powerfully of their lives. Why have so few people heard them? Said (1994, quoted in Wood 1994, p.46) perhaps provides a partial answer:

> It's not that the powerless don't have stories, and it's not only that they don't get to tell the stories they do have. It's that they're scarcely perceived as capable of having stories, their stories are not so much refused as ruled out, unimaginable to us as pieces of recognised history. With no acceptable narrative to rely on, with no sustained permission to narrate, you feel crowded out and silenced.

These women are not powerless in themselves, quite the reverse. But they are made so by the society around them. In this their stories reflect those of other women. After all it is only recently that the achievements and the power of women generally have begun to be explored and acknowledged. The struggle continues.

Cultural differences and common concerns

From the outset this book sought contributions from women across different cultures and countries. It was an ambitious (and looking back an idealistic) enterprise. Women from many continents, countries and cultures have not had their stories included. In part this says something about our networks and our capacities, even in a globalized world, to reach out. It may also say something about the difficulties of gaining access to women with intellectual disabilities in some parts of the world. But two issues have become increasingly apparent to us during the development of this book.

First, cultural differences are important. Cultural attitudes to intellectual disability do shape the life processes of women and can decide whether things like marriage or sexual relationships are matters of fact as, for example, in Janice's life, or dreams and fantasies as in Janka's. Differences in cultures may lead to difficulties for women who belong to minority groups within a dominant culture as for Debra and Teresa. In countries where there are less economic resources and fewer services, life for women with intellectual disabilities may be particularly difficult. Cultural diversity may lead to differences not only in the way women with intellectual disabilities are perceived by those around them, but also in how they see themselves and their places in the community.

Second, despite cultural diversity there are also common concerns and issues which affect the lives of these women. The love of families and their preparedness to include women with intellectual disabilities are highlighted in stories which come from diverse cultures: for example, in Rosemary West's account of the discovery of her sister and in Tamara's loving portrayal of her family members. The need of women to find self-worth and fulfilment in work and in relationships is clear from all countries. The women working in diverse locations in Norway, Tamara's longing for paid work and the constant frustration which women contributors express about the difficulties of living good lives without reasonable incomes emphasize the importance of work. For some of these women poverty is a greater barrier than their disabilities. The pain of motherhood denied, of the struggle to sustain friendships and non-abusive relationships are also heard from women in different countries and with vastly different lives.

Importance of gender

The failure to take account of gender issues in relation to women with intellectual disabilities and the lack of any documentation of their lives were strong motivations in developing this book. The excitement with which the book proposal was greeted by potential contributors and the enthusiasm with which many women developed their chapters over long periods of time are a testament to the need that they felt.

For us, the importance of gender has been reinforced by the chapters of this book. Gender is not a simple issue. It does not sit like a separate part of someone's life; a neat compartment which can be discussed out of the wider context in which one lives. Rather we have found gender issues permeating the styles used in the chapters and in their content. For some of the women in this book gender has been fundamentally important in their lives. For Verna the time at which she was born and her status as an illegitimate child contributed strongly to her placement in an institution where she remained for most of her life. These were gender issues. For other women gender and their perceived skills in taking on a caring role led them out of institutions into lives in the community. The kinds of friendships which women discuss in this book are gender related. As Rannveig Traustadóttir shows, more women than men become friends with women with intellectual disabilities. The frightening issues of sexual abuse documented in Michelle McCarthy's chapter are common not only to this group of women but to all women. Dilemmas of choice and restriction of lifestyle which confront the older women in Chris Bigby's chapter reflect issues that confront older women who are not labelled as having intellectual disabilities.

Many of the women in this book are political activists and they come to their work from a particular women's perspective. They are concerned not only with their own lives, but also with other women who may not be able to speak up for themselves. Behind the stories printed in this book are countless others about the mutual support, caring and solidarity within the group of women with intellectual disabilities. The kind of mutual support once well known as 'sisterhood'.

The chapters in this book call for a refocusing by services, families, friends and people with intellectual disabilities themselves on gender issues.

Collaboration between women with intellectual disabilities and other women

This book has been a work of collaboration, co-operation and sometimes conflict between women across the world. As we note in the introduction, women with intellectual disabilities have not been heard clearly in the past, either by other women or by those in the disability field, partly because of the difficulties many of them have in using written words but also because they have not been perceived as having stories to tell. This book demonstrates vividly that women with intellectual disabilities do have stories to tell and that collaborative work with other women is an exciting way to recount them.

Each of the chapters in the book has involved collaboration between women. Sometimes a woman with an intellectual disability has written the chapter, sometimes women have reported on their life experiences or on particular areas in their lives and these have been written up with the assistance of a non-disabled woman. Sometimes the women with intellectual disabilities have been in long-term contact with the women researchers. Some of the chapters have confirmed friendships or led to them. Others have brought women across the world into contact with each other for the first time. Women have learned from each other in the process of writing. Some have become advocates, others have provided support and friendship during personal crises. Sometimes the advocacy and the support have been reciprocal. The learning has always been so. We believe that the process of the book has been as important as the end product. It provides evidence that women from very different countries and cultures, and of diverse abilities, can work together to tell stories, to learn from each other and to take action together. In this there is a hope that as the stories of women with intellectual disabilities are included in the stories of other women, the possibilities for joint action for social change and social justice will increase.

In conclusion we hope and intend that this book will be a means to increase the power of women with intellectual disabilities to find places in the world; that it will assist in educating other women and community members about the strengths and abilities of this group of women. We hope that it will be a focus for debates and discussions.

The Contributors

Christine Bigby is a lecturer in the Department of Social Work and Social Policy at La Trobe University, Australia. Her primary research and practice interest for the last ten years has been older carers and ageing people with disabilities. She has published widely in key disability journals both in Australia and overseas and is the author of *When Parents Relinquish Care: Sources of Support for Older Adults with Intellectual Disability* (Melbourne: Maclennan and Petty, 2000).

Maria Cerna lives in Prague in the Czech Republic and teaches at Charles University. She has worked with people with intellectual disabilities as a teacher, a researcher and as a member of organizations concerned with disability issues. She has written widely on issues affecting the lives of people with intellectual disabilities both within the Czech Republic and internationally. She has a special interest in education.

Maude Davey is an actor, writer and director working in theatre, film and television. With her music theatre company, Crying in Public Places, she has performed all around Australia, in South East Asia, Britain and Europe. Maude directed *Gina's Story* for Back to Back Theatre Company, as well as *Mr September*, a musical. She is currently a member of the Board of Management.

Pat Felt spent 30 years in institutions. She has lived in the L'Arche community in Syracuse, New York, since 1975. She is a member of Self-Advocates of Central New York and a past member of the New York State Self-Advocacy Steering Committee. She has done both writing and speaking about her own life as well as life in the L'Arche community.

Ellen S. Fisher is a Disabilities Consultant who lives outside of Philadelphia, Pennsylvania. She works in the areas of inclusion and self-determination. She currently serves as a director at Tyler Associates, an agency that serves people through self-determination, and is also conducting research as part of the national initiative on self-determination for people with disabilities.

Janka Hanková lives in Žilina, Slovakia. From 6 years of age she spent 12 years in a special school living away from home. Now she is home again and wants to live like other people, have friends, a name on her door, a real job and know how to do things for herself.

Jana Hanková lives in Žilina, Slovakia, with her daughter, Janka, in a two-roomed flat. She is a teacher. Through her teaching she has found many friends and they have helped her to take care of her daughter. She would like her daughter to be more independent and to have her own life.

Sonja Holubková lives in Žilina, Slovakia. She is the mother of three children and is a psychologist working with people with intellectual disabilities. She believes that inclusion is the only way for all people to live together. Everyone is so unique it is a pity if we cannot share space, activities and time together. She works especially with young people to create festivals and creative workshops. She is a member of the Land of Harmony Foundation.

Kelley Johnson lives in Melbourne, Australia, where she teaches and does research at The Australian Research Center in Sex, Health and Society, La Trobe University. She has worked with women with intellectual disabilities for about 15 years as an advocate and a researcher. She is the author of *Deinstitutionalising Women: An Ethnographic Study of Institutional Closure* (Melbourne: Cambridge University Press, 1998) about the closure of a large institution for people with intellectual disabilities and what happened to some of the women who lived there.

Tamara Kainova lives with her parents and sister in Prague. She has been handicapped from early childhood. Her parents were employed in a nuclear factory and it created her handicaps. Her father is Czech and her mother is Russian. She understands both Czech and Russian. She worked in a sheltered workshop but now it is closed. She likes music, books and songs. Her biggest happiness is that she can write her stories.

Kristjana Kristiansen is a teacher and researcher living in Trondheim, Norway. Her major research interests are listening to and writing down the voices, experiences and situations of marginalized groups in society. She is currently Associate Professor at the University in Trondheim, where she teaches research methodology and gender issues in health and social work at the postgraduate level.

Michelle McCarthy is a feminist and a lecturer in learning disability at the Tizard Centre, University of Kent, England. She has worked with women with learning disabilities on sexuality and sexual abuse issues for the past ten years. She has published widely in this field and most recently has written a book called *Sexuality and Women with Learning Disabilities* (London: Jessica Kingsley, 1999) which summarizes her research and practice experience.

Amanda Millear lives in Melbourne, Australia. She works as a peer educator with people with intellectual disabilities, teaching them about housing rights and issues. She has a strong interest in the laws and has studied about them at a college for adult education. She has used the laws to stop people (including herself) being discriminated against. She has been a strong self-advocate and an advocate for people with intellectual disabilities for more than 19 years. Amanda has been an active member of management committees for advocacy organizations over the years.

Missy Morton lives in Aotearoa/New Zealand. Her passions include feminist and disability rights and quality inclusive education for all children. She is finishing off a long-distance doctoral dissertation, parenting two gorgeous kids and doing some freelance, teaching, research and writing.

Susan O'Connor is an Assistant Professor of Education at Augsburg College in Minneapolis, Minnesota. She is interested in issues of inclusion and multi-culturalism as they relate to schools and community. She has conducted research on these issues as well as issues related to families. She is currently involved in a national initiative on self-determination for people with disabilities, looking specifically at the issues of multiculturalism as it relates to self determination.

Debra Robinson is a self-advocate for people with disabilities who lives in Philadelphia, Pennsylvania. She is a leader in the self-advocacy movement at the local, state and national levels in the USA. She is currently serving a two-year presidential appointment on the National Council on Disability and has received many awards for her service. She has appeared in the US media on numerous occasions. She works as a resource to people in Philadelphia and throughout the USA.

Bonnie Shoultz is the Associate Director of the Center on Human Policy at Syracuse University, Syracuse, New York. She is involved in research, technical assistance, training and information dissemination at the Center. Before she moved to Syracuse in 1986, she worked in the disability field in Nebraska for 11 years, both as a professional and as a volunteer. She has two adult children, one of whom has significant disabilities. Nancy Ward and Bonnie met in Nebraska in 1979 and became friends and supporters of each other. They have written several chapters together, and they still see each other four or more times a year, even though both have moved away from Nebraska.

Hanna Björg Sigurjónsdóttir lives in Reykjavík, Iceland. She is a Research Fellow at the University of Iceland. She has worked as an advocate and a researcher with people with disabilities for many years. Most recently her work has focused on mothers with intellectual disabilities. Together with Rannveig Traustadóttir she has published a book in Icelandic titled *Contested Families: Parents with Intellectual Disabilities and their Children* (Reykjavík: University of Iceland, Social Science Research Institute, 1998).

Janice Slattery lives in Melbourne, Australia. She works as a peer educator with women with disabilities, teaching them about women's health. She also does some other part-time work. She has worked in the past as a co-ordinator for a self-advocacy organization. She has been an active self-advocate and an advocate for people with intellectual disabilities for more than 15 years. Janice is a board member on a number of different advocacy organizations.

Sonia Teuben is 25 years old and has been working as a professional actor for the last seven years. She has worked with a number of Melbourne-based companies. In 1993 she joined Back to Back, a theatre company with a permanent ensemble of intellectually disabled actors, based in Geelong, Australia. In 1997 she was elected to the company's Board of Management, and in 1998 she was made Associate Director in recognition of her contribution to the company. In 1997 Sonia was a semi-finalist in the Australian Young Achievers Award. *Gina's Story* is a piece of theatre that she wrote and performed which tells the story of Sonia's life before she left home.

Rannveig Traustadóttir lives in Iceland. She is Associate Professor at the University of Iceland where she teaches about research methods, gender, disability and multiculturalism, and does research with women with disabilities and other minority women. She has worked with women with intellectual disabilities for more than two decades as an advocate, a direct care worker and researcher. Her most recent book (together with Hanna Björg Sigurjónsdóttir) is *Contested Families: Parents with Intellectual Disabilities and their Children* (Reykjavík: University of Iceland, Social Science Research Institute, 1998).

Pam Walker is a Research Associate at the Center on Human Policy, Syracuse University, Syracuse, New York. She has worked at the Center since 1985. Her research interests include community living, community building and recreation and leisure. She is a co-editor of *Housing, Support and Community: Choices and Strategies for Adults with Disabilities* (Baltimore: Paul H. Brookes, 1993).

Jan Walmlsey lives in Milton Keynes, England, and works at the Open University. She enjoys cycling, long-distance walking, reading, cinema and writing poetry. What she enjoys most about her work is the chance it has given her to open university courses to people with intellectual disabilities.

Nancy Ward was the founding chairperson of Self Advocates Becoming Empowered (SABE), the national self-advocacy organization in the USA, serving from 1992 to 1996. Nancy worked for People First of Nebraska for nine years. In 1997 she moved to Oklahoma to work for Oklahoma People First. Nancy has spoken at many national and international conferences and meetings about how people with disabilities want to be treated and can be contributing members in their communities. She has also written many book chapters and newsletter articles about self-advocacy and her involvement in it. She has influenced many professionals, parents and people with disabilities to see people's capabilities rather than their disabilities.

Rosemary West is a journalist who lives in Melbourne, Australia, and has spent 15 years working at the *Age Newspaper*. She has had an ongoing commitment to social and welfare issues throughout her career and is now working as a freelance journalist. She is an advocate for her sister Verna who has an intellectual disability and lives in a community residential unit. Rosemary is writing a book about her experience of finding her sister.

References

Aldridge, J. and Becker, S. (1993) *Children Who Care: Inside the World of Young Carers.* Loughborough: University of Loughborough.

Amado, N.A. (ed) (1993) *Friendships and Community Connections Between People With and Without Disabilities.* Baltimore: Paul H. Brookes.

Amado, N.A., Conklin, F. and Wells, J. (1990) *Friends: A Manual for Connecting Persons with Disabilities and Community Members.* St. Paul: Human Service Research and Development Center.

Andersen, M.L. (1993) *Thinking About Women: Sociological Perspectives on Sex and Gender.* New York: Macmillan.

Anderson, D. (1989) 'Health care needs and residential settings: A national survey and policy perspectives.' *Australian and New Zealand Journal of Developmental Disabilities 15,* 289–302.

Andron, L. (1983) 'Sexuality counselling with developmentally disabled couples.' In M. Craft and A. Craft (eds) *Sex Education and Counselling for Mentally Handicapped People.* Tunbridge Wells: Costello.

Andron, L. and Tymchuk, A.J. (1987) 'Parents who are mentally retarded.' In A. Craft (ed) *Mental Handicap and Sexuality: Issues and Perspectives.* Tunbridge Wells: Costello.

Andron, L. and Ventura, J. (1987) 'Sexual dysfunction in couples with learning handicaps.' *Sexuality and Disability 8,* 1, 25–35.

Asch, A. and Fine, M. (1988) 'Introduction: Beyond pedestals.' In M. Fine and A. Asch (eds) *Women with Disabilities: Essays in Psychology, Culture, and Politics.* Philadelphia: Temple University Press.

Asch, A. and Fine, M. (1992) 'Beyond pedestals: Revisiting the lives of women with disabilities.' In M. Fine (ed) *Disruptive Voices: The Possibilities of Feminist Research.* Ann Arbor: University of Michigan Press.

Ashman, A., Suttie, J. and Bramley, J. (1993) *Older Australians with an Intellectual Disability: A Report to the Department of Health, Housing and Community Services, Research and Development Grants Committee.* Fred and Eleanor Schonnell Special Education Research Centre. Queensland: University of Queensland.

Atkinson, D. and Walmsley, J. (1996) 'Using autobiographical approaches with people with learning difficulties.' *Disability and Society 14,* 2, 203–216.

Atkinson, D. and Williams, F. (eds) (1990) *Know Me As I Am: An Anthology of Prose, Poetry and Art by People with Learning Difficulties.* Sevenoaks: Hodder and Stoughton.

Baladerian, N.J. (1985) 'Prevention of sexual exploitation of developmentally disabled adults.' Paper presented at the Convention of the California Association of Post-Secondary Educators of the Disabled, Sacramento CA.

Barnes, C. and Mercer, G. (eds) (1996) *Exploring the Divide: Illness and Disability.* Leeds: Disability Press.

Bassaro, J.C. (1990) *Making Friends, Keeping Friends.* New Canaan: Mulvey Books.

Beach Center on Families and Disability (1997) *Amistad: Stories of Hispanic Children with Disabilities and their Friendships.* Lawrence: Beach Center on Families and Disability.

Bell, R.R. (1981) *Worlds of Friendships.* Beverly Hills: Sage.

Between Ourselves (1988) Video. Brighton: Twentieth Century Vixen.

Bigby, C. (1995) 'Is there a hidden group of older people with intellectual disability and from whom are they hidden? Lessons from a recent case-finding study.' *Australia and New Zealand Journal of Developmental Disabilities 20,* 15–24.

Bigby, C. (1997) 'When parents relinquish care: The informal support networks of older people with intellectual disability.' *Journal of Applied Intellectual Disability Research 10,* 4, 333–344.

Bigby, C. (2000) 'When parents relinquish care: Planning, transitions and sources of support for middle-aged and older adults with intellectual disability.' Melbourne: Maclennan and Petty.

Block, J.D. (1980) *Friendship: How To Give It, How To Get It.* New York: Collier.

Bogdan, R. (1995) 'Singing for an inclusive community.' In S.J. Taylor, R. Bogdan and Z.M. Lutfiyya (eds) *The Variety of Community Experience: Qualitative Studies of Family and Community Life.* Baltimore: Paul H. Brookes.

Bogdan, R. and Taylor, S.J. (1984) *Inside Out: The Social Construction of Mental Retardation.* Toronto: Toronto University Press.

Booth, T. and Booth, W. (1994) *Parenting Under Pressure: Mothers and Fathers with Learning Difficulties.* Buckingham: Open University Press.

Booth, T. and Booth, W. (1996) 'Supported parenting for people with learning difficulties: Lessons from Wisconsin.' *Representing Children 9,* 2, 99–107.

Booth, T. and Booth, W. (1997) *Exceptional Childhoods, Unexceptional Children: Growing Up with Parents who have Learning Difficulties.* London: Family Policy Studies Centre.

Booth, T. and Booth, W. (1998) *Growing Up with Parents who have Learning Difficulties.* London: Routledge.

Boylan, E. (ed) (1991) *Women and Disability.* London: Zed Books.

Bowe, F. (1984) *Disabled Women in America: A Statistical Report Drawn from Sensus Data.* Washington DC: President's Committee of the Employment of the Handicapped.

Brantlinger, E. (1995) *Sterilization of People with Mental Disabilities: Issues, Perspectives, and Cases.* Westport: Auburn House.

Breakwell, G. (1986) *Coping with Threatened Identities.* London: Methuen.

Brown, H. (1994) 'Lost in the system: Acknowledging the sexual abuse of adults with learning disabilities.' *Care In Place 1,* 2, 145–157.

Brown, H. (1996) 'Ordinary women: Issues for women with learning disabilities.' *British Journal of Learning Disabilities 24*, 47–51.

Brown, H. and Turk, V. (1992) 'Defining sexual abuse as it affects adults with learning disabilities.' *Mental Handicap 20*, June, 44–55.

Brown, H., Stein, J. and Turk, V. (1995) 'The sexual abuse of adults with learning disabilities: Report of a second two-year incidence survey.' *Mental Handicap Research 8*, 1, 3–24.

Browne, S. E., Connors, D. and Stern, N. (eds) (1985) *With the Power of Each Breath: A Disabled Women's Anthology.* Pittsburgh: Cleis Press.

Buchanan, A. and Wilkins, R. (1991) 'Sexual abuse of the mentally handicapped: Difficulties in establishing prevalence.' *Psychiatric Bulletin 15*, 601–605.

Bulmer, M. (1987) *The Social Basis of Community Care.* London: Allan and Unwin.

Burke, P. and Signo, K. (1996) *Support for Families.* Aldershot: Avebury.

Bytheway, B. and Johnson, J. (1997) 'The social construction of "carers".' In A. Symonds and A. Kelly (eds) *The Social Construction of Care in the Community.* London: Macmillan.

Card, H. (1983) 'What will happen when we've gone?' *Community Care 28*, 20–21.

Chamberlain, A., Rauh, J., Passer, A., McGrath, M. and Burket, R. (1984) 'Issues in fertility control for mentally retarded female adolescents. Sexual activity, sexual abuse and contraception.' *Pediatrics 73*, 4, 445–450.

Chappell, A.L. (1998) 'Still out in the cold: People with learning difficulties and the social model of disability.' In T. Shakespeare (ed) *The Disability Reader: Social Science Perspectives.* London: Cassell.

Craft, M. and Craft, A. (1979) *Handicapped Married Couples.* London: Routledge and Kegan Paul.

Daniels, A.K. (1988) *Invisible Careers.* Chicago: University of Chicago Press.

Danish Ministry of Social Affairs (1996) *Parenting with Intellectual Disability.* Copenhagen: Danish Ministry of Social Affairs.

Davies, A. (1978) 'Rape, racism and the capitalist setting.' *Black Scholar 9*, 7, 24–30.

Deegan, M.J. and Brooks, N.A. (eds) (1985) *Women and Disability: The Double Handicap.* New Brunswick: Transaction Books.

Downs, C. and Craft, A. (1996) 'Sexuality and profound and multiple impairment.' *Tizard Learning Disability Review 1*, 4, 17–22.

Driedger, D., Feika, I. and Batres, E.G. (eds) (1996) *Across Borders: Women with Disabilities Working Together.* Charlottetown: Gynergy Books.

Dunne, T. and Power, A. (1990) 'Sexual abuse and mental handicap: Preliminary findings from a community based study.' *Mental Handicap Research 3*, 111–125.

Eayrs, C.B., Ellis, N. and Jones, R.S.P. (1993) 'Which label? An investigation into the effects of terminology on public perceptions of and attitudes towards people with learning difficulties.' *Disability, Handicap and Society 8*, 2, 111–127.

Edgerton, R. (1989) 'Ageing in the community: A matter of choice.' In A. Brechin and J. Walmsley (eds) *Making Connections*. Sevenoaks: Hodder and Stoughton.

Edgerton, R. (1994) 'Quality of life issues: Some people know how to be old.' In M. Seltzer, M. Krauss, and M. Janicki (eds) *Lifecourse Perspectives on Adulthood and Aging*. Washington DC: American Association on Mental Retardation.

Edgerton, R. (1999) 'Foreword.' *Journal of Intellectual and Developmental Disability 24*, 1, 1–2.

Elkins, T., Gatford, L., Wilks, C., Muram, D. and Golden, G. (1986) 'A model clinic for reproductive health concerns of the mentally handicapped.' *Obstetrics and Gynecology 68*, 2, 185–188.

Eyman, R. and Borthwick-Duffy, S. (1994) 'Trends in mortality rates and predictors of mortality.' In M. Seltzer, M. Krauss and M. Janicki (eds) *Lifecourse Perspectives on Adulthood and Old Age*. Washington DC: American Association on Mental Retardation.

Feldman, M.A. (1986) 'Research on parenting by mentally retarded parents.' *Psychiatric Clinics of North America 9*, 4, 777–796.

Feldman, M.A. (1994) 'Parenting education for parents with intellectual disabilities: A review of outcome studies.' *Research in Developmental Disabilities 15*, 4, 299–332.

Fine, M. and Asch, A. (1985) 'Disabled women: Sexism without the pedestal.' In M.J. Deegan and N.J. Brooks (eds) *Women and Disability: The Double Handicap*. New Jersey: Transaction Books.

Fine, M. and Asch, A. (eds) (1988) *Women with Disabilities: Essays in Psychology, Culture, and Politics*. Philadelphia: Temple University Press.

Fisher, B. and Galler, R. (1988) 'Friendship and fairness: How disability affects friendship between women.' In M. Fine and A. Asch (eds) *Women with Disabilities: Essays in Psychology, Culture, and Politics*. Philadelphia: Temple University Press.

Flynn, R.J. and Nitch, K.E. (eds) (1980) *Normalization, Social Integration, and Community Services*. Baltimore: University Park Press.

Forest, M. (1989) *It's About Relationships*. Toronto: Frontier College Press.

Forest, M. and Lusthaus, E. (1989) 'Promoting educational equality for all students: Circles and maps.' In S. Stainback, W. Stainback and M. Forest (eds) *Educating All Students in the Mainstream of Regular Education*. Baltimore: Paul H. Brookes.

Four Stories. A sex education video for people with intellectual disabilities. Published by Family Planning Association, New Zealand. Available from FPA Resource Unit, Level 3, Newpark Centre, 5 Short Street, Newmarket, Auckland, NZ.

Gavey, N. (1992) 'Technologies and effects of heterosexual coercion.' *Feminism and Psychology 2*, 3, 325–351.

Gibson, J., Rabkin, J. and Munson, R. (1992) 'Critical issues in serving the developmentally disabled elderly.' *Journal of Gerontological Social Work 19*, 35–49.

Gilligan, C. (1982) *In a Different Voice: Psychological Theory and Women's Development*. Cambridge MA: Harvard University Press.

Gouldner, H. and Strong, M.S. (1987) *Speaking of Friendship: Middle-class Women and their Friends.* New York: Greenwood Press.

Graham, H. (1983) 'Caring: A labour of love.' In J. Finch and D. Groves (eds) *A Labour of Love: Women, Work and Caring.* London: Routledge and Kegan Paul.

Hammersley, M. and Atkinson, P. (1994) *Ethnography: Principles in Practice.* London: Tavistock.

Hanna, W.I. and Rogovsky, E. (1991) 'Women with disabilities: Two handicaps plus.' *Disability, Handicap and Society 6,* 1, 49–63.

Hard, S. and Plumb, W. (1986) 'Sexual abuse of persons with developmental disabilities: A case study.' Unpublished manuscript.

Harry, B. (1992) *Cultural Diversity, Families, and the Special Education System: Communication and Empowerment.* New York: Teachers College Press.

Health and Community Services (1993a) *Annual Report 1992/3.* Melbourne: Health and Community Services.

Health and Community Services (1993b) 'Review of placement of eligible aged clients into aged care facilities.' Draft, unpublished paper. Melbourne: Health and Community Services.

Health and Community Services (1993c) *Disability Services Branch Priorities 1993/4.* Melbourne: Health and Community Services.

Health and Community Services (1995) *Report to the Hon Michael John MP, Minister for Community Services of the Intellectual Disability Services Taskforce.* Melbourne: Health and Community Services.

Hite, S. (1976) *The Hite Report.* London: Pandora.

Hoffman, C. and Mandeville, H. (1998) 'Welfare reform and parents with disabilities.' *Impact 11,* 1, 20–21.

Hogg, J., Moss, S. and Cooke, D. (1988) *Ageing and Mental Handicap.* London: Croom Helm.

Holland, J., Ramazanoglu, C., Scott, S., Sharpe, S., and Thomson, R. (1991a) *Pressure, Resistance, Empowerment: Young Women and the Negotiation of Safer Sex.* WRAP Paper 6. London: Tufnell Press.

Holland, J., Ramazanoglu, C. and Sharpe, S. (1991b) *Pressured Pleasure: Young Women and the Negotiation of Sexual Boundaries.* WRAP Paper 7. London: Tufnell Press.

hooks, b. (1996) 'Refusing to be a victim: Accountability and responsibility.' In b. hooks *Killing Rage: Ending Racism.* London: Penguin.

Huberman, A. and Miles, M. (1994) 'Data management and analysis methods.' In N. Denzin and Y. Lincoln (eds) *Handbook of Qualitative Methods.* Newbury Park: Sage.

Hutchison, P. (1990) *Making Friends: Developing Relationships Between People with a Disability and Other Members of the Community.* Toronto: G. Allan Roeher Institute.

Israel, P. (1985) 'Editorial.' *Resources for Feminist Research 14,* 1, 1–3.

Janicki, M., Otis, J., Puccio, P., Rettig, J. and Jacobson, J. (1985) 'Service needs among older developmentally disabled persons.' In M. Janicki and H. Wisniewski (eds) *Aging and Developmental Disabilities.* Baltimore: Paul H. Brookes.

Janko, S. (1992) 'Beyond harm: A case study of the social construction of child abuse.' In P.M. Ferguson, D.L. Ferguson, and S.J. Taylor (eds) *Interpreting Disability: A Qualitative Reader.* New York: Teachers College Press.

Johnson, K. (1998) *Deinstitutionalising Women: An Ethnographic Study of Institutional Closure.* Melbourne: Cambridge University Press.

Johnson, K. and Nadazdyova, M. (1996) 'Working cross-culturally: Australia and Slovakia.' Paper presented at the 10th Congress of the International Association for the Scientific Study of Intellectual Disability. Helsinki, Finland, July.

Johnson, M. (1993) 'Dependency and interdependency.' In J. Bond, P. Coleman and S. Peace (eds) *Ageing in Society.* London: Sage.

Kalyanpur, M. (1996) 'The influence of western special education on community-based services in India.' *Disability and Society 11,* 2, 249–270.

Kaufman, A., Adams, J. and Campbell, V. (1991) 'Permanency planning by older parents who care for adult children with mental retardation.' *Mental Retardation 29,* 293–300.

Keith, L. (1992) 'Who cares wins? Women, caring and disability.' *Disability, Handicap and Society 7,* 2, 167–175.

Keith, L. (ed) (1994) *Mustn't Grumble: Writing by Disabled Women.* London: Women's Press.

Keith, L. and Morris, J. (1995) 'Easy targets: A disability rights perspective on the "children as carers" debate.' *Critical Social Policy,* Autumn, 36–57.

Kelly, L. (1988) *Surviving Sexual Violence.* Cambridge: Polity Press.

Kelly, L. and Radford, J. (1996) '"Nothing really happened": The invalidation of women's experiences of sexual violence.' In M. Hester, L. Kelly and J. Radford (eds) *Women, Violence and Male Power.* Buckingham: Open University Press.

Keltner, B.R., Wise, L.A. and Taylor, G. (1999) 'Mothers with intellectual limitations and their 2-year-old children's developmental outcomes.' *Journal of Intellectual and Developmental Disability 24,* 1, 45–57.

Kiehlbauch Cruz, V., Price-Williams, D. and Andron, L. (1988) 'Developmentally disabled women who were molested as children.' *Social Casework: The Journal of Social Work,* September, 411–419.

King's Fund Centre (1988) *Ties and Connections: An Ordinary Community Life for People with Learning Difficulties.* London: King's Fund Centre.

Kirner, J. and Rayner, M. (1999) *The Women's Power Handbook.* Melbourne: Penguin.

Knowlton, H.E. (1989) *Natural Ties.* Lawrence: University of Kansas, Beach Center on Families and Disability.

Kvist, A. (1998) 'Two decades of parent support: Rueben Lindh Parenting Program.' *Impact 11,* 1, 11.

Kvist, A. (1999) Personal conversation, May.

Lakin, K., Anderson, S., Hill, B., Bruininks, R. and Wright, E. (1991) 'Programs and services received by older persons with mental retardation.' *Mental Retardation 29*, 65–74.

Laslett, P. (1989) *A Fresh Map of Life.* London: Weidenfield and Nicholson.

Lees, S. (1993) *Sugar and Spice: Sexuality and Adolescent Girls.* London: Penguin.

Lewis, J. and Meredith, B. (1988) *Daughters Who Care.* London: Routledge.

Lister, R. (1990) 'Women, economic dependency and citizenship.' *Journal of Social Policy 19*, 4, 445–467.

Llewellyn, G. (1993) 'Parents with intellectual disability: Facts, fallacies and professional responsibilities.' *Community Bulletin 17*, 1, 10–19.

Llewellyn, G. (1994) 'Generic family support services: Are parents with learning disabilities catered for?' *Mental Handicap Research 7*, 1, 64–77.

Llewellyn, G. (1998) 'Strengthening families of older children.' *Impact 11*, 1, 16–17.

Llewellyn, G., McConnell, D. and Bye, R. (1995) *Parents with Intellectual Disability: Support and Services Required by Parents with Intellectual Disability.* Sydney: University of Sydney.

Lloyd, M. (1992) 'Does she boil eggs? Towards a feminist model of disability.' *Disability, Handicap and Society 7*, 3, 207–221.

London Rape Crisis Centre (1988) *Sexual Violence: The Reality for Women.* London: Women's Press.

Lutfiyya, Z.M. (1989) 'The phenomenology of relationships between typical and disabled people.' Unpublished PhD dissertation, Syracuse University.

McCarthy, M. (1991) 'I don't mind sex, it's what the men do to you: Women with learning difficulties talking about their sexual experiences.' Unpublished MA dissertation, Middlesex Polytechnic.

McCarthy, M. (1993) 'Sexual experiences of women with learning difficulties in long-stay hospitals.' *Sexuality and Disability 11*, 4, 277–286.

McCarthy, M. (1998) 'Sexual violence against women with learning disabilities.' *Feminism and Psychology 8*, 4, 544–551.

McCarthy, M. (1999a) 'Interviewing people with learning disabilities about sensitive topics: A discussion of ethical issues.' *British Journal of Learning Disabilities 26*, 4, 140–145.

McCarthy, M. (1999b) *Sexuality and Women with Learning Disabilities.* London: Jessica Kingsley Publishers.

McCarthy, M. and Thompson, D. (1996) 'Sexual abuse by design: An examination of the issues in learning disability services.' *Disability and Society 11*, 2, 205–217.

McCarthy, M. and Thompson, D. (1997) 'A prevalence study of sexual abuse of adults with intellectual disabilities referred for sex education.' *Journal of Applied Research in Intellectual Disability 10*, 2, 105–124.

McCarthy, M. and Thompson, D. (1998) *Sex and the 3R's: Rights, Responsibilities and Risks*, 2nd edn. Brighton: Pavilion.

MacDonald, M. and Tyson, P. (1988) 'Decajeopardy – the aging and aged developmentally disabled.' In A. Marchetti (ed) *Developmental Disabilities: A Lifespan Perspective*. San Diego: Grune Stratton.

MacKinnon, C. (1987) 'Feminism, Marxism, method and the state: Towards feminist jurisprudence.' In S. Harding (ed) *Feminism and Methodology*. Bloomington and Milton Keynes: Indiana University Press and Open University Press.

McNeill, P. (1992) '…doin' it on my own.' In P. McNeill, B. Freeman and J. Newman (eds) *Women Talk Sex: Autobiographical Writing on Sex, Sexuality and Sexual Identity*. London: Scarlett Press.

Mandeville, H. and Snodgrass, P. (1998) 'Helping parents be parents.' *Impact 11*, 1, 2–3.

Marks, G. (1996) 'Coming out as gendered adults: Gender, sexuality and disability.' In C. Christensen and F. Rizvi (eds) *Disability and the Dilemmas of Education and Justice*. Buckingham: Open University Press.

Mattinson, J. (1970) *Marriage and Mental Handicap*. London: Duckworth.

Merton, R. (1968) *Social Theory and Social Structure*. New York: Free Press.

Millard, L. (1994) 'Between ourselves: Experiences of a women's group on sexuality and sexual abuse.' In A. Craft (ed) *Practice Issues in Sexuality and Learning Disabilities*. London: Routledge.

Morris, J. (1991) *Pride Against Prejudice: Transforming Attitudes to Disability*. London: Women's Press.

Morris, J. (1995) 'Creating a space for absent voices.' *Feminist Review 51*, 69–93.

Morris, J. (ed) (1996) *Encounters with Strangers: Feminism and Disability*. London: Women's Press.

Morton, M. and Munford, R. (1998) 'Re/presenting difference: Women with intellectual disabilities.' In R. DuPlessis and L. Alice (eds) *Feminist Thought in Aotearoa/New Zealand*. London: Oxford University Press.

Mount, B., Beeman, P. and Durcharme, G. (1988) *What Are We Learning About Circles of Support?* Manchester: Communitas.

Newton, S.J. (1989) *Social Support Manual*. Eugene: University of Oregon, Specialised Training Program.

Nisbet, J. and Hagner, D. (1988) 'Natural supports in the workplace: A re-examination of supported employment.' *Journal of the Association for Persons with Severe Handicaps 13*, 4, 260–267.

O'Connell, M. (1990) *Community Building in Logan Square*. Evanston: Center for Urban Affairs and Policy Research, Northwestern University.

Oliver, M. (1996) *Understanding Disability: From Theory to Practice*. London: Macmillan.

Orlando, J. and Koss, M. (1983) 'The effect of sexual victimisation on sexual satisfaction: A study of the negative-association hypothesis.' *Journal of Abnormal Psychology 92*, 1, 104–106.

Owen, M.J. (1986) 'Women's studies.' *The Disability Rag*, July–August, 28–29.

Owen, M.J. (1988) 'Women's studies revisited: An immodest expectation.' *Kaleidoscope*, Winter–Spring, 20–21.

Pateman, C. (1980) 'Women and consent.' *Political Theory 8*, 2, 149–168.

People First (undated) *Women First: A Book by Women with Learning Difficulties about the Issues for Women with Learning Difficulties*. London: People First.

Perske, R. (1988) *Circles of Friends*. Nashville: Abingdon Press.

Pierpoint, J. (1990) *Judith Snow ... Pioneer, Prophet and Friend*. Toronto: Inclusion Press.

Pixa-Kettner, U. (1999) 'Follow-up study on parenting with intellectual disability in Germany.' *Journal of Intellectual and Developmental Disability 24*, 1, 75–93.

Pogrebin, L.C. (1987) *Among Friends: Who We Like, Why We Like Them and What We Do with Them*. New York: McGraw-Hill.

Powerhouse (1996a) 'Power in the house: Women with learning difficulties organising against abuse.' In J. Morris (ed) *Encounters with Strangers: Feminism and Disability*. London: Women's Press.

Powerhouse (1996b) 'What women from Powerhouse say about sexual abuse.' *Tizard Learning Disability Review 1*, 4, 39–43.

Quilliam, S. (1994) *Women on Sex*. London: Quality Paperbacks Direct.

Ramcharan, P., Roberts, G., Grant, G. and Borland, J. (1997) 'Citizenship, empowerment and everyday life: Ideal and illusion in the new millennium.' In P. Ramcharan, G. Roberts, G. Grant and J. Borland (eds) *Empowerment in Everyday Life: Learning Disability*. London: Jessica Kingsley Publishers.

Raymond, J.G. (1986) *A Passion for Friends: Toward a Philosophy of Female Affection*. Boston: Beacon Press.

Richardson, A. and Ritchie, J. (1989) *Letting Go: Dilemmas for Parents whose Son and Daughter has a Mental Handicap*. Milton Keynes: Open University Press.

Rolph, S. (1997) 'Surprise journeys and border crossings: A way of understanding community care 1930–1970.' Paper presented at Social History of Learning Disability Conference, Open University, 2 July.

Rose, N. (1979) 'The psychological complex: Mental measurement and social administration.' *Ideology and Consciousness 5*, 5–68.

Rubin, L.B. (1985) *Just Friends: The Role of Friendship in our Lives*. New York: Harper and Row.

Saxton, M. and Howe, F. (eds) (1987) *With Wings: An Anthology of Literature by and about Women with Disabilities*. New York: Feminist Press.

Schaffner, C.B. and Buswell, B.E. (1992) *Connecting Students: A Guide to Thoughtful Facilitation for Educators and Families*. Colorado Springs: Peak Parent Center.

Scheerenberger, R.C. (1983) *A History of Mental Retardation*. Baltimore: Paul H. Brookes.

Scheerenberger, R.C. (1987) *A History of Mental Retardation: A Quarter Century of Promise*. Baltimore: Paul H. Brookes.

Seltzer, M. and Krauss, M. (1987) *Ageing and Mental Retardation: Extending the Continuum*. Washington DC: American Association on Mental Retardation.

Senn, C.Y. (1988) *Vulnerable: Sexual Abuse and People with an Intellectual Handicap*. Toronto: G. Allan Roehr Institute.

Shoultz, B. (1995) '"My heart chose freedom": The story of Lucy Rider's second life.' In S.J. Taylor, R. Bogdan and Z.M. Lutfiyya (eds) *The Variety of Community Experience: Qualitative Studies of Family and Community Life*. Baltimore: Paul H. Brookes.

Smith, D.E. (1987) *The Everyday World as Problematic: A Feminist Sociology*. Boston: Northeastern University Press.

Sobsey, D. (1994) *Violence and Abuse in the Lives of People with Disabilities*. Baltimore: Paul H. Brookes.

Sobsey, D. and Doe, T. (1991) 'Patterns of sexual abuse and assault.' *Sexuality and Disability 9*, 3, 243–259.

Sobsey, D., Gray, S., Wells, D., Pyper, D. and Reimer-Heck, B. (1991) *Disability, Sexuality and Abuse: An Annotated Bibliography*. Baltimore: Paul H. Brookes.

Souza, A. with Ramcharan, P. (1997) 'Everything you ever wanted to know about Down's Syndrome but never bothered to ask.' In P. Ramcharan, G. Roberts, G. Grant and J. Borland (eds) *Empowerment in Everyday Life: Learning Disability*. London: Jessica Kingsley Publishers.

Spelman, E. (1988) *Inessential Woman: Problems of Exclusion in Feminist Thought*. Boston: Beacon Press.

Spender, D. (1985) *Man Made Language*, 2nd ed. London: Routledge and Kegan Paul.

Strauss, D. and Zigman, W. (1996) 'Behavioral capabilities and mortality risk in adults with and without Down syndrome.' *American Journal on Mental Retardation 101*, 3, 269–281.

Strully, J. and Strully, C. (1985) 'Friendships and our children.' *Journal of the Association for Persons with Severe Handicaps 10*, 4, 224–227.

Taylor, S.J. and Bogdan, R. (1998) *Introduction to Qualitative Research Methods: A Guidebook and Resource*, 3rd edn. New York: Wiley.

Thompson, D. (1994) 'Sexual experience and sexual identity for men with learning disabilities who have sex with men.' *Changes 12*, 4, 254–263.

Thompson, D. (1997) 'Profiling the sexually abusive behaviour of men with learning disabilities.' *Journal of Applied Research in Intellectual Disability 10*, 2, 125–139.

Thompson, S. (1990) 'Putting a big thing into a little hole: Teenage girls accounts of sexual initiation.' *Journal of Sex Research 27*, 3, 341–361.

Traustadóttir, R. (1990) 'Obstacles to equality: The double discrimination of women with disabilities.' In R. Traustadóttir (ed) *Women with Disabilities: Issues, Resources, Connections.* Syracuse: Center on Human Policy, Syracuse University.

Traustadóttir, R. (1992) 'Mothers who care: Gender, disability and family life.' *Journal of Family Issues 12,* 2, 211–228.

Traustadóttir, R. (1996) 'Diversity of female experience and the exclusion of women with disabilities.' Paper presented at a Nordic conference on women's studies. University of Oslo, Norway, November.

Traustadóttir, R. (1997) 'Kvenleiki og fötlun' (Womanliness and disability). In H. Kress and R. Traustadóttir (eds) *Íslenskar kvennarannsóknir* (Icelandic women's studies). Reykjavík: Centre for Women's Studies, University of Iceland.

Traustadóttir, R. (1998) 'Líka fyrir fatlaðar konur?' (What about women with disabilities?). In F.H. Jónsson (ed) *Rannsóknir í félagsvísindum* (Research in social sciences). Reykjavík: Social Science Research Institute and the University of Iceland Press.

Traustadóttir, R. (1999) 'Gender, disability, and community life: Toward a feminist analysis.' In H. Bersani Jr (ed) *Responding to the Challenge: Current Trends and International Issues in Developmental Disabilities.* Cambridge: Brookline Books.

Traustadóttir, R. and Sigurjónsdóttir, H.B. (1998) *Umdeildar fjölskyldur: Sein-færir/proskaheftir foreldrar og börn þeirra* (Contested families: Parents with intellectual disabilities and their children). Reykjavík: Social Science Research Institute, University of Iceland.

Trupin, L., Sebesta, D.S., Yelin, E. and LaPlante, M.P. (1997) 'Trends in labor force participation among persons with disabilities, 1983–1994.' *Disability Statistics Report (10).* Washington DC: Department of Education, National Institute on Disability and Rehabilitation Research.

Turk, V. and Brown, H. (1993) 'The sexual abuse of adults with learning disabilities: Results of a two year incidence survey.' *Mental Handicap Research 6,* 3, 193–216.

Tymchuk, A.J. (1992) 'Predicting adequacy of parenting by people with mental retardation.' *Child Abuse and Neglect 16,* 165–178.

Tymchuk, A.J. (1999) 'Moving towards integration of services for parents with intellectual disabilities.' *Journal of Intellectual and Developmental Disability 24,* 1, 59–74.

Tymchuk, A.J. and Andron, L. (1990) 'Mothers with mental retardation who do or do not abuse or neglect their children.' *Child Abuse and Neglect 14,* 313–323.

Tymchuk, A.J. and Feldman, M.A. (1991) 'Parents with mental retardation and their children: Review of research relevant to professional practice.' *Canadian Psychology 32,* 3, 486–496.

Tymchuk, A.J., Llewellyn, G. and Feldman, M. (1999) 'Parenting by persons with intellectual disabilities: A timely international perspective.' *Journal of Intellectual and Developmental Disability 24,* 1, 3–6.

United Nations (1991) *The World's Women 1970–1990: Trends and Statistics.* New York: UN.

Walmsley, J. (1993) 'Contradictions in caring: Reciprocity and interdependence.' *Disability, Handicap and Society 8,* 2, 129–141.

Walmsley, J. (1995) 'Gender, caring and learning disability.' Unpublished PhD thesis, Milton Keynes, Open University.

Walmsley, J. (1997) 'Doing what mum wants me to do: Looking at family relationships from the point of view of adults with learning disabilities.' *Journal of Applied Research in Intellectual Disability 9,* 4, 324–341.

Walmsley, J. and Downer, J. (1997) 'Shouting the loudest: Self advocacy, power and diversity.' In P. Ramcharan, G. Roberts, G. Grant and J. Borland (eds) *Empowerment in Everyday Life: Learning Disability.* London: Jessica Kingsley Publishers.

Walsall Women's Group (1994) *No Means No.* Walsall: Learning For Living Scheme.

Wates, M. and Jade, R. (eds) (1999) *Bigger than the Sky: Disabled Women on Parenting.* London: Women's Press.

Wearing, B. (1996) *Gender: The Pain and Pleasure of Difference.* Melbourne: Longman.

Wendell, S. (1996) *The Rejected Body: Feminist Philosophical Reflections on Disability.* New York: Routledge.

Williams, D. (1992) *Nobody Nowhere: The Extraordinary Autobiography of an Autistic.* New York: Avon Books.

Wilmuth, M. and Holcomb, L. (eds) (1993) *Women with Disabilities: Found Voices.* New York: Haworth Press.

Withman, B. and Accardo, P. (eds) (1990) *When a Parent is Mentally Retarded.* Baltimore Paul H. Brookes.

Wolfensberger, W. (1975) *The Origin and Nature of our Institutional Models.* Syracuse Human Policy Press.

Wolfensberger, W. (1992) *A Brief Introduction to Social Role Valorization as a Higher-ord Concept for Structuring Human Services,* 2nd edn. Syracuse NY: Training Institu Syracuse University.

Wood, M. (1994) 'Lost paradises.' *New York Review of Books,* 3 March, 469.

Wyatt, G., Newcomb, M. and Riederle, M. (1993) *Sexual Abuse and Consensual S Women's Developmental Patterns and Outcomes.* Newberry Park: Sage.

Subject Index

ability levels, sexual abuse 148–9
accessibility, of the book 23
activities, L'Arche 225–6
Activities of Daily Living (ADL) 109
aged care accommodation 82–3
ageing, perceptions of 72
Alanna 192, 205–9, 211
Alice 191–2, 198–201, 210
AMIDA 103–5
appearance, Jenny 110–11
ARC-US 181
Aslaug 182–3, 189–90
attitudes
  cultural 275–6
  fighting against 242
Australia
  Disability Discrimination Act 246–52
  employment, Sonia Teuben 162–71
  families, Rosemary West 34–51
  older women 69–85
  relationships, Janice Slattery 90–105
autobiographies 18

Bauer, Michelle 118–31
beliefs, intellectual disabilities 115–16
Beryl 192, 201–5, 210–11

bifurcated consciousness 129
Birna 268–9
Braňo 58
bribery, sexual abuse 151

careers
  Jenny 114–15
  Nancy Ward 172–81
carers 194–5
caring 191–212
  feminist position 195–7
  women and 193–5
  women with intellectual disabilities 197–212
case studies 18–19
celebrations, at L'Arche 224
Citizen Advocacy 225
Clark, Susan 118–31
collaboration, between women 277–8
collaborative writing 17
colonization, issue of 22–3
colour, women of 229–38
communities
  diversity of places in 274–5
  involvement in 214–15
competency development 116
complaint, against Scout Association of Australia 246–8
concerns, common 275–6
consent, sexual abuse 152–3
coping, with sexual abuse 154–5
countries, including voices from different 15–16
creativity 159

cultures
  differences in 275–6
  including voices from different 15–16
  intersecting 229–38
Czech Republic, Tamara Kainova 28–33
Daughters Who Care 194
decisions
  about children 244–5
  about sex 142
  L'Arche 222
dependency, in friendships 127–8
disability
  feminism 12–13
  fighting against 241–2
  language and labelling 21–2
  learning about, Nancy Ward 174–5
  social discrimination 273–4
Disability Discrimination Act
  after the decision 252
  agreement 252
  attempted conciliations 248–9
  complaint 246–8
  conciliation meetings 250–2
  hearings 249–50
disability movement, inclusion within 14–15
discrimination see Disability Discrimination Act; social discrimination

elderly mothers 260–1

employment
  access to paid 116, 158
  creative 162–71
  fighting for 243–4
  relationships at 102–3
  sheltered workshops
    160–1
  supported 182–90
  see also careers
exclusion 12, 13, 16

families
  finding strength in 246
  Janice Slattery 92–6
  Janka and Jana Hanková
    52–62
  parents with intellectual
    disabilities 255–6
  Pat Felt, L'Arche 226–7
  Rosemary West 34–51
  Tamara Kainova 28–33
  traditional view of 26
  unhappy 63–8
fathers, sexual abuse 148,
  153–4
fear, of sexual abusers 150
Felt, Pat 217–28
feminism
  on caring 192, 195–7
  inclusion within 12–14
  view of families 26
Ferguson, Bronwyn 75–7
fighting
  against disability 241–2
  discrimination 245
  for independence 244
  loneliness 242–3
  people's attitudes 242
  to decide about
    children 244–5
  under Disability
    Discrimination Act
    246–52

for work 243–4
financial incentives, sexual
  abuse 151
friendship
  finding strength in 246
  Janice Slattery 101
  Michelle and Susan
    118–31
    difficulties 122–3
    ideals and reality
      127–31
    love or work 126–7
    rewards 123–4
    Susan's perspective
      124–5

gender
  disability movement
    14–15
  importance of 276–7
  as source of power 151
Gina's Story 162–71
God, finding strength in
  245–6
group research studies 19
Gudrun 183, 185–9

Halladóra 265–7
Hanková, Jana 52–62
Hanková, Janka 52–62
help
  at L'Arche 221–2
  living alone 108–10
higher order discussions
  113–14
housing moves 81–2
human rights, focus on 15

Iceland, motherhood
  study 258–69
ideals, of friendship
  127–31
identity
  dual, Teresa 233

through caring 192,
  194
ideologies, imposition of
  inappropriate 16
independence, fighting for
  244
Independent Living
  Movement 21–2
informal carers 194–5
informal networks,
  support 74, 83
intellectual disability,
  medical discourse 14
Intellectually Disabled
  Person's Services Act
  (1986), Australia 40
international interest,
  motherhood 255–6
IQ, parental success 257
Ireland, sexual abuse
  study 145

Jenny 106–17
Johnson, Amy 77–8
Jónína 263–4
Journal of Intellectual and
  Developmental Disability
  256

Kainova, Tamara
  at Blue Door day centre
    17–18
  employment 160–1
  family life 28–33
Know Me As I am: An
  Anthology of Prose,
  Poetry and Art by People
  with Learning
  Difficulties 197
Kristina 182, 184–5

labelling 21–2, 174,
  232–3
Land of Harmony 59

language 21–2
L'Arche 217–28
leadership career 172–81
learning
    about one's disability
        174–5
    from and with women
        106–17
life expectancy 71
life history research 197
literature
    by women on
        disabilities 15
    on relationships 130
living alone, Jenny
    108–10
loneliness, fighting 242–3
loss
    minimising 83–5
    older women 81–3
Louise 63–8

Marián 61
marriage, Janice Slattery
    96–101
masturbation 132, 136–7
medical discourse,
    intellectual disability
    14
men
    learning about 111–12
    relationships with 133,
        140–3
middle-aged mothers
    261–2
Millear, Amanda 239–52
motherhood 253–70
    Icelandic study 258–69
    international interest in
        255–6
    research findings
        256–8
multiculturalism 229–38

New Zealand, Louise
    63–8
Norway, Jenny 106–17

older women 69–85
opportunity
    ensuring 83–5
    for older women 80–1
oppression 153
othering 22
ownership, of women's
    stories 22–3

parenting
    international interest in
        255–6
    research findings
        256–7
    violence 67–8
parents, life without
    69–85
People First of Nebraska
    178
perpetrators, sexual abuse
    146–8
personal development
    older women 74
    Pat Felt, L'Arche 227
prayer, at L'Arche 224
privacy, at L'Arche 221

relationships 88–9
    desire for sexual 133
    Janice Slattery 90–105
    with men 140–3
    with non-disabled
        people 177–8
    Pat Felt, L'Arche 222–3
    see also friendship
representativeness, of the
    book 22
research
    on motherhood
        findings 256–8

study in Iceland
    258–69
older women
    findings 74–85
    study in Melbourne
        73–4
residential mobility 81–2
rewards, of friendship
    123–4
rights see human rights
Robinson, Debbie 235–8
Rowley, Beatrice 78–80
rules
    at L'Arche 222
    rewriting 112–13

Scout Association of
    Australia, complaint
    against 246–8
Self Advocates Becoming
    Empowered (SABE)
    179–80
self-advocacy
    discovery of 176–7
    finding strength in 246
    influence of 159
    jobs and positions
        178–9
    Pat Felt 225–6
self-esteem 234
self-fulfilling prophecies
    116
services
    for older women 83,
        84–5
    women of color 233–4
sexual abuse 133, 143
    coming to terms with
        153–5
    consent 152–3
    dynamics of 148–51
    impact on other sexual
        experiences 151–2

nature and extent of
144–6
perpetrators 146–8
speaking out about
155–6
sexual activity, with other
women 137–9
sexual attraction, to other
women 132–3
sexual lives, speaking
about 135–43
sexual pleasure 139
sexual relationships, desire
for 133
sheltered workshops 158,
160–1
Slattery, Janice 90–105
Slovakia, Janka and Jana
Hanková 52–62
social discrimination
disability 273–4
fighting 245
women of color 231
social meaning, of work
182–90
social model, of disability
21–2
socialization 115
State Disability Services
system 83
stepfathers, sexual abuse
148
styles, *Women with
Intellectual Disabilities*
20
Summer Dialogues 59
support, informal
networks 74, 83
supported employment
159, 182–90

Teresa 231–4
terminology 21–2

Teuben, Sonia 162–71
themes, *Women with
Intellectual Disabilities*
20
Third Age, notion of 84
Thorbjörg 264–5
travelling, at L'Arche 225
trust, relationships with
men 141

UK General Household
Survey 194–5
United States
Nancy Ward 172–81
Pat Felt 217–28
unpaid care 194–5

Verna 34–51
violence 63–8
vulnerability, older women
81–3

Ward, Nancy 172–81
West, Rosemary 34–51
women
and caring 193–5
with intellectual
disabilities
caring 197–212
collaboration with
other women
277–8
color 229–38
creativity 162–71
diverse places in the
world 274–5
experiences of older
women 69–85
friendship with
118–31
involvement in com-
munities 214–28
leadership career
172–81

learning from other
women 106–17
motherhood 253–70
parenting 67–8
sexuality 132–56
sheltered workshops
158, 160–1
social meaning of
work 182–90
sexual activity with
137–9
sexual attraction to
132–3
*Women with Intellectual
Disabilities*
contested issues 21–3
reasons for book 12–17
structure of the book
19–21
writing the book
17–19
Women's Support Group
65
work
involved in friendship
127, 128, 129
see also employment

young carers 196
young mothers 262–3

Name Index

Aldridge, J. and Becker, S. 196
Amado, N.A. 127
Amado, N.A., Conklin, F. and Wells, J. 130
Andersen, M.L. 26, 158
Anderson, D. 72
Andron, L. 139
Andron, L. and Tymchuk, A.J. 270
Andron, L. and Ventura, J. 139
Asch, A. and Fine, M. 12, 14
Ashman, A., Suttie, J. and Bramley, J. 72
Atkinson, D. and Walmsley, J. 18
Atkinson, D. and Williams, F. 197

Baladerian, N.J. 66
Barnes, C. and Mercer, G. 22
Bassaro, J.C. 131
Beach Center on Families and Disability 130
Bell, R.R. 127, 128
Between Ourselves 155
Bigby, C. 72, 73, 82
Block, J.D. 128
Blytheway, B. and Johnson, J. 194
Bogdan, R. 214
Bogdan, R. and Taylor, S.J. 65

Booth, T. and Booth, W. 197, 255, 257, 258, 270
Bowe, F. 158
Boylan, E. 15
Brantlinger, E. 11, 14
Breakwell, G. 154
Brown, H. 146, 153
Brown, H., Stein, J. and Turk, V. 145, 146, 147
Brown, H. and Turk, V. 145, 146
Browne, S.E., Connors, D. and Stern, N. 15
Buchanan, A. and Wilkins, R. 144
Bulmer, M. 127, 128
Burke, P. and Signo, K. 196

Card, H. 71
Chamberlain, A., Rauh, J., Passer, A., McGrath, M. and Bucket, R. 144
Chappell, A.L. 15
Craft, M. and Craft, A. 149

Daniels, A.K. 214
Danish Ministry of Social Affairs 255, 256, 258
Davies, A. 155
Deegan, M.J. and Brooks, N.A. 15
Downs, C. and Craft, A. 135
Driedger, D., Feika, I. and Batres, E.G. 15, 16
Dunne, T. and Power, A. 145

Eayrs, C.B., Ellis, N. and Jones, R.S.P. 21
Edgerton, R. 72, 73, 205, 256
Elkins, T., Gatford, L., Wilks, C., Muram, D. and Golden, G. 144
Eyman, R. and Borthwick-Duffy, S. 71

Feldman, M.A. 255, 257
Fine, M. and Asch, A. 13, 15, 66
Fisher, B. and Galler, R. 89
Flynn, R.J. and Nitch, K.E. 261
Forest, M. 130
Forest, M. and Lusthaus, E. 130
Four Stories 139

Gavey, N. 153
Gibson, J., Rabkin, J. and Munson, R. 71
Gilligan, C. 88
Gouldner, H. and Strong, M.S. 127
Graham, H. 193, 195, 211

Hammersley, M. and Atkinson, P. 19, 259
Hanna, W.I. and Rogovsky, E. 158
Hard, S. and Plumb, W. 144, 145, 146, 153
Harry, B. 232
Health and Community Services 72
Hite, S. 136
Hoffman, C. and Mandeville, H. 257

Hogg, J., Moss, S. and Cooke, D. 71, 72
Holland, J., Ramazaloglu, C., Scott, S., Sharpe, S. and Thomson, R. 153
Holland, J., Ramazaloglu, C. and Sharpe, S. 153
hooks, b. 12, 16
Huberman, A. and Miles, M. 73
Hutchison, P. 127, 130

Israel, P. 13

Janicki, M., Otis, J., Puccio, P., Rettig, J. and Jacobson, J. 71
Janko, S. 68
Johnson, K. 11, 14, 88
Johnson, K. and Nadazdyova, M. 16
Johnson, M. 211, 212

Kalyanpur, M. 16
Kaufman, A., Adams, J. and Campbell, V. 71
Keith, L. 12, 13, 15, 196
Keith, L. and Morris, J. 196
Kelly, L. 144, 153, 155
Kelly, L. and Radford, J. 147
Keltner, B.R., Wise, L.A. and Taylor, G. 257
Kiehlbauch Cruz, V., Price-Williams, D. and Andron, L. 151
King's Fund Centre 130
Kirner, J. and Rayner, M. 12, 214
Knowlton, H.E. 129
Kvist, A. 234

Lakin, K., Anderson, S., Hill, B. and Bruininks, R. and Wright, E. 71
Laslett, P. 84
Lees, S. 140
Lewis, J. and Meredith, B. 194
Lister, R. 211
Llewellyn, G. 257, 270
Llewellyn, G., McConnell, D. and Bye, R. 255
Lloyd, M. 196
London Rape Crisis Centre 144
Lutfiyya, Z.M. 129

McCarthy, M. 135, 137, 138, 150, 151, 257
McCarthy, M. and Thompson, D. 137, 138, 145, 146, 147, 148, 149
MacDonald, M. and Tyson, P. 72
MacKinnon, C. 152
McNeill, P. 136
Mandeville, H. and Snodgrass, P. 258
Marks, G. 66
Mattinson, J. 149
Merton, R. 116
Millard, L. 154
Morris, J. 12, 13, 15, 196
Morton, M. and Munford, R. 66, 68
Mount, B., Beeman, P. and Ducharme, G. 130

Newton, S.J. 130
Nisbet, J. and Hagner, D. 129

O'Connell, M. 130
Oliver, M. 22

Orlando, J. and Koss, M. 151
Owen, M.J. 13

Pateman, C. 152
People First 155
Perske, R. 130
Pierpoint, J. 130
Pixa-Kettner, U. 257
Pogrebin, L.C. 128
Powerhouse 155, 214

Quilliam, S. 136

Ramcharan, P., Roberts, G., Grant, G. and Borland, J. 15
Raymond, J.G. 131
Richardson, A. and Ritchie, J. 71
Rolph, S. 199
Rose, N. 14
Rubin, L.B. 128

Saxton, M. and Howe, F. 15
Schaffner, C.B. and Buswell, B.E. 130
Scheerenberger, R.C. 14, 261
Seltzer, M. and Krauss, M. 72
Senn, C.Y. 66
Shoultz, B. 214
Smith, D.E. 129
Sobsey, D. 257
Sobsey, D. and Doe, T. 66
Sobsey, D., Gray, S., Wells, D., Pyper, D. and Reimer-Heck, B. 66
Souza, A. with Ramcharan, P. 214
Spelman, E. 12
Spender, D. 88

Strauss, D. and Zigman, W. 72

Strully, J. and Strully, C. 130

Taylor, S.J. and Bogdan, R. 19, 259

Thompson, D. 138, 153

Thompson, S. 137

Traustadóttir, R. 11, 12, 13, 158, 214, 257

Traustadóttir, R. and Sigurjónsdóttir, H.B. 270

Trupin, L., Sebesta, D.S., Yelin, E. and LaPlante, M.P. 158

Turk, V. and Brown, H. 146, 147

Tymchuk, A.J. 257, 258

Tymchuk, A.J. and Andron, L. 257

Tymchuk, A.J. and Feldman, M.A. 256, 257, 270

Tymchuk, A.J., Llewellyn, G. and Feldman, M. 255, 256

United Nations 158

Walmsley, J. 12, 13, 81, 196, 210

Walmsley, J. and Downer, J. 214

Walsall Women's Group 155

Wates, M. and Jade, R. 15

Wearing, B. 26

Wendell, S. 15

Williams, D. 65

Wilmuth, M. and Holcomb, L. 15

Withman, B. and Accardo, P. 255

Wolfensberger, W. 14, 116

Wood, M. 275

Wyatt, G., Newcomb, M. and Riederle, M. 147, 151